Teaching and Social Justice

Teaching and Social Justice

Integrating Multicultural and Feminist Theories
in the Classroom

Edited by Carolyn Zerbe Enns and Ada L. Sinacore

American Psychological Association
Washington, DC

Published by
American Psychological Association
750 First Street, NE
Washington, DC 20002
www.apa.org

To order
APA Order Department
P.O. Box 92984
Washington, DC 20090-2984
Tel: (800) 374-2721; Direct: (202) 336-5510
Fax: (202) 336-5502; TDD/TTY: (202) 336-6123
Online: www.apa.org/books/
E-mail: order@apa.org

In the U.K., Europe, Africa, and the Middle East, copies may be ordered from
American Psychological Association
3 Henrietta Street
Covent Garden, London
WC2E 8LU England

Typeset in Goudy by Stephen McDougal, Mechanicsville, MD

Printer: Edwards Brothers, Inc., Ann Arbor, MI
Cover Designer: Naylor Design, Washington, DC
Technical/Production Editor: Gail B. Munroe

The opinions and statements published are the responsibility of the authors, and such opinions and statements do not necessarily represent the policies of the American Psychological Association.

Library of Congress Cataloging-in-Publication Data

Teaching and social justice : integrating multicultural and feminist theories in the classroom / Edited by Carolyn Zerbe Enns and Ada L. Sinacore.
    p. cm.
Includes bibliographical references and index.
ISBN 1-59147-167-2
1. Social justice—Study and teaching. 2. Multicultural education. 3. Feminism and education. 4. Critical pedagogy. I. Enns, Carolyn Zerbe. II. Sinacore, Ada L.

LC192.2.T43 2005
370.11'5—dc22   2004012197

British Library Cataloguing-in-Publication Data
A CIP record is available from the British Library.

Printed in the United States of America
First Edition

CONTENTS

PREFACE

The purpose of this book is to provide a rationale, theoretical foundations, and general guidelines for implementing multicultural feminist theories and pedagogies in psychology and related disciplines. Each of the three words in the phrase *multicultural feminist pedagogy* is highly relevant to the social sciences. During the past several decades, multicultural and global perspectives have pointed to the limitations and ethnocentrism of many psychological practices and theories and have become catalysts for the development of a more inclusive psychology of diversity. Likewise, feminist psychology has become an influential approach for understanding the psychological experiences of women and other marginalized people. The third word, *pedagogy*, encompasses a very important activity of psychologists as educators. Multicultural, feminist, critical, and liberatory theories and pedagogies are associated with a wide range of theoretical foundations that first emerged in the 1970s and have continued to mature and increase in complexity over the past 35 years. Our major goals are to summarize these varied theoretical perspectives on social justice education, suggest general guidelines for integrating these theories of pedagogy, and discuss the challenges and rewards of teaching from multicultural and feminist frameworks.

We use the phrase *social justice* in the title of this book to highlight the importance of infusing scholarship and practice relevant to diversity in both the process and the content of education. More specifically, social justice in education includes (a) centralizing and affirming the perspectives of those whose experiences have been marginalized or ignored, (b) transforming the manner in which education occurs such that power differences are minimized and the empowerment of learners and educators is optimized, (c) working toward the full and equal participation of all learners, and (d) rethinking the institutional structures in which learning occurs. We seek to provide theoretical and practical roadmaps for engaging in these activities.

Many approaches to teaching about oppression and diversity, though related, currently exist in isolation of each other. For example, there has been little cross-fertilization about pedagogical practices among scholars and educators in women's and gender studies, ethnic studies, multicultural education and training, and international education. When dialogue among contributors to these diverse literatures has occurred, the relationships and communications between feminist and multicultural scholars and scholarship have sometimes been uneasy (e.g., Okin, 1999; Volpp, 2003). This book summarizes how various frameworks construe issues of diversity, identifies the contributions of each, and discusses common as well as divergent implications and strategies. Our first objective, then, is to provide readers with tools for creating multicultural feminist pedagogies. Given the complexity and richness of pedagogical theory, we do not propose a single multicultural feminist pedagogy, but, rather, we propose a foundation that allows educators to formulate their own positions.

A second goal is to help psychologists and educators integrate theory and practice. Professors often apply strategies to implement pragmatic goals and to capture student interest but frequently neglect to formulate a clear theoretical framework for guiding their choice of techniques. We believe that it is essential for multicultural feminist educators to consider the compatibility of the teaching tools they use and specific feminist and multicultural and critical theoretical approaches. If educators do not clarify connections between theory and strategy, they may operate without a clear rationale and may experience limited self-awareness, blank spots, and diminished effectiveness. By articulating a personal theory of pedagogy, the multicultural feminist educator is able to express her or his classroom identity in a coherent and goal-directed manner.

A third goal of this book is to bring the literature of pedagogy, particularly pedagogy about diversity, to psychology. Despite the clear relevance of feminist multicultural pedagogy to the teaching of psychology, limited discussion of these practices has occurred within psychology. Most writings on feminist and multicultural and critical pedagogy have emerged in disciplines such as education, women's and gender and sexuality studies, and the humanities. Although many psychologists have written about teaching strategies for conveying content regarding controversial issues or multicultural and gender content (e.g., articles published in *Teaching of Psychology*), dialogue about the theoretical models that inform practices or how teaching strategies can contribute to a transformed educational experience has been limited (Forrest & Rosenberg, 1997). Our objective is to begin filling this gap.

This volume is divided into two sections that address both theoretical (chaps. 1–6) and application (chaps. 7–11) aspects of multicultural and feminist pedagogies. In the first section (chaps. 1–6), authors convey definitions of feminist and multicultural pedagogies and compare theoretical foundations and training methods that are based in a variety fields such as multicultural education, women's studies, critical studies, ethnic studies, queer studies, and multicultural counseling. These chapters provide an overview of the theoretical frameworks, explore the intersections among different frameworks and disciplines, address the links between theory and teaching, and encourage educators to assess how their theoretical positions inform teaching as it relates to social justice. The second section of the book (chaps. 7–11) offers selective reviews of research and practice related to the application of multicultural and feminist pedagogy. Authors discuss the impact of multicultural and feminist pedagogies on students and educators, clarify some of the challenges of and barriers to teaching for social justice, introduce specific applications of pedagogy such as mentoring, and consider the impact of historical themes and institutional structures that influence pedagogy.

A major premise of this book is that the social locations and social identities (e.g., race, class, sexual orientation, gender, age, and nationality) of educators and students contribute substantially to how education about diversity is articulated and experienced. Consistent with our belief that the positionalities and life experiences of educators are crucial considerations in the implementation of pedagogy, chapters are written by teams of individuals who represent different areas of expertise, life experiences, social identities, educational roles, and stages of career development. Our goal is to communicate the importance of flexibility, ongoing reflection and lifelong learning, and attentiveness to the complexities and shifting dynamics among educators and students. To highlight this objective, we have based the final chapter on the personal reflections of book contributors. It discusses the ways in which personal identity intersects with the content one teaches as a multicultural feminist educator and explores the challenges and benefits of integrating multicultural and feminist perspectives in psychology and education.

ACKNOWLEDGMENTS

This book has been a work in progress for 6 years and was inspired by the 1998 working conference entitled "Advancing Together: Centralizing Feminism and Multiculturalism in Counseling Psychology." The conference explored the intersections of multiculturalism and feminism and was sponsored by the American Psychological Association's Division of Counseling Psychology (17) Section for the Advancement of Women (SAW). One of the 10 conference working groups, which focused on pedagogy, provided the impetus for this book. The original group consisted of 15 persons: Julie Ancis, Karyn Boatwright, Beth Cohen, James Croteau, Carolyn Zerbe Enns, Pat Healy, Carolyn Heineman, Brenda Karns, Terri Lance, Dinah Meyer, Sarah Nehring, Julia Phillips, Ada Sinacore, Merideth Tomlinson, and Denise Twohey. We thank group members for challenging our thinking about pedagogy, considering the ways in which diverse life experiences and social identities influence education, and reinforcing our commitments to teaching that is informed by social justice perspectives. We also owe special thanks to 1998 Advancing Together conference coordinators, Linda Forrest and Freda Ginsberg, and conference program chair, Ruth Fassinger.

The voices of some original group members are not represented in this book because of life transitions, career changes, new priorities, or major illnesses. In their place, additional psychologists, who are committed to the integration of multicultural and feminist perspectives, wrote chapters for this project. We appreciate the efforts of persons who contributed to this project at its various stages: those who helped articulate the original framework, those who invested energy in its evolution, and those who joined the project at later stages to expand the range of perspectives and topics this book explores.

Teaching and Social Justice

1

TOWARD DEFINING AND INTEGRATING MULTICULTURAL AND FEMINIST PEDAGOGIES

CAROLYN ZERBE ENNS AND LINDA M. FORREST

During the past 30 years, a variety of multicultural and feminist approaches to diversity training and pedagogy have emerged. These approaches have often developed independently of each other, and there has been limited communication among contributors to these feminist and multicultural literatures. In their comparison of feminist and multicultural approaches, Elizabeth Sparks and Aileen Park (2000) proposed that feminism has addressed issues of power and gender and examined a wide range of oppressions related to gender and patriarchy as they intersect with "isms" such as racism, classism, heterosexism, colonialism, and ageism. Multiculturalism has emphasized the impact of culture, ethnicity, race, and other related aspects of identity on human experience. The values of diversity and pluralism are highlighted by multicultural educators, along with the importance of examining the influence of ethnocentrism, stereotypes, racism, prejudice, and nationalism on one's own attitudes and the values of the larger society.

In this chapter, we explore definitions and strategies of multicultural and feminist pedagogies and identify shared and unique features as well as converging themes. Our summary is informed by a variety of traditions, including critical and liberatory pedagogy (e.g., Freire, 1970, 1994a; Giroux, 1992; Giroux & McLaren, 1994), antiracism pedagogies (e.g., Kailin, 2002; Ng, Staton, & Scane, 1995), feminist pedagogy (e.g., Fisher, 1981, 2001; Forrest & Rosenberg, 1997), engaged pedagogy or education as the practice of freedom (hooks, 1994), radical pedagogies (Gore, 1998), and pedagogies associated with multicultural education and counselor training (e.g., Adams, Bell, & Griffin, 1997; Banks & Banks, 2003; Nieto, 1999a, 1999b; Sleeter, 1996, 1999). Although the phrase *critical pedagogy* is usually associated with multicultural pedagogies, some authors (e.g., Ng, 1995) use terms such as *critical teaching* to encompass all methods that "question and challenge existing knowledge base and power relations" (p. 130), including feminist pedagogy, antiracism education, and liberatory pedagogies.

We begin by exploring the range of multicultural and critical pedagogies and summarizing the principles and strategies of feminist pedagogy. We then review similarities and converging themes among these perspectives and discuss ideas for integrating these perspectives. We conclude by proposing important concepts and features of multicultural feminist pedagogies.

MULTICULTURAL, LIBERATION, AND CRITICAL PEDAGOGIES

In the following section, we briefly describe the varied approaches that are identified as critical, liberation, and multicultural pedagogies. We define the role of conscientization in these teaching approaches, and summarize major principles and strategies of critical pedagogies.

An Overview of Multicultural and Critical Approaches

Civil rights movements (Banks, 1995, 2000) and human rights movements associated with class-related struggles (Freire, 1970) provided the primary foundations for contemporary multicultural approaches. The phrase *multicultural education* is "a free floating signifier" (Sleeter & McLaren, 1995) representing an array of approaches that emphasize the following dimensions to differing degrees: (a) content integration about multicultural issues and diversity, (b) prejudice reduction efforts, (c) pedagogies that support equity, (d) the critical examination of assumptions supporting the traditional *canon* and *hidden curriculum*, and (e) an educational culture that empowers all students (Banks, 2000). The definitions we explore are most closely associated with approaches to multicultural education that address issues of power and social justice within education. These pedagogies are typically labeled by terms such as *liberation pedagogy, antiracism pedagogy, critical pedagogy,* or *pedagogy for social justice.*

Sonia Nieto's (1999b) and Goli Rezai-Rashti's (1995) descriptions of multicultural pedagogy integrate multiculturalism, social justice, and critical pedagogical approaches. Nieto views multicultural education as antiracist at its core and as permeating all aspects of educational experience, including the placement and tracking of students in classes, educational climate, physical surroundings, and educator interactions with students and the community. Multicultural educators teach about the nature and impact of racism to ensure that students are prepared to confront racism. As noted by Nieto, "multicultural education is a philosophy, a way of looking at the world, not simply a program or a class or a teacher" (1999b, p. 11).

Second, multicultural competency and literacy are central to basic education and indispensable to the successful negotiation of life tasks. Third, multicultural education is about and for all people, not only those who are identified as disadvantaged or *at risk*. Students from dominant groups are often misinformed about diversity, power, and privilege and, consequently, are important recipients of multicultural education efforts. These students may identify themselves as having no cultural identity other than being American and thus believe that their experiences are normative and all other life experiences represent deviations from the norm. Fourth, multicultural education is a process that is ongoing, dynamic, involves relationships among people, and emphasizes intangibles, such as expectations as well as complex and ever-changing perceptions and beliefs. A final component of Nieto's definition is her characterization of multicultural education as a critical pedagogy that is empowering, liberating, and active.

Goli Rezai-Rashti (1995) described a critical emancipatory multicultural approach as providing a systematic critique of how knowledge is constructed, including the privileging of Western and Eurocentric perspectives. Second, critical multiculturalism promotes not only cultural diversity but also the relational implications of content. In other words, the curriculum pays attention to relationships among different social groups within countries and continents as well as throughout the world. It calls on educators to see inequality in global and relational terms. Third, critical multiculturalism does not conceptualize racial or ethnic identities in static terms but as dynamic, complex self-understandings that include variations, discontinuities, and contradictions in the needs and actions of majority and minority group members. Finally, critical emancipatory multiculturalism promotes democratic pedagogies.

Patti Lather (1998) depicted critical pedagogy as a *big tent* or a home for a wide range of educational perspectives that emphasize social justice goals. Well-known theorists include Paulo Freire (1970, 1994a), Henry Giroux (1992; Giroux & McLaren, 1994), Peter McLaren (1997, 2000a, 2000b), and Ira Shor (1987a, 1987b). A number of feminist pedagogy theorists, including bell hooks (1994), Elizabeth Tisdell (1995, 1998), Elizabeth Ellsworth (1989), Kathleen Weiler (1988, 1991, 2001), and Nina Wallerstein (1987), also draw substantially from critical pedagogy to inform their work. The following section discusses the shared features of critical pedagogies.

Conscientization: Foundation for Critical and Liberation Pedagogy

Paulo Freire (1970, 1994a) is considered a major founder of liberation pedagogy and built his theory on experiences of teaching peasants and disenfranchised persons in Brazil. His work was informed by Marxist–Socialist thought, liberation theology, and the belief that capitalism is the foundation of domination (McLaren, 1997, 2000a). As Freire's students developed literacy skills, they also gained a new sense of themselves, participated in a critical examination of the social situations in which they were embedded, and developed skills for social change. Freire used the term *conscientização*, which is often translated as conscientization or critical consciousness, to conceptualize the changed awareness that students develop during the educational process. *Conscientização* refers to "learning to perceive social, political, and economic contradictions, and to take action against the oppressive elements of reality" (Freire, 1970, p. 19). Conscientization can also be defined succinctly as "coming to a consciousness of oppression and a commitment to end that oppression" (Weiler, 1991, p. 454). Critical consciousness is the process by which individuals recognize the systems of oppression in which they exist, articulate their roles and places in these systems, and develop concrete strategies to empower themselves and others to engage in social action (Burbules & Berk, 1999).

Freire (1970, 1994a, 1994b) noted that a crucial component of critical consciousness is helping students understand how they learned to define themselves as their colonizers viewed them (i.e., internalized oppression). For example, coping and passive resistance mechanisms that members of nondominant groups may develop in response to colonization include silence, accommodation, evasiveness, ingratiation, and manipulation (Maher, 1987b). Through conscientization, learners gain awareness of cultural invasion or the colonizing effects of the dominant culture and how they have become unsuspecting *hosts* to the oppressive aspects of culture. Recognizing this internalized oppression is central to the recovery of one's voice and the beginning of decolonization (Adams, 1997; hooks, 1994; Locke & Faubert, 1999).

Principles and Strategies Associated With Critical Pedagogies

Paulo Freire (1970) identified three overlapping activities as central to empowerment: (a) listening to the needs and perspectives of those who are oppressed, (b) using a problem-posing participatory dialogue to draw out the knowledge and build the confidence of participants, and (c) building on the knowledge acquired from this questioning and dialogue process to engage in positive changes and action (Freire, 1970, 1994a). Principles based on these activities are explored more fully in the next paragraphs.

Principle 1: Problem Posing and Participatory Dialogue

Freire (1970) contrasted a liberation approach with traditional banking education, a process in which learners become passive recipients or receptacles of knowledge that is deposited by expert teachers. In banking education, "knowledge is a gift bestowed by those who consider themselves knowledgeable upon those whom they consider to know nothing" (p. 58). It stifles inquiry, eliminates creativity, promotes passivity, and reinforces alienation and oppression. In contrast, the revolutionary educator uses problem posing or liberating education, which consists of "acts of cognition, not transferals of information" (p. 67). Education becomes the practice of freedom rather than domination. Liberatory education is associated with demythologizing and reinventing reality. It supports creativity and transformation rather than the *domestication* of individuals and breaks down the vertical hierarchies associated with banking teaching (Darder, 2002).

Nancy Wallerstein (1987) defined problem posing as "a group process that draws on personal experience to create social connectedness and mutual responsibility" (p. 34). Through dialogue between colearners and coeducators, participants negotiate shared understandings of oppression and develop knowledge and skills for engaging in collective action. Patricia Hinchey (1998) also described problem posing as questioning unconscious, taken-for-granted beliefs or ideas that both teachers and students have "accepted by default because they are blinded by assumption" (p. 136). Colearners become more knowledgeable about themselves and their circumstances through asking self-reflective questions about everyday experience such as: "What do I do, believe, and experience?" "Where do these ideas come from?" "How does who I am (e.g., my privileges, identity, and oppressions) affect my experience?" and "Who gains and who loses because of my behaviors and those of others?" Integrated with problem posing is the use of a dialectical perspective, which involves adopting an opposite point of view to *try out* the dominant worldview and then challenge it (Thousand et al., 1999). These perspectives are applicable to all educational activities, and the knowledge acquired by answering these questions becomes the basis for activism.

Problem-posing education means that "the teacher is no longer merely the one-who-teaches, but one who is himself [sic] taught in dialogue with the students, who in turn while being taught also teach" (Shor, 1987a, p. 67). Although dialogue is highly valued, more hierarchical pedagogical strategies may be used on those limited occasions when the educator has familiarity with knowledge foundations that are needed by students (Grossberg, 1994). Most common to critical pedagogy are (a) dialogic practice, which encourages those who have been silenced to speak for themselves; (b) praxical pedagogy, which emphasizes skill development that prepares individuals to "understand and intervene into their own history" (p. 17); and (c) a pedagogy of articulation and risk, which focuses on making connections or maps between different practices and theories to find methods that work.

Ideally, students and teachers are coparticipants in a shared learning process. According to Ira Shor (1987a), an important goal is the "withering away of the teacher" (p. 98). Although the teacher is an indispensable agent of change at the beginning of the educational process, the teacher eventually becomes expendable. Over time, the educator may play a "mobile complex of roles" (p. 102) including convener, facilitator, advocate, adversary, lecturer, recorder, mediator, and librarian. During initial phases, the teacher is likely to act as a "provocateur of conceptual inquiry" (p. 102). Eventually, however, "the class can set its own agenda by reflecting on its previous session, thus making each phase of its own development grounded in a recognition of its growth so far" (p. 102).

Principle 2: Self-Reflection and Praxis

As students develop critical consciousness, they typically negotiate four stages related to self-reflection: (a) an intransitive stage, at which time individuals have no sense of their capacity to influence the environment; (b) a semi-intransitive stage, at which time students see their sphere of influence as limited to basic survival needs; (c) a naïve transitive phase, at which time persons develop an expanded worldview, but tend to oversimplify problems, be susceptible to slogans, and engage in polemical dialogue rather than authentic dialogue; and (d) a critically transitive phase, at which time individuals examine issues with greater depth and show the ability to reflect on, test, and modify their perspectives (Freire, 1994b; Locke & Faubert, 1999). Self-reflection is an important tool throughout all phases of the learning process. Reflection leads to action, which then leads to further self-reflection that supports further transformation of oneself, one's reality, and institutional systems (Thousand et al., 1999).

An action–reflection–action cycle is supported by a variety of self-reflection activities, challenges of traditional knowledge, and involvement in activism. Tools that facilitate self-reflection and praxis include journals, reflections about readings and experience, and autobiographical writing. Pedagogies that involve the critique of popular culture and the creation of poetry, drama, photography, and art are also important because they stimulate creativity, imagination, vision, and students' abilities to critique traditional reality (Darder, 2002; Morrell, 2002). A recent application is the use of *rap pedagogy*, which allows students to reflect on and enact their multiple identities and roles, explore how they experience contradictions and the means by which they gain or lose power, and consider how their use of standard or nonstandard English influences their relationships in the community (Morrell, 2002; Scherpf, 2001). In general, educators emphasize the value and importance of exploring students' cultures, using varied learning styles and methods and including self-affirmation experiences that build student skills and confidence (Gay, 2000; Lynn, 1999; Wallerstein, 1987).

Gloria Ladson-Billings's (1998) summary of the process and outcomes of critical pedagogies noted that students whose social, cultural, and economic futures "are most tenuous" (p. 299) are supported and encouraged to become leaders. Students are placed in a learning community rather than being taught skills that appear unrelated and out of context, and the day-to-day lives of learners are considered relevant to the curriculum. Finally, students and teachers work collectively against the status quo and develop knowledge of themselves as political actors.

FEMINIST PEDAGOGY

The next section introduces concepts related to feminist pedagogy. We define the role of consciousness-raising and summarize major principles and strategies of feminist pedagogy.

Consciousness-Raising: Foundation for Feminist Pedagogy

Themes that appear in definitions of feminist pedagogy can be organized under the concept of consciousness-raising (CR). Berenice Fisher's (1981) influential definition of feminist pedagogy identified two aspects of consciousness-raising: (a) the nurturing of self-education and self-definition, which includes the examination and critique of dominant theories that marginalize the lives and self-definitions of members of nondominant groups, and (b) applying emotion as well as cognition to the task of understanding experiences of oppression and liberation. The educator and learner use personal information and the experiences of oppressed or stigmatized people to reinterpret and change the world. Fisher (1981) stated, "CR envisions the liberation of the self, or rather, of a part of the self which is denied by the oppressive conditions under which we live" (p. 22). She also identified diversity as central to feminist pedagogy, emphasizing the importance of paying attention to differences among women, especially women of color, lesbians, and working-class women.

In her recent book on feminist pedagogy, consciousness-raising remains a central aspect of Fisher's (2001) more fully elaborated and complex definition of feminist pedagogy and discourse. Consciousness-raising involves increasing one's awareness of "relations between self and the world through sharing experiences, feelings, and ideas about the needs for and possibilities of liberatory actions" (p. 34). Included in this educational process are (a) "a shift in attention" (p. 34) from the typical content of education related to dominant groups to experiences of nondominant groups that have been obscured, marginalized, or erased and (b) a focus on power dynamics in the service of critiquing oppressive practice. This exploration may involve the examination of (a) how women and other oppressed groups are denied status as meaning makers; (b) how dominance is reinforced through male-centered content and language; or (c) how institutions, families, and classrooms often become microcosms of injustice. The learner examines previously unexamined connections, such as how unequal social power may have affected her or his own diminished sense of self, limited her or his options, or exacerbated her or his personal vulnerability or fear.

As consciousness-raising unfolds, the participant becomes more self-reflective as well as mindful of external social limitations. Such self-reflection provides information about personal injustice and privilege and also calls on educators and learners to "suspend and critique our own point of view and to consider other points of view" (Chin & Russo, 1997, p. 104). To appreciate diversity, participants, especially persons who hold greater power in society, need to "value humility, to be aware of our fallibility, and to avoid arrogance or dogmatism about our own biases" (p. 104). The collaborative process supports participants as "political speakers and actors" (Fisher, 2001, p. 39) who acquire a sense of agency that fosters action.

Berenice Fisher's (2001) "rough definition" (p. 44) of feminist pedagogy encompasses five components: (a) cooperative, collective, and continuous activity that highlights students' actions, experiences, cognitions, and emotions; (b) knowledge of and the willingness to challenge or resist unequal power dynamics; (c) the development of social action skills by examining the *personal* concerns of students and clarifying their connections to political meanings; (d) the examination of diverse experiences as they relate to oppression and liberation; and (e) the implementation of an accepting, nonjudgmental stance that both recognizes women's unique experiences while also nurturing the critical thinking that is necessary for responding to "interwoven forms of injustice" (p. 44).

Principles and Strategies of Feminist Pedagogy

Although many of the influential definitions of feminist pedagogy have been proposed by scholars in women's studies and education, feminist psychologists have also contributed to the clarification and elaboration of feminist pedagogical principles. Participants at the 1993 National Conference on Education and Training in Feminist Practice were among the first psychologists to organize principles of feminist pedagogy and a feminist curriculum for psychology (Chin & Russo, 1997; Kimmel & Worell, 1997). Ellen Kimmel (1999) organized these principles into four basic categories. Other authors, including Maurianne Adams (1997) and Linda Forrest and Freda Rosenberg (1997) have used similar structures and descriptions, which we integrate within the four categories used by Kimmel.

Principle 1: Power

This principle emphasizes the importance of rethinking power and authority in the classroom as well as creating communal and democratic learning environments. Feminist educators reject the notion that power involves domination and, instead, define power as a source of energy, potential, and capacity. Feminist pedagogy addresses authority and power as they relate to the content of study as well as the dynamics within the classroom. Thus, students and educators work toward acknowledging and understanding power differences, privilege, and oppression as they are manifested within and outside of the classroom (Schniedewind, 1987a; Shrewsbury, 1987).

A critical feature of pedagogy is the manner in which the educator deals with her or his power. The feminist teacher acknowledges the power inherent in the teaching role but also strives to model egalitarian behaviors and limit power differences. Teachers and students engage in participatory and mutual learning, recognizing that empowerment is often a two-way, shared experience (Adams, 1997; Forrest & Rosenberg, 1997; Kimmel, 1999). This principle also focuses on the power of language, which can be used to define reality in narrow or accessible ways and can either support egalitarian values or exaggerate power differences. Also, the feminist pedagogue seeks to use language that is as clear and as free of jargon as is possible (Kimmel, 1999; Kimmel & Worell, 1997; Rosser, 1998).

Crucial to the modeling of power sharing is the creation of classroom environments that emphasize participatory and interactive learning. The feminist educator emphasizes the importance of building communication skills that facilitate group decision making, cooperative learning, collaboration, and consensus. Feminist educators implement a wide range of strategies to decrease hierarchies and equalize power. Examples of these tools follow.

The use of student-generated discussion questions based on their readings or experiences (Ballard, 1995) can be used to enhance students' roles as experts and active participants. Strategies for equalizing participation (e.g., Disch, 1999; Jenkins, 1990) may include establishing turn-taking norms and practices, defining the educator as facilitator rather than as discussion leader, allowing students to have *think time* before responding, ensuring that the positive aspect of each person's efforts to speak are recognized, and encouraging students to "share culture-specific knowledge without making them spokespersons for the race" (Jenkins, 1990, p. 11). Small-group work and dyadic interactions (S. N. Davis, 1999; Disch, 1999; Freedman, 1990; Schniedewind, 1985) encourage students to share resources and perspectives, develop expertise in collaborating with each other, and practice cooperative learning.

Another set of strategies providing interpersonal skills training and training in feminist process can help students develop skills related to assertiveness, clear and respectful communication, collaboration, and the giving and receiving of feedback (Disch, 1999; Schniedewind, 1987b). This training may also focus on (a) acquiring democratic and shared leadership styles; (b) learning skills related to networking and organizing; and (c) developing skills for increasing trust, building consensus, and resolving conflict. The teacher's expertise is used effectively when students and educators participate in continuous, mutual feedback and teachers take active leadership in helping students articulate what they need and want to know and how to decide whether they have achieved desired outcomes (S. N. Davis, 1999). Including students in the text selection process can also support student empowerment (Sutphin, 1992).

Some of the dilemmas experienced by the educator include dealing with authority, respect, and power-sharing issues that are related to her or his gender or minority statuses. Susan Friedman (1985) argued, "Any kind of authority is [seen as] incompatible with the feminine" (p. 206). Feminist educators who use nontraditional methods may find that their authority and competence is questioned, undermined, or denied by both students and the institution. Women of color and lesbians often face special challenges. Educators of diversity are still few in number, and because of their token status, their behaviors and methods may be scrutinized more carefully than are the practices of White heterosexual educators. These educators serve as direct reminders of those who have been marginalized and may become the targets of students' racist or homophobic attitudes as well as internalized racism and heterosexism. Their authority and credibility may be devalued. When educators from nondominant groups challenge the canon by centralizing materials and texts related to diversity, students may complain that they are being exclusionary, erasing the experiences of White people, or practicing *reverse discrimination* (Brokes & Twine, 1998; Elenes, 2001; Ng, 1995).

Educators' self-disclosure can be an important method for decreasing power differentials, humanizing the classroom, establishing one's authenticity, facilitating the integration of personal and political perspectives, validating diversity and difference, and empowering students. The teacher's self-disclosure reveals her or his unique views and identity, which encourages students to articulate their unique identities and areas of knowledge. As a part of self-disclosure, the educator demonstrates openness and mutuality by sharing personal reactions and evolving but incomplete ideas as well as mistakes (Adams & Emery, 1994; Beck, 1983; Kimmel & Worell, 1997). Self-disclosure, however, needs to be timed carefully to meet the needs of students and the professor. For example, "to disclose or not to disclose" is often a complicated decision for teachers who are lesbian and women of color because of the attitudes or resistances of students as well as the potential impact and consequences of self-disclosure for both educators and their students (Adams & Emery, 1994; Duncombe, 1998; Elenes, 2001; Wright, 1998).

A final method for decreasing the power differential focuses on the evaluation process (Disch, 1999; A. Ferguson, 1982; Schniedewind, 1985). A variety of grading methods can be used: (a) peer accountability and group grading, an evaluation option in which all members of a group contribute to a product and receive a group grade; (b) student and teacher narrative, non-graded descriptions of students' learning; (c) the *contract*, which allows students to choose the number of assignments they will complete and the level of involvement they will maintain to achieve a specific grade; (d) credit–no credit grading options, which may free students to focus primarily on establishing personal learning goals and free them from competitive concerns; (e) shared grading, in which the professor takes responsibility for some components of grading while giving students control over other aspects of the grading process; and (f) mastery learning, which allows students to complete multiple drafts to demonstrate knowledge.

Principle 2: Holistic Learning and Integrating Dichotomies

The principle of holistic learning involves eschewing bipolar categories (e.g., thinking vs. feeling) and integrating cognition, feelings, and personal experiences as well as multiple sources of knowledge in all aspects of learning. Many authors on the topic of feminist pedagogy (e.g., Bauer, 1990; Boler, 1999; Culley, Diamond, Edwards, Lennox, & Portuges, 1985; Currie, 1992; Enns, 1993a; Forrest & Rosenberg, 1997; Gawelek, Mulqueen, & Tarule, 1994; hooks, 1994; Maher, 1987a) have addressed ways in which traditional educational experiences promote dichotomous thinking and overvalue the type of objective, rational, logical analysis that is typically embedded in a competitive academic environment. Thus, feminist educators integrate rational analysis with emotional and personal learning as well as disparate sources of data and experience to make connections between *objective* textbook learning, self-awareness, and personal growth. Students are encouraged to consider their own experiences and those of marginalized groups in light of social–political realities (i.e., the personal is political).

A holistic approach involves supporting the value of students' subjective experiences as well as knowledge based on the study of general systemic issues and interactions among people and groups. Students and teachers value the personal and place it in a larger context; they work toward authoring and validating individual voice and balancing personal experience with a broader understanding of oppression and the voices of diverse groups of people (Chin & Russo, 1997; Forrest & Rosenberg, 1997; Kimmel, 1999; Kimmel & Worell, 1997).

Journals, autobiographical papers, and creative writing and expression (Ballard, 1995; Berry & Black, 1987; Brunner, 1992; Clinchy, 1995; Cottrell, 1999; Grobman, 2001; Stevenson, 1989) facilitate students' reflections about personal learning and feelings in response to content. For example, students may be encouraged to describe their own situations about which a specific text or theoretical analysis is relevant. Creative expression (e.g., artistic and musical work) and the writing of fiction or poetry may also facilitate holistic learning. Role-playing, storytelling, and dramatic enactments encourage learners to take on and experience the views and feelings of another person (Brown & Gillespie, 1997; Crumpacker & Vander Haegen, 1987; Fisher, 1987; King & Buker, 2001). These *experiencing with* activities increase students' empathy for alternative positions and further enhance the connected learning climate. Role-playing may also be used to increase students' confidence for trying out new behaviors. Exposure to first-person accounts, case studies, and audiovisual materials also facilitates holistic learning (Gardner, 1993; Wood, 1993).

The integration of theoretical reading and conceptual frameworks (e.g., on violence, work, and intimacy) with first-person accounts, films, self-help sources, literary sources, and other creative forms of expression humanizes issues such as violence, helps students gain a deeper understanding of the diversity of human experience, and affirms students who are exploring their own experiences of oppression (Cottrell, 1999; S. Davis & Ratigan, 1999; James, 1998). Finally, the structured discussion of competing perspectives (Elliot, 1993; Walsh, 1997) contributes to students' knowledge base, confidence, and ability to challenge sexist, racist, and classist ideas and can be used to help students support ideas with logical analysis and empirical support as well as connect personal learning with logical analysis. To avoid perpetuating dichotomous thinking, educators must use tools to integrate competing perspectives.

Principle 3: Diversity

The third principle of exploring and respecting diversity entails recognizing multiple and intersecting forms of privilege and oppression. Fostering respect includes increasing an appreciation for difference and nurturing open-mindedness and critical thinking about *taken-for-granted* positions. It involves developing knowledge of and sensitivity to a wide array of cultural realities and fosters healthy and productive forms of disagreement and conflict resolution (Chin & Russo, 1997; Forrest & Rosenberg, 1997; Kimmel & Worell, 1997).

Many of the techniques associated with Principles 1 and 2 are applicable to the exploration of diversity and include first-person accounts, movies, skills for respectful self-disclosure and discussion, and face-to-face interaction. Additional strategies are useful for facilitating an appreciation for diversity, such as examining *isms* related to White privilege, racism, heterosexism, classism, and ableism. Through experiential activities, students begin to think more critically about ways in which their unexamined assumptions about culture have influenced their assumptions about *normal* human experience (Bowleg, 1998; Bronstein & Quina, 1988, 2003; Cross, Klein, Smith, & Smith, 1982; Deay & Stitzel, 1998; DeDanaan, 1990; Frankenberg, 1990; Rothenberg, 1998, 2000). By becoming informed about the worldviews and experiences of women of color, lesbians, and women who are living in poverty, students gain appreciation for the perspectives of those whose lives are unlike their own and are less likely to engage in ethnocentric evaluations of women of diversity.

Structured experiential activities may be used to concretely illustrate how structural patterns of discrimination and differential access to resources are perpetuated and magnified over time. Process analysis of classroom dynamics can also be used to illustrate how power dynamics may operate within day-to-day activities (Romney, Tatum, & Jones, 1992; Weiler, 1988). The feminist educator may also structure activities in which individuals are assigned roles that are inconsistent with their social locations in the world and then encourage them to reflect on what they learned from these experiences. Finally, content analysis can be used to increase student appreciation of diversity (Ballard, 1995; Eichstedt, 1996; Rickabaugh, 1998; Riger, 1978). Through content analysis, students assess the frequency with which individuals from a variety of social locations are depicted in objectified, stereotyped, or biased ways. This objective analysis of bias or unfair treatment raises awareness about how individuals with nondominant statuses are portrayed and provides a foundation from which to challenge discriminatory messages.

Principle 4: Social Change

A fourth principle involves connecting ideas to social action, which may include transforming oneself, the learning process, and the larger society. Within the classroom, the reclamation of the histories, *herstories*, and cultures of people who are oppressed is a form of social change. Social change goals are also reflected through efforts to transform disciplines, such as by (a) moving content about persons with nondominant statuses from the margin to the center of the curriculum; (b) transforming teaching, learning, research, and testing methods; (c) dismantling policies that may be harmful to students; and (d) rethinking relationships between students and teachers. Social change also includes helping students translate their personal learning to concrete, tangible action (Adams, 1997; Forrest & Rosenberg, 1997; Kimmel, 1999; Kimmel & Worell, 1997; Stake, Roades, Rose, Ellis, & West, 1994). For example, including field trips to and guest speakers from women's health services, domestic violence shelters, or rape-counseling centers sensitizes students to the perspectives of feminists who work with women's issues (e.g., Eichstedt, 1996) and fosters their enthusiasm for social change. Internships with feminist service organizations also support skill development in community organization, education, and networking.

Involvement in public rallies (e.g., "Take Back the Night" events), social protest, community consciousness-raising efforts, petitions, and letter writing provide excellent opportunities to experience social change (Rose, 1989; Stake et al., 1994). Activism can also be integrated into class projects and papers (Freedman, 1990; Mussey & Kesselman, 1998; S. Rose, 1989; Scanlon, 1993; Schram, 1976) as students address themes such as a rationale for the project, issues encountered during the project, assessments of the short-

TOWARD INTEGRATING CRITICAL, MULTICULTURAL, AND FEMINIST PERSPECTIVES

We now turn to a discussion of the multiple similarities among the multicultural and feminist pedagogies and the ways in which they can inform and enrich each other (Hughes, 1998; Jackson, 1997; Maher, 1987b; Weiler, 1991). We identify similar and converging themes and recent efforts to integrate these perspectives as *borderland* pedagogies.

Similarities Among Critical, Multicultural, and Feminist Pedagogies

The similarities among the liberation pedagogies can be grouped around three themes: the content, the process, and the goals of education. All of the pedagogies discussed in this chapter are based on interdisciplinary scholarship; they weave together a broad range of ideas and perspectives from multiple sources rather than compartmentalizing them in strict disciplinary boundaries (Jackson, 1997). They also challenge traditional definitions of knowledge and point out gaps and distortions of knowledge that require correction as students and educators create models that are relevant to people who are oppressed and hold limited power (Acker, 1994). This rethinking of traditional knowledge includes the examination of hidden values, shrouded meanings, and unspoken but widely accepted norms that support dominant forms of knowledge and structures of education. Each pedagogy places content about diversity at the center of inquiry (Jackson, 1997). This knowledge base focuses not only on explicating oppression and privilege but also on identifying sources of strength of persons from nondominant groups. Content also highlights contributions of persons whose work has often been ignored or obscured.

In addition to transformed content, a common characteristic of both feminist and multicultural pedagogies is an emphasis on the process of building new forms of awareness and ways of seeing the world. Contributors to feminist pedagogy often refer to this experience as consciousness-raising, and contributors to liberatory pedagogy tend to use the term conscientization or critical consciousness. Educators and learners work toward developing shared awareness, knowledge, and a commitment to challenging oppression (Hughes, 1998; Jackson, 1997). As tools for building new lenses of perception, these radical pedagogies emphasize the importance of dialogue and experiential learning so learners become theorists about their own lives (Weiler, 1991). Members of oppressed groups are encouraged to "name, describe, and then analyze salient features of their world as they experience it" (Maher, 1987b, p. 93). The validation of personal experience, overcoming silence, and "coming to voice" are central to this process. Attentiveness to the power of language is also crucial to changing the dynamics of education.

These pedagogies view the imposition of the colonizer's or masculine language as a tool of domination (Darder, 2002). In contrast, nonoppressive and egalitarian uses of language define experience in ways that reflect the perceptions of people whose reality has been discounted (Jackson, 1997). Honoring a person's original language is also important because one's first language often structures a person's experience, represents the means by which a person comes to know the world, and gives special meaning to her or his cultural realities (Darder, 2002; Freire, 1985).

Related to pedagogical process is a new type of relationship between teachers and students that emphasizes two-way and mutual communication, the coconstruction of knowledge, and the dismantling of traditional boundaries between educators and learners. Recent contributors to feminist pedagogy have been especially attentive to authority within the classroom, have sought to limit power differences between educators and students, and have attended to power issues that may affect interactions among students (Fisher, 2001; Jackson, 1997; Kaufmann, 2000; Kimmel & Worell, 1997; Weiler, 1991). Facilitating the learning of all students, and especially those who have been ignored or marginalized in traditional classrooms, is essential.

These pedagogies also seek to alter the goals of education. Critical and feminist pedagogies view education as a political act and view empowerment and social activism as important outcomes of education (Jackson, 1997). They emphasize group empowerment and structural change rather than individual change alone. Authors who contribute to these literatures provide visions of a better world that is associated with improved personal and societal circumstances, and they use a language of possibilities to convey these goals. These approaches also share an understanding that there is an inseparable, synergistic, and cyclical relationship between self-reflection and action.

Within both the feminist and the critical, multicultural literatures, authors speak about the complex relationship between theory and teaching strategies, and each of the perspectives speaks to the importance of making appropriate connections between theory and practice. Social justice educators agree that the use of strategies without a coherent framework can promote a *tourist* or an *add and stir* approach to diversity. For example, Paulo Freire expressed concern that the social vision of liberatory pedagogy not be reduced to a methodology of teaching, which he believed might strip it of its revolutionary ideas (Darder, 2002; Freire, 1998b).

Unique and Converging Themes Among Critical, Multicultural, and Feminist Pedagogies

The multicultural and feminist literatures share an attentiveness to dynamics of power and privilege, with the feminist pedagogy literature tending to foreground power issues related to gender and the critical and multicultural literatures tending to foreground issues related to class, ethnicity, or race (Tisdell, 1998). Early versions of critical theory paid limited attention to the problems of patriarchy and male White privilege, and Paulo Freire has been criticized for his use of the male referent in much of his writing (hooks, 1994; Jackson, 1997; McLaren, 2000a, 2000b; Weiler, 1991). In contrast, second-wave feminists have been criticized for their limited attention to the impact of race, ethnicity, and class on the lives of women (e.g., Anzaldúa, 1990). Increasingly, however, both of these literatures emphasize the intersections of gender, class, race, and other social identities.

Although personal perspectives are considered an important source of knowledge in each of the liberation pedagogies, there is some variation regarding the aspects of personal experience that are emphasized. The critical pedagogies (e.g., Freire, 1970) have tended to underline the cognitive and rational analysis of personal experience as it is reflected in the public spheres of work and politics (Ellsworth, 1989; Kaufmann, 2000; Luke & Gore, 1992; Maher, 1987b; Tisdell, 1998), whereas the feminist pedagogy literature has highlighted the relevance of more private and affective aspects of personal experience, such as intimacy and emotion, as well as issues of intimate violence and unpaid family work. Increasingly evident in both literatures is the recognition that public and private as well as cognitive and emotional aspects of personal experience and knowledge are relevant to a complete and holistic understanding of the connections between personal and political meanings (Ellsworth, 1989; Kaufmann, 2000).

Conceptualizations of oppression and privilege are complicated and have evolved over time. Although some of the radical education theories have been criticized for adopting a dualistic approach to the dynamics that occur between oppressors and oppressed (Jackson, 1997; Maher, 1999; Weiler, 1991), more recent perspectives in both the multicultural and critical literatures and the feminist literatures have pointed to the complex dynamics of oppression and privilege that vary across contexts (Chin & Russo, 1997; Kanpol & McLaren, 1995; Kimmel & Worell, 1997; Ng, 1995; Sleeter, 1996). Kathleen Weiler (1991) noted "the possibility of simultaneous contradictory positions of oppression and dominance" (p. 453). Thus, White women may oppress women of color while simultaneously experiencing oppression in relationships with men. Likewise, men of color who experience oppression due to economic exploitation and racism may oppress women of color. A "situated theory of oppression" (p. 455) that considers the impact of a person's multiple social identities on her or his experiences of empowerment, privilege, and discrimination is now becoming central to both multicultural and feminist pedagogies.

A common conundrum for feminist and multicultural, feminist educators is how power can be used and shared most effectively. The feminist pedagogy literature has placed significant emphasis on limiting power differentials between students and teachers, managing conflict between students within the classroom, and dealing with resistance and anger on the part of students (Jackson, 1997). A particularly complex issue, however, involves encouraging egalitarianism in the classroom while also acknowledging the power that teachers have over students (Kimmel & Worell, 1997). Paulo Freire, who has been a highly influential critical pedagogy theorist, viewed the educator as transparent, being on the side of the students and encouraging dialogue and interaction. However, he saw the sharing of power with students as less important than the dialogue process and called on educators to use their power in the service of freedom (Darder, 2002). Although critical of banking education that focused only on transferring knowledge, Freire saw directive approaches as acceptable when they helped challenge meanings and reinvent new knowledge (Darder, 2002). He stated, "I have to convince students of my dreams but not conquer them for my own plans" (Shor & Freire, 1987, p. 157).

Meanwhile, Elizabeth Ellsworth (1989) argued that even those who teach for liberation must be cautious about implying that the educator's knowledge and understanding of issues is superior to that of students. She argued that all perspectives need to be seen as "partial, multiple, and contradictory" (p. 312) and as reflecting teachers' and students' "socially constructed positions of privilege . . . [and] subordination" (p. 313). For example, there are occasions when students may know more about the topic of study than the educator, such as when the topic is racism, the educator is White, and the student is a person of color.

Roxana Ng (1995) also noted that the classroom "confers privilege to those members who are from the dominant group" (p. 144), a principle that applies to both students and educators. Individuals bring more or less privilege to the classroom on the basis of their social position in society, which means that tensions among students as well as between students and teachers are common. The race, class, gender, sexual orientation, or minority identity status of the educator may also influence her or his authority in the educational setting as well as how her or his expertise is perceived (Ellsworth, 1989; McLaren, 2000b; Weiler, 1991). As a result, both the critical or multicultural and the feminist pedagogy literatures are increasingly exploring the dynamics of teaching as they relate to the social and power locations of both students and educators.

Borderland Pedagogies as Tools for Integration

Some integration of feminist and critical perspectives has already occurred, as can be seen by the influence of critical theory on the pedagogical practices of some feminist educators (e.g., hooks, 1994; Luke & Gore, 1992; Weiler, 1991). The convergence of perspectives is also found in models that are referred to by terms such as *situated pedagogy* (Grace & Gouthro, 2000; Weiler, 1991) or *pedagogies of positionality* (Grace & Gouthro, 2000; Maher, 1999; Maher & Tetreault, 2001; Tisdell, 1995, 1998). Situated pedagogy "emphasizes the specificities of experience of people living in the intersections of relationships of power where they can be variously privileged or subjugated"

(Grace & Gouthro, 2000, p. 23). The goal of situated pedagogy is to explore the strengths and struggles of individuals as they exist at intersections of the various social locations they inhabit.

Elizabeth Tisdell (1995) used similar language to define positional pedagogy, which involves recognizing that "both the self and others are situated and positioned within social structures in which they are multiply and simultaneously privileged and oppressed" (p. 74). The goal of positional pedagogy is to examine how the positioning of individuals and the power relationships in which they participate inform their knowledge base and experience and how social and political forces affect this process. Another author, Vanessa Sheared (1994), spoke of the "polyrhythmic realities" of educators and their students. At any time, all participants in the educational process have various responsibilities associated with their roles as beings of a certain race and gender and in their roles as workers, students, and teachers. These positions have an impact on how learning activity is experienced and how knowledge is constructed. Central to this process is the discussion of how power relations influence the outside world as well as the world of the classroom.

Frances Maher (1999) argued that the complex identities individuals bring to the classroom (e.g., learning style, cultural background, class, religion, sexual orientation, age, race, and gender) should not be viewed as fixed identities that need to be bridged or transcended. Identity statuses shift across contexts, and the intersections of these differences become the major focus of attention in the classroom as students and teachers seek to create complex yet incomplete or partial models of oppression, reality, and empowerment. The goal, then, of a multicultural feminist pedagogy is to explore the intersections, borders, and boundaries among identities.

During the past decade, an increasing number of authors have described their educational practices with phrases such as "border pedagogy" (Giroux, 1992; Scherpf, 2001), "border crossings" (Humm, 1991), "crossing borders" (Tisdell, 1998), "between borders" (Giroux & McLaren, 1994), "teaching at the crossroads" (Grobman, 2001), and "border/transformative pedagogy" (Elenes, 2001). Elizabeth Sparks and Aileen Park (2000) also suggested that integrating feminist and multicultural perspectives requires working at and highlighting the borderlands that exist at the multiple intersections where feminism and multiculturalism meet. As is the case with many borderlands, boundaries are sometimes unclear, messy, ambiguous, and contested. Thus, exploring intersections and borders requires that we live with perspectives on diversity that are useful, yet partial. Jennifer Obidah (2000) identified her primary pedagogical role as that of a border guide who helps students to acquire necessary skills to negotiate unfamiliar territory and consider their life experiences in light of class readings and discussions.

One possibility for implementing border pedagogies that integrates multicultural and feminist pedagogies is to emphasize content and experiences that are by, about, and for women from diverse and nondominant social locations and people of color who are sexual minorities. For example, Johnnella Butler (2000) proposed, "When we study women of color, we raise our awareness and understanding of the experiences of all women either implicitly or directly" (p. 177). The scholarship of women of color is placed at the center of inquiry, which transforms the nature of knowledge acquisition and production and decenters the lives of privileged persons. An important approach to "understanding the oppressor is to study the oppressed" (p. 177).

To understand the lives of women of color and of people of color who are sexual minorities, one needs to explore their relationships with privileged persons, and this examination provides a rich perspective on the complexities of gender, race, and other social identities. By placing women of color or people of color who are sexual minorities at the center of inquiry, educators and their students highlight the multiplicity of perspectives that individuals hold. There is no need for "a neutral or dominant center" (Butler, p. 183), which often becomes the case (usually inadvertently) when the lives of White people are the focus of attention. Finally, class, gender, race, sexual orientation, and other aspects of social identity are seen as aspects of complex lives and realities. Race, gender, class, ethnicity, or sexual orientation are relinquished as primary definers of reality, but instead, become aspects of complex realities.

SUMMARY OF INTEGRATIVE CONCEPTS AND CONCLUSIONS

We conclude by summarizing important integrative concepts arising from both the multicultural and the feminist pedagogies. Multicultural feminist pedagogies include (a) an emphasis on holistic learning based on conscientization and consciousness-raising and designed to build connections between personal experience and social structural issues as well as emotional and cognitive learning; (b) a reliance on egalitarian methods that include self-reflection, dialogue, the coconstruction of knowledge, and participatory methods of learning; and (c) an intentional effort to address, redistribute, and equalize dynamics of power and privilege as they influence individuals and groups, the dynamics of classroom interaction, the structure and content of knowledge, and educational and other institutional structures.

Concepts associated with border pedagogies are especially relevant to the flexible integration of multicultural and feminist principles. Multicultural feminist pedagogy needs to be based on the assumption that all students and educators bring multiple and dynamic social identities (e.g., race, gender, ethnicity, sexual orientation, age, disability, class, and nationality) to the classroom and that these multiple dynamic identities are associated with varying levels of oppression and privilege that vary in salience over time and across contexts. Conceptualizing and negotiating the complex intersections, borders, and boundaries of these identities are central concerns to multicultural feminist pedagogy and are relevant to educator–student relationships, classroom dynamics, and social relationships beyond the classroom. Educators and students should not feel compelled to choose one identity over others or to claim a *feminist* or *multicultural* identity. Instead, their efforts to occupy multiple places, to explore contradictions and ambiguities within and between perspectives and identities, and to explore flexible ways of integrating or foregrounding various aspects of their identities are facilitated by integrated multicultural feminist approaches (Bernal, 1998). Educators and learners learn to practice "differential consciousness," which allows persons to "privilege or de-emphasize different aspects of themselves in different situations" (Moya, 2001, p. 461). We believe that it is important to emphasize classroom content and processes that consistently heighten awareness of perspectives by and for persons with diverse social identities and locations to encourage integrative and flexible awareness; to support the consistent exploration of multiple identities, intersections, and borders; and to ensure that marginalized perspectives are centralized.

Finally, multicultural feminist pedagogies are built on the assumption that knowledge is socially constructed and shaped by life experience, sociodemographic variables and social locations, access to power, cultural values, language, social contexts, and historical and global perspectives. As a result, any one perspective is partial and limited by specific contexts or circumstances. Multicultural feminist educators are border guides who assist learners as they explore intersections among these variables and help students explore dynamic social identities or positionalities that influence their knowledge and understandings. Developing an understanding of intersections furnishes the sturdy foundation necessary for building social change alliances among and between groups.

RECOMMENDED READING

Cohee, G. E., Däumer, E., Kemp, T. D., Krebs, P. M., Lafky, S., & Runzo, S. (Eds.). (1998). *The feminist teacher anthology: Pedagogies and classroom strategies*. New York: Teachers College Press.

Darder, A. (2002). *Reinventing Paulo Freire: A pedagogy of love*. Boulder, CO: Westview Press.

Darder, A., Baltodano, M., & Torres, R. D. (Eds.). (2003). *The critical pedagogy reader*. New York: Routledge.

Davis, S. N., Crawford, M., & Sebrechts, J. (Eds.). (1999). *Coming into her own: Educational success in girls and women*. San Francisco: Jossey-Bass.

Fisher, B. M. (2001). *No angel in the classroom: Teaching through feminist discourse*. Lanham, MD: Rowman & Littlefield.

Forrest, L., & Rosenberg, F. (1997). A review of the feminist pedagogy literature: The neglected child of feminist pedagogy. *Applied and Preventive Psychology, 6,* 179–192.

Freire, P. (1993). *Pedagogy of the oppressed.* (Rev. 20th anniv. ed., M. B. Ramos, Trans.). New York: Continuum.

hooks, b. (1994). *Teaching to transgress: Education as the practice of freedom.* New York: Routledge.

hooks, b. (2003). *Teaching community: A pedagogy of hope.* New York: Routledge.

2

SECOND-WAVE FEMINISMS AND THEIR RELATIONSHIPS TO PEDAGOGY

CAROLYN ZERBE ENNS AND ADA L. SINACORE

At the most basic level, feminist pedagogy involves the "infusion of feminist values into the process and methods of teaching" (Forrest & Rosenberg, 1997, p. 180). Beyond this basic area of agreement, authors who write about feminist pedagogy interpret the principles and practices of feminist pedagogy through a variety of lenses. In chapters 2 and 3, we summarize the ways in which the many feminist theoretical frameworks influence how educators may define and interpret pedagogical goals, articulate and fulfill their roles as educators, choose course content, create optimal learning environments, and clarify desired outcomes. This chapter provides brief overviews of four second-wave feminisms: liberal feminism, cultural feminism, radical feminism, and socialist feminism (see Table 2.1). These perspectives informed many of the early statements about feminist pedagogy that were written during the 1970s and 1980s.

Although the feminisms that highlight diversity among women are most relevant to educational practice that is multicultural and feminist, the second-wave feminisms provided basic foundations for feminist social justice and equity pedagogies. Knowledge of these feminisms helps educators articulate enduring values and constructs, identify blank spots not addressed by

TABLE 2.1
Second-Wave Feminisms and Pedagogy

Dimension of theory	Liberal feminism	Cultural feminism	Radical feminism	Socialist feminism
Causes of oppression	Gender role conditioning and irrational prejudice	Devaluation of women's ways of knowing and connection, overvaluation of masculine values	Patriarchy and male control over women's bodies	Multiple oppressions based on class, race, and gender and embedded in institutional structures
Tools for change and learning	Educational reform, gender-neutral policies, affirmative action, gender role flexibility	Support for unique learning and relational strengths of women	The personal is political, social activism, challenge all forms of violence against women	Transform institutional structures that reinforce classism, racism, and sexism
Pedagogy	Cooperative learning, increase skills and self-esteem, gender-fair teaching, support student success in nontraditional areas of study	Learning through connection and relationships, *midwife* teaching	Consciousness-raising, linking learning to social change, integration of affective and cognitive learning	Consciousness-raising, examining hidden assumptions, challenging educational and social structures that reproduce inequality

second-wave theories, and clarify roadmaps for creating more comprehensive and inclusive feminist and multicultural theories. In chapter 3, we focus on the diversity feminisms, which build on and transcend some of the limitations and omissions of these early models.

LIBERAL FEMINIST THEORY AND FEMINIST PEDAGOGY

Liberal feminism has its roots in liberal enlightenment thought, rationalism, and natural rights philosophies. Liberal feminists have historically promoted the ideals of human rationality, the importance of critical thinking, and the conviction that men and women share the same inherent rights and capacity to make productive individual choices. The ideals of individual dignity, autonomy, equality, and right to seek self-fulfillment are central to liberal feminist analyses. Oppression is viewed as the consequence of rigid or inflexible gender role conditioning as well as irrational beliefs that women are less capable than men. The solutions to these problems are achieved through engaging in rational argument; overcoming traditional gender role injunctions that have limited individual achievement; and enacting institutional, legal, and legislative reforms and gender neutral policies designed to ensure that all individuals have access to equal opportunities to exercise their free choice and skills (Berkeley, 1999; Donovan, 2000; Freedman, 2002; Tong, 1998; Whelehan, 1995). Liberal feminists have focused primarily on reforming existing systems and institutions, and in general, have not challenged the basic structures of these institutions.

A major goal of liberal feminist pedagogy is to help women gain access to educational resources that have been denied to women because of prejudiced attitudes and institutional structures that limit women's achievement and to help women overcome socialization experiences that have limited their aspirations (Acker, 1994). Liberal feminists view education as "an instrument for gaining power" (Fisher, 1981, p. 20). This power is achieved when individual women are provided with opportunities and support to achieve at levels consistent with their abilities.

The elimination of discriminatory practices that result in unequal opportunity is of central importance to liberal feminist pedagogy. Consistent with a liberal feminist approach is the American Association of University Women's (AAUW) 1992 report (Franzosa, 1993) regarding how education shortchanges girls. The report described how girls are overlooked, experience discrimination because women's contributions are excluded from the curriculum, encounter testing bias, experience competitive classroom formats that diminish self-esteem and achievement goals, and receive less attention from teachers than their male peers. The report recommended strategies for humanizing the classroom environment by (a) emphasizing more cooperative learning, (b) strengthening the power of Title IX, (c) including more experiences of women in curriculum materials, (d) encouraging women to value math and science education, (e) incorporating testing procedures that are gender fair, and (f) increasing girls' skills for achieving success in education.

Although many women may not have encountered overtly sexist attitudes, they often encounter a null academic environment (Betz, 1989, 2002; Freeman, 1979), which is characterized by the absence of support rather than opposition to women's advancement. This environment, combined with socialization experiences that limit women's aspirations, decreases women's likelihood of realizing their full educational potential. As a result, the liberal feminist educator seeks to create a classroom environment in which students are encouraged to become familiar with the full range of their skills and opportunities. For example, the liberal feminist educator may be especially attentive to the fact that women are underrepresented in classrooms and professions that focus on mathematical and scientific domains and may attempt to raise consciousness about possibilities for success in these domains.

The feminist classroom also becomes a location where students clarify and understand the socialization experiences faced by men and women. When students explore their gender role socialization, they experience increased awareness about the ways in which their individual aspirations may be limited by low confidence, low self-esteem, math anxiety, the fear of success, or the *imposter syndrome*. Once aware of these problems, students are able to challenge and transcend these difficulties.

Coeducational learning environments are likely to be most attractive to the liberal feminist teacher because they replicate the real world in which women and men interact. If women develop confidence to speak and achieve in this environment, they are likely to be successful in other endeavors. Liberal feminists tend to believe that separate educational experiences for women and men may result in access to inferior facilities and resources and the *ghettoization* of women's intellectual endeavors (Fisher, 1981).

The activities of the liberal feminist teacher include serving as a role model, providing encouragement to students, and teaching the skills necessary to achieve personal goals. Rather than challenging the validity of traditional teaching practices, the educator attempts to reform these practices, decrease occasions when students are forced to compete with each other, and incorporate teaching strategies that enhance cooperation. The feminist teacher also engages in periodic self-reflection to increase awareness of subtle biases that she or he may impose on students and makes efforts to apply authority equitably and evaluate student work fairly. A major goal is to ensure that each class member has equal access to the teacher's expertise and resources and equal opportunity to participate in classroom interaction.

What type of content in psychology is likely to support the educational goals of liberal feminist education? Given the liberal feminist belief that differences between men and women are minimal, exposure to the research in gender similarities and differences is important, especially meta-analyses of this research that reveal that many gender differences are minimal (Crowley-Long, 1998; Hyde, 1990, 1994). Furthermore, the educator may expose students to research studies and perspectives that reveal how differential training and access to resources can account for the few gender differences that emerge consistently. For example, the discussion of studies of how men and women are treated from cradle to grave (see Crawford & Unger, 2004; Matlin, 2004, for reviews) supports students' increasing awareness of how they may have been treated differently as well as their growing knowledge that they are capable of achieving at levels they have not realized in the past. Research on the benefits of gender role flexibility and the way in which gender role conflict creates obstacles for both men and women also supports these goals.

Liberal feminism has not challenged existing academic methodologies and assumptions but has been concerned about eliminating biases in how they are applied or practiced. Thus, helping students develop the skills of critical thinking and rational analysis are important goals. Research conducted in accordance with nonsexist research methods (Denmark, Russo, Frieze, & Sechzer, 1988; McHugh, Koeske, & Frieze, 1986) and "feminist empiricism" (Harding, 1986) is especially consistent with liberal feminism. Feminist empiricism challenges the incomplete way in which scientific inquiry is conducted and attempts to eliminate sexism by adhering more strictly to rules of good research design and the scientific method. Objective, scientific inquiry is used to challenge knowledge that is based on biased assumptions, questions, or interpretations.

In summary, liberal feminist educators are likely to emphasize the importance of developing critical thinking tools that allow students to achieve their educational and career goals. They also attempt to reform educational practices by identifying ways that teachers and institutions can implement gender neutral and gender fair practices that ensure women's access to intellectual stimulation and achievement (Acker, 1994). Kathleen Crowley-Long (1998) proposed that the psychology of women is dominated by a liberal feminist framework, perhaps because this perspective is most compatible with the structures of most academic disciplines.

CULTURAL FEMINISM AND FEMINIST PEDAGOGY

In contrast to liberal feminists who emphasize rational analysis and contend that women and men are essentially alike, cultural feminists highlight the special, unique qualities of women and the importance of intuitive, nonrational aspects of human experience. Cultural feminists have envisioned social transformation that calls for the infusion of feminine or maternal values into society; the promotion of relatedness and connectedness among humans; and an appreciation of altruistic, cooperative, nonviolent values that support harmony and peace. Cultural feminist goals are consistent with social reforms that focus on revaluing communal roles and relationally based ethics (Donovan, 2000; Freedman, 2002; Tong, 1998; Whelehan, 1995).

In general, feminist educators who are influenced by cultural feminism are likely to highlight the value of communal learning that helps women clarify how they experience personal and intellectual growth in the context of relationships. The goal of cultural feminist teaching is to empower women to understand themselves as knowers and creators, not just as receivers of information. A major assumption of cultural feminism is that women often feel silenced, paralyzed, or deficient through their exposure to traditional or *separate* ways of knowing (Clinchy, 1995). Women are empowered to speak when they learn within a connected framework that is built on relationship values and designed to help students see themselves as capable of constructing knowledge (Belenky, Clinchy, Goldberg, & Tarule, 1986; Clinchy, 1995).

Women's lives and women's ways of knowing are placed at the center of inquiry.

The primary goal of the feminist teacher is not to transmit knowledge, but to help the learner discover what she already knows as someone who has been involved in the "naturalistic study of the social world" since childhood (Clinchy, 1995, p. 103) and to empower her by creating an environment in which she can tap her strengths as well as claim and elaborate on her inner personal knowledge. Affirmation of the learner's strengths is important at the beginning of the educational experience because it increases the connected knower's confidence and motivates her to take risks because she is free of the "tyranny of expectation" (Belenky et al., 1986, p. 205). Blythe Clinchy (1995) also contrasts "real questions" with "teacher type" questions, noting that students often hear teachers' questions as challenges to the validity of their views rather than as a genuine "quest for understanding" (p. 101). Real questions arise from students' experiences and encourage students to elaborate and develop support for their perspectives. Although cultural feminists emphasize the relevance of connected knowing for women, these principles are relevant to all learners who have felt disempowered by traditional learning methods.

Mary Belenky et al. (1986) labeled the role of the feminist teacher as that of a midwife, who facilitates the expression and clarification of knowledge, rather than that of a banker, who imparts knowledge as deposits of information that the learner absorbs. Other cultural feminists describe the teaching role as one in which maternal, nurturing skills become the foundation for helping students claim their personal knowledge (Culley, Diamond, Edwards, Lennox, & Portuges, 1985; Grumet, 1988; Jipson, 1995b; Noddings, 1984; Ruddick, 1989). Nel Noddings depicted the teacher as a responsive and receptive person who values the feelings and reactions of each person and cares "completely and non-selectively" (1984, p. 176).

In contrast to liberal feminist perspectives that rely primarily on helping individuals achieve by applying rational, objective strategies, the cultural feminist teacher challenges the androcentric culture's message that to succeed, individuals must "learn to think like a man" (Goldberger, 1997, p. 256). The cultural feminist educator assists learners in revaluing forms of knowing that been devalued in an androcentric world and applying these affiliation skills to further their knowledge and competence. According to Clinchy (1989), although separate knowing and most educational systems train persons to take nothing at face value, relational learners take everything at face value. Rather than attempting to immediately evaluate and critique what she is learning, the connected learner forms a relationship with ideas and attempts to empathize with and understand these ideas as understood by the person conveying ideas. Instead of looking for flaws, the connected knower looks first for aspects of a person's views that make sense. The learner emphasizes *thinking with* and believing rather than *thinking against* and doubting (Clinchy, 1995; Goldberger, 1997). Nancy Goldberger (1997) noted that "the heart of connected knowing is active imagination, that is, figuratively climbing into the head of another. In connected knowing, objectivity is achieved by entering the perspective of the other and by reasoning along with the other" (p. 255). In contrast to traditional forms of learning, this form of thinking is often highly personal and calls on the individual to value her emotional reactions. Clinchy (1989) stated, "Connected knowers are not dispassionate, unbiased observers. They deliberately bias themselves in favor of the thing they are examining. They try to get right inside it, to form an intimate attachment to it" (p. 651).

The cultural feminist teacher implements teaching strategies that affirm and revalue the centrality of connected experiences. The cultural feminist educator does not reject the value of separate knowing and assumes that once learners have developed basic self-confidence, it is beneficial for learners to integrate the strengths of separate and connected knowing (Belenky et al., 1986). Once trust is established, participants in a connected learning environment are free to engage in a wide range of learning roles including listening, affirming, challenging, and disagreeing with each other. Within the supportive feminist classroom, the learner is able to adopt an ethic of knowing that integrates the truth of subjective and connected knowledge with objective and rational reason (Belenky et al., 1986; Goldberger, 1997).

Given the assumption that men and women may learn in different ways, some cultural feminist teachers may prefer teaching single-sex classes in which all students are women. Within a supportive, connected environment, women and girls may build on their inherent strengths as learners and place women's lives at the center of inquiry. Within coeducational environments, women may feel silenced by the separate voices of male knowers, whose greater tendency to criticize and challenge ideas may limit women students' willingness to articulate their ideas. However, the cultural feminist teacher may also enjoy working within the mixed-gender classroom. In this context, the teacher can observe and comment on the gendered communication and thinking patterns of students and can use these spontaneous expressions to illustrate the different goals of connected and separate communication, help men and women honor and respect differences, and assist them with building skills for talking across gender boundaries (Wood, 1993).

In addition to supporting relational knowing, feminist teachers may place priority on conveying theories regarding women's relational morality, ethics, and identity. These works include writings about women's unique moral voice (Gilligan, 1982), relational–cultural models of identity (Miller & Stiver, 1997), the different languages of men and women (Tannen, 1990, 1997), women's maternal, relational caring and thinking (Noddings, 1984; Ruddick, 1989), feminist peace perspectives (Forcey & Swerdlow, 1995), and women's relational self and psychological distress (Jack, 1991). Readings in feminist identity, spirituality, and mythology that have been inspired by

Jungian archetypal psychology present additional perspectives about women's connected strengths that are consistent with cultural feminist views (Enns, 1994).

Cultural feminist teachers are likely to rely on feminist standpoint epistemologies to inform their teaching. Standpoint epistemologies assume that because of their outsider status in patriarchal society, women are more capable than privileged men of identifying the harmful nonconscious and androcentric aspects of theory and culture. Given the reality that traditional methods of inquiry have been based entirely on separate, objective knowing, many cultural feminists view empirical methods as inadequate for providing a comprehensive perspective on women's experience. Feminist standpoint researchers reject the notion that inquiry can be value free and objective, place women and other marginalized groups at the center of inquiry, attempt to erase the boundaries between researchers and the persons who are studied, and make efforts to understand participants' experiences on their own terms (Harding, 1986).

RADICAL FEMINISM AND FEMINIST PEDAGOGY

Radical feminists believe that social transformation can only be accomplished through social activism and the dramatic alteration of cultural values. Initial forms of radical feminism, which were born during the *new* feminist movement of the 1960s, identified women's oppression as the most fundamental and pervasive form of oppression and articulated how patriarchal power and control over women's bodies have dominated every area of life including paid employment, housework, love and intimate partnerships, violence, childbearing, and child rearing. To enact social change, radical feminists have sought to uncover, illuminate, and question the ways in which they believe patriarchy dominates virtually all aspects of human experience at both conscious and nonconscious levels (e.g., thinking patterns, social relationships, dress and physical appearance, and work). Given the ubiquitous nature of patriarchal values, radical feminists view the reformation of social institutions (liberal feminism) and the revaluing of traditional *feminine* strengths (cultural feminism) as inadequate methods for altering society at its roots. According to a radical perspective, constructs such as masculinity and femininity should be abolished and new, nongendered categories for organizing personal and social life should be formulated and adopted (Donovan, 2000; Tong, 1998).

Similar to cultural feminists, many radical feminists believe that women hold special strengths for reconstructing a world in which oppression will disappear. In contrast to cultural feminist views, however, it is women's experiences as oppressed beings within patriarchy and not necessarily their relational characteristics that provide the basis for women's more complete knowledge. References to feminine or masculine qualities are seen as perpetuating traditional gendered categories and contributing to polarized and distorted perceptions of gender. Collective social action is an essential vehicle for achieving radical feminism's goal of transforming gender rules and the culture (Donovan, 2000; Tong, 1998; Whelehan, 1995).

Given the difficulty of achieving a transformed social order within current structures, radical feminists have sometimes advocated the creation of separatist communities or organizations in which new values can be clarified within egalitarian experimental environments. Within these environments, women's energies can be directed toward making creative contributions to new forms of religion, art, poetry, science, and literature, rather than being diverted into fighting the inevitable and insidious tentacles of patriarchal values.

The radical feminist educator brings a radical critique to the teaching–learning environment and designs methods to disrupt the ways in which patriarchal values infuse classroom dynamics, educational content, and the outcomes of education. A variety of works on feminist pedagogy underline these goals, as reflected by article titles that include the following phrases: "feminist pedagogy as a subversive activity" (Bezucha, 1985, p. 81), "interrupting patriarchy" (Lewis, 1990, p. 467), and "keeping our activist selves alive in the classroom" (Scanlon, 1993, p. 8). Major goals of radical feminist pedagogy emphasize raising consciousness about the pervasive nature of patriarchy and male domination and helping students become "agents of social change" (A. Ferguson, 1982, p. 28).

The major goal of radical feminist education is to create a transformed world free of patriarchal domination and violence. Within the feminist classroom, educators and learners focus on how women's contributions have been devalued and how male dominance is reproduced. The act of naming oppression involves overcoming silence and is seen as empowering in and of itself (Romney et al., 1992). Knowledge of oppressive dynamics provides students with new understandings for combating these dynamics in significant interpersonal relationships within the classroom, within institutions, and in the culture at large.

The assumption that "the personal is political" is of great importance to radical feminist educators. The consciousness-raising group or classroom experience is a context in which women explore their experiences, develop theories about women's lives, and propose methods of enacting social change on behalf of all women. Given the centrality of group process to increasing awareness and transforming society, the development of feminist group process skills is central to radical feminist learning, as is using these skills to implement social change (Schniedewind, 1987b).

Radical feminists may prefer teaching women-only classes to ensure that patterns of male dominance are not replicated within the learning environment. For the radical feminist educator, the classroom environment is as nonhierarchical as possible, places women and girls at the center of inquiry, and emphasizes the importance of participation and dialogue in preparation for resistance and action. Magda Lewis (1990) noted that women often learn to express their own interests within the "parameters of patriarchic meaning-making" (p. 474). This tendency may be especially pronounced in mixed-gender classes. For example, women may inadvertently play *woman-as-caretaker* roles when they show concern for male students' feelings during discussions of male violence against women or when women's concerns and perspectives are placed at the center of inquiry. From a radical feminist perspective, the classroom is a laboratory in which students and teachers gain increased awareness about how they may be nonconsciously influenced by dominant, patriarchal ways of thinking.

The radical feminist classroom is a transformed classroom. The radical feminist teacher is cognizant that throughout history, the classroom has been dominated by men and the manner in which most men have defined learning. Patriarchal models of thinking are seen as contributing to a world in which dichotomous thinking is pervasive. Thinking is seen as the opposite of feeling. Masculine is contrasted with feminine. Objectivity is considered the opposite of subjectivity. Rationality is contrasted with irrationality (Boler, 1999; Culley et al., 1985). Teachers and learners work toward transcending these dichotomies by validating emotion and subjective perspectives as important components of learning. The goal of such activity is not to categorize emotion and subjectivity as women's modes of thinking but to integrate these processes and heal the fragmentation that occurs when the worlds of men and women are understood in polarized ways (Boler, 1999; Culley et al., 1985).

For the radical feminist educator, the freedom to express emotion gives women permission to name fears and reveal secrets, secrets that may be related to violence, abuse, or experiences of oppression or subordination. By naming their realities, learners validate their personal realities and are free to respond to oppression and injustice in new and empowered ways. In addition to providing more complete information about experience, emotions such as anger can nurture new awareness and insights, which can then be directed toward productive activity that challenges injustice. Margo Culley (1985) proposed that "anger is the energy mediating the transformation from damage to wholeness" (p. 212). Anger facilitates "the transition from passivity to action" (p. 216). The study of theory is important; however, theory is tested against subjective experience, and new personal discoveries become the basis for theory and action (Fisher, 1981, 2001).

As a part of her efforts to decrease hierarchical aspects of education, the radical feminist teacher does not give up power but participates in the classroom as a "potent agent of change" (Culley, 1985, p. 211). She must "claim her authority if her students are to claim their own" (p. 211). The teacher's modeling of energy, willingness to challenge traditional authority and knowledge, and ability to facilitate a feminist cooperative environment are catalysts for helping students claim their own power. The educator not only provides information about the global and extensive impact of patriarchy but also fulfills roles as coparticipant and facilitator to decrease power differentials between students and teachers. In other words, "the teacher is an organizer of the resources rather than a self-contained expert" (Schram, 1976, p. 161). Students are also experts who facilitate one another's learning.

More than any other feminist approach to pedagogy, radical feminist teachers are likely to question whether male teachers can offer a radical transformative experience to female students. Margo Culley (1985) stated, "No amount of knowledge, insight and sensitivity on the part of a male instructor can alter the deep structures of privilege mirrored in the male as teacher, female as student model" (p. 211). This teacher cannot be the "agent of the deepest transformation" in a culture in which women have been trained to look to men for approval, validation of their self-worth, and affirmation that they are adequate learners.

Given the reality that radical feminism has been especially attentive to the reproduction of male dominance through the objectification of women and violence against women, content about violence and its consequences receives special emphasis in the radical feminist classroom. The radical feminist teacher may also devote attention to the manner in which patriarchy is often reproduced through researcher–participant relationships, therapist–client relationships, and other relationships of unequal power. The educator challenges students to reject models that subtly reinforce any form of oppression. In general, radical feminist teachers share with cultural feminists a preference for standpoint theories and epistemologies that seek to transform the topics of research, the manner in which studies are conducted, and the nature of researcher–participant relationships.

SOCIALIST FEMINISM AND FEMINIST PEDAGOGY

Socialist feminists share the radical feminist views that gender oppression is a major form of oppression and that social activism is an essential feminist activity. However, they have also sought to develop a more complete analysis of oppression, one that examines the manner in which oppression is shaped by and intersects with class, economics, nationality, race, and history. Socialist feminists attempt to integrate analyses of (a) the structure of production, class, and capitalism (Marxist feminism); (b) the control of women's bodies, reproduction, and sexuality, and how this control is shaped by patriarchy (radical feminism); and (c) the impact of gender role socialization on individual choices and activity (liberal feminism). Socialist feminists believe that individual opportunity alone will not lead to an egalitarian world; the realization of human potential can only be achieved through the restructuring of personal and public experiences of men and women. Universal access to economic and work options, education, housing, birth control, and child care is essential (Donovan, 2000; Freedman, 2002; Tong, 1998; Whelehan, 1995).

Whereas radical and socialist feminists share the conviction that social transformation is essential, radical feminists have focused primarily on issues of patriarchy and male dominance, and socialist feminists have examined ways in which sexism, classism, and racism are reinforced through economic means. The goal of redistributing power through the transformation of economic structures, including the educational systems that prepare individuals for work, represents a central objective of socialist feminism (Donovan, 2000; Freedman, 2002; Tong, 1998). Thus, the socialist feminist classroom examines the ways in which social policy and capitalism reproduce systems of domination. More specifically, socialist feminist educators explore how educational systems prepare students to accept their assigned roles as paid and unpaid workers as well as fulfill roles that are consistent with their gender, class, and racial backgrounds. Socialist feminist educational theory also emphasizes how some individuals, especially women, are required through structural arrangements to play nurturing and caregiving roles in family contexts, educational settings, and other paid employment roles. The concentration of women in service jobs, low-paying jobs, and caregiving jobs (e.g., as primary and elementary school teachers) and men in administrative roles reflects the division of labor within private households in which women are expected to be primary caregivers and men are given executive or decision-making power.

Educational policies often reinforce these structures. One of the roles of the feminist educator is to clarify for students the *hidden* curriculum and educational policies that reproduce inequality and determine women's and men's *proper* roles (Deem, 1980; Weiler, 1988). Socialist feminist educators are attentive to the way in which the hidden curriculum reinforces inequities and make these hidden problems explicit to challenge and change them. Eric Margolis and Mary Romero (1998) articulated eight issues that reproduce gender, race, and class inequities including (a) being stigmatized and identified as an *affirmative action* student rather than as a person with specific types of academic interests; (b) experiencing victim-blaming attitudes or receiving messages that encourage the personalization of problems that should be attributed to the structure of the educational program; (c) being encouraged to *cool out*, or lower personal expectations and redefine unjust situations as normal and unchangeable; (d) being stereotyped or defined solely in terms of one's race, class, or gender characteristics; (e) being isolated, tokenized, or expected to represent particular minority perspectives; (f) encountering the absence of gender- and race-related content in the curriculum; (g) being excluded or ostracized for being critical of inequities or desiring to conduct research in minority communities; and (h) being *tracked* or receiving differential access to research experiences, published opportunities, and employment options. Socialist feminists believe that structural aspects of the curriculum will not be altered through individual change alone but require institutional transformation.

Socialist feminist pedagogy has been influenced by critical educational theories (Freire, 1970; Shor, 1987b), which seek to analyze and interrupt the reproduction of social, gender, and class relationships by helping students develop a *critical consciousness* that empowers them to initiate social change. Paulo Freire's (1970) problem-posing method is used to help oppressed groups understand barriers and obstacles and work toward transformation. Individuals not only become aware of the ways in which they are determined but "are also able to reflect on that determination and to begin to 'free themselves'" (Weiler, 1988, p. 147). Participants articulate their personal experiences of oppression, place these encounters within the larger economic, cultural, and social context, and discuss strategies and solutions for change (see chap. 1, this volume, for further discussion of problem posing). The socialist feminist educator recognizes that her students are *multilayered* beings who are influenced by a variety of ideologies and cultures as well as their race, class, and gender statuses. Conflict and negotiation among class members about their different understandings of the world are inevitable (Weiler, 1988).

Some of the important questions that the feminist educator introduces into the classroom include the following: How can the production of services be restructured to allow men and women of all classes and races to participate in production? How can power be redistributed in the workplace? How can the resources and rewards of society be redistributed so that all people have access to education, fulfilling work, and leisure? How can family life and reward systems be restructured so that both men and women engage in satisfying work and receive appropriate rewards for their work, both paid and unpaid? What structural changes are necessary to ensure that both public (paid) and private (unpaid) *provider* roles are valued? What structural changes are necessary to ensure that nurturing roles and jobs are as valued and well compensated as traditional scientific roles? Psychological and sociological theories and studies about the realities of diverse men and women in economic roles and the inequities of men and women in family life support the exploration of these questions. Ethnographic and qualitative research studies that reveal hidden structural inequities are central to the content of socialist feminist pedagogy, as is clarification of how standpoint and qualitative perspectives reveal race, class, and gender intersections that cannot be adequately understood through quantitative methods alone.

Socialist feminist educators meet many of their pedagogical goals by providing structural analyses of the social institutions that affect students, by helping individuals understand how they take up assigned identities to survive in the communities in which they are embedded (Rakow, 1992), and by encouraging students to resist these assigned identities and inequitable structures. They also help students articulate how their educational, family, and socialization experiences reveal power, race, class, and gender-related arrangements that reinforce oppression or confer privilege (Kenway & Modra, 1992).

IMPLICATIONS FOR THEORY AND PEDAGOGY THAT IS FEMINIST AND MULTICULTURAL

The second-wave feminisms discussed in this chapter represent prominent theoretical viewpoints of the late 1960s, 1970s, and early 1980s. The strategies of liberal feminism have paralleled tools that have supported civil rights policies, and together, these equal rights approaches have provided basic foundations for gender- and race-neutral policies and affirmative action programs that seek to *level the playing field* and increase the educational opportunities and skills of disadvantaged groups. Early liberal second-wave-feminist efforts were often inattentive to issues of diversity and tended to equate the needs of White heterosexual middle-class women with the needs of all women. Women of color and lesbians pointed out hypocrisies of White feminists and have been influential in putting forth the needs and perspectives of women of color and lesbians while also advancing the civil rights and educational needs of all women (Hartmann, 1998).

Cultural feminisms have revalued relational, connected, and subjective ways of learning and pointed to the importance of integrating *separate* and *connected* approaches to knowing. Although initial notions about relational knowing were based on assumptions about *generic* women and did not attend to the diversity within and between groups of women, Yvonne Jenkins (2000) proposed that culturally sensitive relational models can be useful for understanding the needs of many African American women and other women of color.

Radical feminist thought highlights aspects of patriarchy that permeate all cultures. Problematic to this approach are some radical feminist theorists' assumptions that patriarchy and gender-related oppression are the first and foremost forms of oppression. This point of view alienated many women of color who have experienced racism as a more extensive and consistent form of oppression than sexism and who have viewed men of color as allies against racism rather than as enemies associated with patriarchy. Despite these deficiencies, a reconstructed radical perspective may lend insight about the mechanisms of androcentrism and patriarchy that remain intact across contemporary cultures despite substantial shifts toward more egalitarian social structures (Wood & Eagly, 2002). In addition, the assumption that the personal is political and the tool of consciousness-raising represent central features of most liberation pedagogies.

Socialist feminists were among the first feminists to recognize the intersections of racism, classism, and sexism as they relate to oppression and privilege. Nellie Wong (1991) proposed that socialist feminism attends simultaneously to race, gender, sexual orientation, and class problems and stated, "Socialist feminism lives in the battles of all people of color, in the lesbian and gay movement, and in the class struggle" (p. 290). Class issues have often received limited attention within multicultural and feminist literatures, and socialist feminism reminds educators and social activists of the importance of integrating class issues within analyses of oppression. Whereas early socialist feminist models tended to frame oppression as triple jeopardy and examined race, class, and gender as additive components, more recent models have conceptualized privilege and oppression as related to multiple, complex, and intersecting social identities (Kim, 2000). Socialist feminist educators also emphasize the importance of examining and challenging hidden assumptions and unexpressed norms that permeate education.

The theories discussed in this chapter not only have provided a solid foundation for feminist educational practice but also include blank spots and significant limitations. In recent years, authors from within each of these theoretical traditions have reformulated these models to be more inclusive than their original versions. The basic pedagogical tools and strategies associated with these feminisms are not bound to a single theoretical tradition and represent useful techniques for teaching about oppression and social justice in diverse contexts.

The diversity feminisms, which are summarized in the next chapter, provide a rich source of information for transforming inadequate theories and supporting new models of social justice. The works of lesbian feminists, women-of-color feminists, international feminists, third-generation feminists, antiracist feminists, and postmodern feminists have revealed how subtle racism, colonialism, classism, heterosexism, and other isms have sometimes been embedded in the frameworks of feminist theory. The creation of feminisms by and for women and men of diversity is one of the most exciting trends in feminist theory and can be used to inform comprehensive models of pedagogy that are both multicultural and feminist.

3

DIVERSITY FEMINISMS: POSTMODERN, WOMEN-OF-COLOR, ANTIRACIST, LESBIAN, THIRD-WAVE, AND GLOBAL PERSPECTIVES

ADA L. SINACORE AND CAROLYN ZERBE ENNS

Feminists of color, antiracist feminists, lesbian feminists, postmodern feminists, third-wave feminists, and global feminists share the view that second-wave feminist theories have ignored or paid inadequate attention to diversity issues such as race, social class, generational difference, and sexual orientation. This chapter summarizes central themes of recent diversity feminisms and reviews implications of these theories for an integrated multicultural and feminist pedagogy (see Table 3.1). Diversity feminisms have much to offer because they attend to the intersections of multiple identities, focus on the impact of power structures on experience, examine the impact of specific contexts on people's lives, and provide insights about the complex dynamics within and between different groups of women. It is beyond the scope of this chapter to analyze all diversity theories; thus, we have focused specifically on those theories that hold major significance for pedagogies that are both feminist and multicultural.

TABLE 3.1

Diversity Feminisms and Pedagogy

Points of comparison	Postmodern feminisms	Women-of-color feminisms	Lesbian feminisms	Global feminisms	Third-wave feminisms
Key concepts	Knowers are fallible; truth is socially constructed; language is a method of expressing power.	Sexism intersects with racism and other "isms"; racism is often more virulent, visible, and constant than sexism.	Oppressions result from heterosexism; compulsory heterosexuality and other rigid sexual categories are critiqued and challenged	Emphasis is on oppressions of colonialism, nationalism, and multinational corporations; stresses importance of exploring differences and interconnectedness of women throughout the world.	Emphasis is on uniqueness and intersections of oppressions; rejects "politically correct" feminisms; values flexible feminisms that are tolerant of ambiguity and contradictions.
Goals	Question "fixed" truths; reveal how power is attained and maintained.	Place women of color at center of inquiry; eliminate all forms of oppression and privilege; create inclusive and antiracist feminisms.	Eliminate heterosexism; affirm diverse sexual identities; transform concepts of "normal" emotional and sexual expression.	Recognize global implications of local choices; encourage global cooperation among feminisms; stress gender equality throughout the world.	Create feminisms relevant to young generations; create "hybrid" feminisms that transcend early divisions.
Tools and methods	Use deconstruction; question dualistic constructs.	Analyze privilege and multiple oppressions; encourage activism.	Deconstruct heterosexuality; encourage activism and coming out as a political act.	Challenge ethnocentrism of Western feminists; implement global and grassroots efforts by and for women.	Encourage activism directed toward diverse forms of injustice; use autobiography to reveal complexity of women's lives.

42   SINACORE AND ENNS

Pedagogy	Positional pedagogies	Decolonization, critical consciousness, education as liberation	Identity affirming and transforming pedagogies	Decolonization and critical consciousness, multicultural and multinational content, global awareness	Use of zines, cyberspace, and the Internet to augment traditional forms of communication

POSTMODERN FEMINIST PERSPECTIVES

Since the 1980s, poststructural or postmodern approaches to feminism have been promoted as ways of transcending the limitations of other feminisms (e.g., Maher & Tetreault, 2001; Tisdell, 1995, 1998). In general, postmodernism is linked to a "bewilderingly diverse" array of approaches, and "is best thought of as a 'mood' arising out of a sense of the collapse of all those foundations of modern thought which seemed to guarantee a reasonably stable sense of Truth, Knowledge, Self and Value" (Waugh, 1998, p. 178). Consistent with this mood, postmodern feminisms reject "broad-brush" theories of feminism and examine the "particularity" of women's experiences as they occur in cultural and historical contexts (Kirk & Okazawa-Rey, 2001). Postmodern perspectives highlight the limitations of knowledge and the fallibility of knowers (both educators and students), including the tendency for knowers to misunderstand reality, to engage in ethnocentric thinking, and to draw flawed generalizations about human experience. Instead, feminist postmodernist theorists seek to understand how meaning is negotiated, how people in power maintain control over meanings, and how meaning and truth are invented, shaped, and modified by history, the social context, and the views and life experiences of the knower (Bohan, 2002; Cacoullos, 2001; Morrow, 2000; Waugh, 1998).

A primary tool of feminist postmodern analysis is deconstruction, which involves challenging bipolar or binary definitions of constructs (e.g., masculine and feminine), showing how reality is created rather than something that exists in a "natural" or "true" state, and showing how reality is often defined by hierarchies of power. According to this position, all "truth" and meaning systems (including feminist theories) are (a) socially constructed, (b) mediated and modified by specific contexts, (c) influenced by power structures, and (d) fallible. Thus, no truth is all-encompassing or invariable. Deconstruction reveals the fallibility of truth by analyzing power relations and revealing the multiplicity and diversity of positions that exist. For this reason, dualistic concepts or binary constructs are particularly problematic. Deconstruction reveals that these concepts only have meaning when juxtaposed against each other. In exploring the various meanings of truth, postmodern feminist theorists focus primarily on the connections between meaning and power, and their inquiries emphasize the power of language as it represents ideas, concepts, and power (Hare-Mustin & Marecek, 1990). Postmodern theorists frequently use the technique of discourse analysis to examine the functions of language concepts such as metaphors, paradoxes, and dualistic constructs.

Postmodern Feminisms and Pedagogy

In contrast to feminisms that have been centered in social activism, postmodern feminism emerged within academic disciplines and has become a method for understanding the limitations of knowledge and the changing nature of knowledge. Consistent with this view, the postmodern educator stresses the importance of examining the "situatedness" of all knowledge, how power shapes knowledge, and how these realities can be used to develop more complex and relevant views of reality and gender. Consequently, postmodernism is consistent with educational approaches that raise questions, point to the uncertainty and changing nature of knowledge and identity, and emphasize differences rather than commonalities and uniformity.

Many recent publications on feminist pedagogy have built on postmodern or poststructuralist positions (e.g., Lather, 1991; Luke & Gore, 1992; Maher & Tetreault, 1994, 2001; Ropers-Huilman, 1998; Tisdell, 1995, 1998), perhaps because postmodern perspectives provide insights about the complexity and diversity of learners, teachers, and the contexts in which learning interactions occur. A postmodern approach reminds us that it is important to explore students' varying identities not only as women and men in general but also as members of other marginalized or powerful groups. It also reminds feminist educators to be consistently aware of power dynamics; to be mindful of the reality that most academic feminism has been produced by relatively privileged women; and to continually ask how power influences knowledge, classroom dynamics, and student–teacher interactions.

Four interrelated themes are typically linked to postmodern feminist pedagogies: knowledge structure and construction, voice, authority, and positionality (Maher & Tetrault, 2001; Tisdell, 1998). The preceding summary of postmodern theory reveals that knowledge, the first theme, is considered to be variable and unstable and thus, the exploration of differences among persons takes center stage. Second, feminist postmodern pedagogy deconstructs or problematizes concepts such as "coming to voice," "safety," "authenticity," and "empowerment." Early models of feminist pedagogy may have overestimated the degree to which students and teachers can speak from a fully conscious, informed, coherent, "authentic" sense of self. The notion of an "authentic voice" can promote dualistic visions of what constitutes student growth, when in reality, people experience shifting identities, multiple identities, and contradictions across contexts and time (Orner, 1992). Whereas early writers on pedagogy emphasized the importance of establishing safety in the feminist classroom, educators influenced by postmodern views recognize that students from dominant groups are more likely to feel safety than are students from marginalized groups. Rather than attempting to guarantee safety or a sense of security, the educator is more likely to ask, Who is likely to feel safe and unsafe? When and in what contexts are students more and less likely to experience safety? Likewise, empowerment has a variety of subjective meanings, may be facilitated by a variety of different people and circumstances, is shaped by the characteristics and constraints of institutions, and may be connected to a range of desired end states or outcomes. If authentic voice, safety, and empowerment are defined in unitary "feminist" ways, teachers may inadvertently replicate oppressive power dynamics (Ellsworth, 1989; Gore, 1992, 1998; Orner, 1992; Tisdell, 1998).

A third theme of postmodern feminist pedagogy is authority. Of particular importance is the need for educators to scrutinize their own practices and beliefs. Mimi Orner (1992) stated the following:

> Educators concerned with changing unjust power relations must continually examine our assumptions about our own positions, those of our students, the meanings and uses of student voice, our power to call for students to speak, and our often unexamined power to legitimate and perpetuate unjust relations in the name of student empowerment. (p. 77)

Educators need to be self-reflective about their own sources of power and authority and how these are influenced by their own characteristics, values, and social identities. As noted by Elizabeth Tisdell (1998), questioning or problematizing one's own identity may be much more risky for some educators than for others. For example, a White male married professor can critique his own identity and privileges with relative safety. He may also support lesbian and gay rights, affirmative action, and various other human rights and be seen as a hero. In contrast, when a lesbian woman of color discusses her identity or provides public support for the same rights, she is more likely to be seen as "having an agenda."

Postmodern theory does not suggest a particular set of strategies, but rather poses critical questions. Which identities of students are being promoted in the feminist classroom? How does the identity of a student connect with the identities of others? How do the multiple identities of students and teachers influence who listens and who speaks, who is comfortable, and how interactions between individuals are interpreted? For what time and context is the text relevant? For whom is this text empowering? To what identities does it speak? These questions are also relevant to the full range of diversity feminisms we discuss in this chapter.

A fourth characteristic of feminist postmodern pedagogy is positionality. Positionality is the reality that "people are defined not in terms of fixed identities, but by their location within shifting networks of relationships, which can be analyzed and changed" (Maher & Tetreault, 1994, p. 164). The goal of positional pedagogy is for educators and students to develop a "third eye" or self-reflective awareness of the "constantly shifting contexts" (p. 164) in which oppression and empowerment occur; to be observant of the complex intersections of power, privilege, race, class, gender, sexual orientation, and other aspects of identity and how they affect the learning process; and to use this information to deal with difference effectively and develop flexible, "situated" ways of seeing themselves and the world. The knowledge that emerges in the positional classroom helps students and educators develop theory that is embedded in the "dynamic evolution of the group's consciousness," and must be "continually and consciously rediscovered and remade" (p. 205). For example, an assignment that may increase sensitivity to positionality asks each class member to become an expert on one of the socially defined categories of identity that shape meanings about a particular issue (e.g., violence against women). Students then compare their findings about how different social identities may influence the worldviews, realities, and truths of individuals (Ginorio, 1998).

Another tool that is consistent with postmodern thought is reflexivity, a practice that shares many commonalities with positionality. Feminist scholars initially used reflexivity as a means to critically examine and locate themselves within the research process and soon adapted it to teaching (Allen & Farnsworth, 1993; Cook & Fonow, 1986; Harding, 1987). In the classroom, reflexivity promotes self-awareness, scholarly accountability, and recognition of a range of human truths. Teachers and students learn to observe and locate themselves as knowers within certain cultural and sociohistorical contexts (Allen & Farnsworth, 1993; MacDermid, Jurich, Myers-Walls, & Pelo, 1992) and to avoid reifying their own and others' lives and experiences (Lather, 1991). Students use their personal experience to critique accepted knowledge in a field, while also making sense of personal experience through the lens of that accepted knowledge. By "refusing to let others do your thinking, talking, and naming for you" (Rich, 1979, p. 231), students become involved with class material on cognitive, affective, and experiential levels and become aware of the link between personal lives and the social world (Sinacore, Blaisure, Justin, Healy, & Brawer, 1999).

A social constructionist model, which is one form of postmodern thought (Bohan, 2002), has become a dominant perspective within feminist psychology (Gergen, 2001; Morrow, 2000). From a feminist social constructionist perspective, gender is a verb. Gender is about doing; it is not permanent, nor is it a unitary set of characteristics. Gender is shaped and changed by context. According to Stephanie Riger (1992), gender "is a pattern of social organization that structures the relations, especially the power relations, between women and men" (p. 737). Likewise, many other social identities (e.g., race, class, culture, and sexual orientation) are not fixed identities but are modified by context and perceptions.

Some feminist critics have argued that postmodernism can promote a *slide into relativism* because all realities are placed into question. If all truth is relative, no group can legitimately make specific claims or create new knowledge; efforts to explore the nature of specific oppressions become obsolete; and "once again, underneath we are all the same" (Alcoff, 1988, p. 421). Mary Gergen (2001) proposed, however, that postmodernism is associated with both deconstructive and reconstructive aspects. Deconstruction involves dissolving meanings, but social constructionism offers opportunities to create meanings that highlight how social influences are integrated within and between persons and communities of persons. Although meanings associated with experiences and events vary, phenomena such as racist acts occur and are not made up or constructed (Bohan, 2002). Although reality may be complex, a basis for activism and social change remains.

WOMEN-OF-COLOR FEMINISMS

Women-of-color feminists share many of the concerns articulated by socialist feminists (see chap. 2, this volume), but also argue that feminist theory must become more inclusive. According to bell hooks (1984), the liberal feminist assertion that "all women are oppressed" (a) led to "endless analogies between 'women' and 'blacks'" (hooks, 1982, p. 139); (b) implied that all women experience common oppressions, problems, and challenges; and (c) ignored the lack of choices and unique oppressive forces faced by women of diverse ethnic, racial, religious, and sexual minorities (hooks, 1989). When feminists propose that gender oppression is central to understanding all other oppression, they may leave women of color with the impossible choice of choosing between their identities as women or as people of color. Alternatively, women of color may feel forced to prioritize their identities. bell hooks (1984) noted that "suggesting that a hierarchy of oppression exists, with sexism in the first place, evokes a sense of competing concerns that is unnecessary" (p. 35). For many women of color, the personal experience of racism is far more visible, virulent, and commonplace than is the experience of sexism. Thus, the concept of differential oppression is a primary tenet of women-of-color feminism.

In keeping with their rejection of the "false homogenizing" of women (Higgenbotham, 1992, p. 273), many feminists of color prefer the term *womanist* rather than *feminist* because it highlights the uniqueness of their commitment to women of color. Alice Walker (1983) defined womanist as "a black feminist or feminist of color" (p. xi). Womanist also refers to women who love other women and appreciate women's culture, women's strength, and women's emotional flexibility. A womanist is committed to the "survival and wholeness of an entire people, male *and* female" (Walker, 1983, p. xii).

Many feminists of color believe that exploring differential access to privilege is essential to the creation of feminisms that are relevant to women of color. Because of their relatively privileged status as White people, White women are "seduced into joining the oppressor under the pretense of sharing power" (Lorde, 1984, pp. 118–119). In contrast, sharing power has not been an option available to many women of color; being involved with a man of color cannot lead to sharing power if there is little or no power to be shared. Instead,

> for poor or working-class men of color, asserting dominance over women and children may be nothing but a last desperate gesture to "prove their manhood" in a world that both expects all men to achieve certain suc-

cess and systematically destroys the chances of some men to achieve that position. (Espín, 1994, p. 266)

Feminisms for women of color need to include an understanding of the oppression and double binds faced by men of color of different socioeconomic statuses (Espín, 1994).

Depending on the context, White women and men of color may act as oppressors or be oppressed (hooks, 1984). For example, men of color can be victims of racism but exploit women, and White women can be victims of sexism but exploit people of color. Knowledge of the multiple oppressions of women of color can be used to most directly challenge racist, sexist, and classist notions. Thus, a feminist theory of women of color can enhance the feminist struggle to develop a "liberatory ideology and liberatory movement" (hooks, 1984, p. 15).

Women of color have also been critical of radical White women for identifying men as enemies rather than as potential allies. For example, the radical feminist separatist view that it is impossible for women to resist male supremacy while maintaining personal connections with men has fueled antagonism between women of color and White women. Many women of color have worked simultaneously for the rights of their racial and ethnic groups as well as women's rights and see the need for a connection between civil rights and feminism. Paula Giddings (1984) stated, "In times of racial militancy, Black women threw their considerable energies into that struggle—even at the expense of their feminist yearnings" (p. 7). In less militant times, they demanded rights in their relationships with Black men. They did not see these demands "in the context of race *versus* sex" (p. 7) but as rights that were necessary for ensuring the well-being of all Black people.

Feminists of color have been playing central roles in creating more inclusive and pluralistic feminisms by proposing theories that reflect their personal experiences and worldviews. For example, Patricia Hill Collins (2000) articulated basic characteristics of Black feminist thought, which emphasizes the centrality of self-definition and self-valuation, the analysis of the interlocking aspects of oppression, and the integration of Black women's culture and Afrocentric values with feminism. Black feminist thought builds on the concrete everyday experiences of Black women by (a) highlighting the centrality of dialogue, which is connected to African and African American oral traditions, to explore and articulate knowledge about women; (b) integrating feminism with a humanistic ethic of care; and (c) practicing an ethic of accountability, which involves using reason, emotion, and ethics to evaluate the character and ethics of persons who propose knowledge claims. The standpoints of Black women are used to rethink feminism and place the life experiences of Black women at the center of inquiry.

Other women-of-color feminists, such as Chicana feminists, have proposed approaches that incorporate the complex experiences and concerns of

Chicanas, which include language issues, immigration and migration, generation of residence in the United States, and religion. According to Dolores Delgado Bernal (1998), embedding one's perspective within Chicana experience "means that we deconstruct the historical devaluation of Spanish, the contradictions of Catholicism, the patriarchal ideology that devalues women, and the scapegoating of immigrants" (p. 562). Also unique to Chicana feminism are concepts such as borderlands and *mestiza* status or being a woman of mixed ancestry who "straddles cultures, races, languages, nations, sexualities, and spiritualities" (Bernal, 1998, p. 561). The term borderlands refers to the emotional, psychological, and geographical spaces that mark the boundaries between cultures and the sixth sense that is required to juggle cultures and contradictions associated with these spaces (Anzaldúa, 1987). Chicanas work toward negotiating the borders of multiple identities, and thus, can serve as examples of how to integrate complex identities of difference.

Central to Chicana epistemology is the construct of differential or oppositional consciousness, which is defined as a personal subjectivity or set of survival skills for persons facing multiple oppressions (Sandoval, 1991). Differential consciousness allows one to emphasize specific aspects of personal identity to achieve important goals. For example, the woman-of-color feminist working within a race-based group learns to strategically privilege race-related issues; when working with White feminists, however, she develops the capacity to foreground gender issues. Thus, women-of-color feminists develop flexibility and strength and become adept at "shifting their ideologies and identities in response to different configurations of power" (Moya, 2001, p. 461). Similarly, many women of color develop *la facultad*, which is informed by their painful experiences of marginalization (Anzaldúa, 1987) and involves developing an intuitive perceptiveness of power dynamics that allows a person to "adjust quickly and gracefully to changing (and often threatening) circumstances" (Moya, 2001, p. 469). For many feminists of color, feminist pedagogy involves teaching about border issues and practicing *la facultad* and differential consciousness within the classroom environment.

In contrast to feminists of color who emphasize the unique contributions of specific groups of women, antiracist feminists emphasize the importance of analyzing multiple identities, with race and gender central to that analysis (Calliste, Dei, & Agular, 2000). The individual is not seen as having a single-dimensional identity but as experiencing multiple selves. Consistent with postmodern feminism, antiracist feminists argue that individuals are socialized into identities that are dependent on the meanings applied to race, gender, class, and sexuality. Conceptualizing issues as multiple oppressions, such as intersecting and interlocking oppressions rather than as competing oppressions, is central to antiracist feminist discourse. Thus, gender and race are considered to be interlocking and vital to understanding social identities and knowledge construction (Calliste et al., 2000).

Antiracist feminism emerged from theories of antiracist education and integrates many of the tenets of postmodern feminism such as empowerment, deconstruction, and discourse analysis. A primary area of analysis is that of *knowledge generation*, which involves analyzing the construction of knowledge and how that construction is supported within societal institutions. Thus, antiracist feminists suggest that knowledge is gained through the intersections of one's multiple identities with personal, social, political, and educational systems. It is through the analysis of these intersections that an understanding of difference, including how difference is either marginalized or centralized, is supported and refined through discourse analysis.

An important component of both feminisms of women of color and antiracist feminism is activism. For many feminists of color, theorizing about the oppression of women of color is important, but engaging in social change is more important; feminist theory must be dynamic, not static. The feminisms of women of color are embedded in real life issues, and "without activism informing the theory, positive social change will not occur" (Saulnier, 1996, p. 115). Consistent with the views of feminists of color, antiracist feminists argue that agency is a necessary activity to bring about social change. Thus, individuals are encouraged to be involved in activities that confront racism, colonialism, sexism, and classism and to be participants in movements and interventions that confront alienation, marginalization, and exploitation of oppressed groups (Calliste et al., 2000; Ng, 1995). Feminists of color have demonstrated that although "all women are women, there is no being who is only a woman" (Spelman, 1988, p. 102). Appreciating difference and using difference to inform multiple feminisms are central values associated with feminisms of color and antiracist feminisms.

Women-of-Color and Antiracist Feminisms and Pedagogy

As summarized in the previous paragraphs, feminist theorists of color and antiracist feminists call for (a) an analysis of multiple oppression, (b) an assessment of access to privilege and power, (c) an inclusion of the personal experiences and worldviews of women of color, and (d) activism. Feminists of color and antiracist feminists argue that education can either contribute to the oppression of others or can serve a "liberatory function" (hooks, 1989). Pedagogy needs to be transformative to bring about lasting change. Feminist educators aim to analyze oppression, appreciate difference, include multiple perspectives and voices, use knowledge of pluralism to construct useful feminisms, and use this theory to bring about change.

The pedagogy of many feminists of color and antiracist feminists is informed by the critical pedagogy of Paulo Freire (e.g., hooks, 1994; see chap. 1, this volume, for definitions and discussion). Feminists of color state that critical pedagogy needs to be empowering (Ng, 1995) and focus on decolonization (Comas-Díaz, 1994; Valle, 2002). Education is "the practice of freedom" (hooks, 1994, p. 13); both students and teachers need to "transgress those boundaries that confine each pupil to a rote, assembly line approach to learning" (p. 13). Educators must be willing to let go of their traditional teaching methodologies and to relinquish power so that students have a critical voice in their learning. Thus, a liberatory pedagogy requires that one teach from a standpoint that includes an awareness of race, sex, class, and sexual preference. Although it does not allow traditional White male pedagogy to be the sole voice, it does not necessarily exclude that voice (hooks, 1994; Ng, 1995).

Many people of color have experienced the suppression or eradication of their own cultures, and to survive, have been required to accommodate themselves to dominant colonizing cultures. Common consequences of colonization include victimization, alienation, self-denial, assimilation within the dominant culture, and ambivalence about one's role in a dominant culture (Comas-Díaz, 1994; Ng, 1995). *Conscientizaçao*, or the development of a critical consciousness (Freire, 1970), is a central component of feminist pedagogy for people of color. Through decolonization, students become aware of how they have internalized the racist and sexist beliefs of the culture and learn skills for countering these beliefs. To address the effects of colonization, teachers and students must examine the ways in which women of color have been marginalized and use this information to propose feminisms and visions of equality that place women of diversity at the center of inquiry (Omolade, 1987; Valle, 2002).

Feminists of color and antiracist feminists argue that an important aspect of deconstructing traditional pedagogies involves examining the learning environment and power dimensions of the teacher–student relationship. Educators act as consultants rather than controllers of the learning process (Omolade, 1987; hooks, 1994). The classroom becomes a place where information is shared and students learn to "generalize their life experiences within a community of fellow intellectuals" (p. 39). In contrast to the model in which the educator imparts information and provides the *right answers*, the classroom becomes a democratic community where each individual is responsible for contributing to discussion (hooks, 1994). Collins (2000) proposed that those individuals who remain quiet but have something to say are *cheating* because they have withheld information from others. However, it is also important for educators to help establish a democratic classroom so that the voices of students with stronger personalities do not exclude the voices of others. Thus, mutual dialogue becomes an essential component of the antiracist classroom.

The notion that the classroom is a community of knowers is assumed by numerous feminist writers (e.g., Clinchy, 1989; Romney, Tatum, & Jones, 1992). However, bell hooks (1989, 1994) questioned the feminist notion of the classroom as a place of safety, suggesting that safety in the classroom may result in a pedagogy that supports the "politics of domination" by those who are most vocal and assertive. She argued that students from exploited groups may be afraid to speak even when the feminist classroom is identified as a place where they can gain their voices. These students need support as they come to voice in an atmosphere in which they see themselves at risk or are afraid to speak. Thus, "the goal is to enable all students, not just an assertive few, to feel empowered in a rigorous critical discussion" (hooks, 1989, p. 53).

Feminists of color believe that a truly transformational pedagogy needs to be attentive to the power between student and teacher as well as institutional power both in and outside the classroom. Feminist teachers seek to avoid the position of "all knowing professor" (e.g., hooks, 1989), explain their pedagogical strategies and feminist views, and are open to criticism. The educator opens herself up to being seen as "not knowing." This type of dialogue or analysis serves to deconstruct power in the classroom (hooks, 1989; Omolade, 1987).

Many of these strategies are also consistent with postmodern and positional pedagogies, which call for constant self-reflective attention to issues of power, position, and difference in the classroom. For example, Alejandra Elenes's (2001) proposal for a transformative Chicana feminist pedagogy focuses on undoing dualistic and oversimplified thinking and facilitates the exploration of complex analyses of race, class, gender, and sexual orientation intersections at the borderlands. As a *mestiza* who has negotiated many complex circumstances and identities, Elenes works with students to forge a "'common language' through which multiple and even contradictory discourses can be discussed, respected, and understood" (p. 693).

Feminists of color and antiracist feminists clearly state that course content needs to be inclusive and pluralistic. When integrating literature about women of color into course content, academics need to be cognizant of the writer's perspective, avoid the add-and-stir approach, and resist relying on content about women of color that is built primarily on the scholarship of White women (Greene & Sanchez-Hucles, 1997). To ensure that content demonstrates an appreciation for women of color on their own terms, texts and readings (both academic and autobiographical) should explore the lives of women from the perspectives of women of color, be based on culturally sensitive definitions of constructs such as gender roles, and focus on the strengths and coping functions of behaviors rather than as actions that represent weaknesses or exceptional patterns when compared to dominant groups (Ginorio & Martinez, 1998).

Another issue relevant to women of color and antiracist pedagogy is the ongoing presence of racism, sexism, or other "isms" in the classroom. By placing the works and lives of marginalized individuals at the center of inquiry, teachers provide opportunities for students to understand difference in revolutionary ways. At least in some educational settings, however, students may believe that people of color and lesbians are no longer marginalized and that centralizing the voices of women of color represents a form of "reverse discrimination." A major challenge for educators is helping these students understand that "naming one's position in the world is not the same as erasing others' existence" (Elenes, 2001, p. 697; see also Maynard, 1996; Ng, 1995). Some of these students may begin to understand the value of exploring the lives of people of color by first exploring their own cultural identities and the complex social locations and identities that contribute to their own lives (TuSmith, 1989–1990).

To summarize, feminists of color and antiracist feminists call for a pedagogy that is inclusive of multiple voices and encourages women of color and other marginalized groups to hold a central role in the learning environment. In addition, all individuals in the classroom must struggle together to learn new ideas and models of scholarship. The classroom becomes a place where "students engage in political struggle to learn enough and know enough to transform our mutual futures within and without the academy" (Omolade, 1987, p. 39).

LESBIAN FEMINISM AND QUEER THEORY

Lesbian feminist theory first emerged as a reaction to exclusionary practices of second-wave feminism. It has roots in radical feminism, which emphasizes oppression based on patriarchy; and identity politics, which involves efforts to seek justice for individuals who share a specific identity. From an identity politics position, being lesbian may be viewed as a self-definition that supercedes other identities. The view, which was held by some heterosexual liberal feminists, that lesbians would undermine the goals of the women's liberation movement was a major catalyst for lesbian feminism (Ross, 1995). Betty Friedan (1969, as cited in Berkeley, 1999) argued that lesbians were a "lavender herring," and detracted from the real cause of liberating women. Other liberal feminists believed that women needed to prove they were equals to men rather than choosing a lesbian identity and appearing to reject the system in which they hoped to achieve equality and power (Kitzinger, 1996; Ross, 1995). Similar to many feminists of color, lesbian feminists were often placed in a position of choosing between identities. They felt pressure to choose invisibility within the women's movement or join the mixed lesbian and gay movement and focus on the oppression of "female homosexuals." These factors formed the foundation for a lesbian feminist movement.

Lesbian feminists view women's sexuality and sexualized images of women as central to the analysis of women's oppression and have provided an important analysis of how heterosexuality contributes to patriarchy and oppression. Adrienne Rich's (1980) classic commentary about "compulsory heterosexuality" pointed out that heterosexuality is presumed to be normative for all people and represents a key component of heterosexism, which is defined as the belief that heterosexuality is the only natural form of emotional and sexual expression. Lesbian feminists highlight the necessity of analyzing heterosexuality as an institution rather than as merely a sexual preference. More specifically, lesbian feminism examines the manner in which heterosexuality dictates how and why some members of society, especially heterosexual men, hold greater power than others. Maintaining an almost universal female heterosexuality is an important mechanism of male domination because it guarantees women's sexual availability to men. Women's subordination to men is solidified through various heterosexual norms and traditions, including heterosexual romantic traditions and rites of passage, women's acts of caring for men, prohibitions against cross-dressing, heterosexual pornography and erotica, and heterosexualized humor and dress. Concerns such as violence against women and children, sexual harassment, and physical enslavement are also functions of patriarchal power, and women are required to be heterosexual to sustain these oppressive acts.

Lesbian feminists also evaluate heterosexuality as an ideology that subtly erases or prohibits lesbianism and homosexuality. Heterosexism promotes the view that male–female relationships are a fundamental building block of society; in contrast, same-sex intimate relationships are seen as holding no social reality. The critical analysis and deconstruction of heterosexist assumptions in society and feminist theory are essential for creating truly liberating feminisms (Calhoun, 1997; Kitzinger, 1996). One of Adrienne Rich's (1980) central concerns, addressed in her essay on compulsory heterosexuality, was that traditional feminist theorists do not question heterosexual norms and do not address the societal forces that shape women's sexual and psychosocial development. Despite lesbian critiques, heterocentric and ethnocentric feminist theories (e.g., some cultural feminist theories) remain popular, and to a certain extent, the phrase "compulsory heterosexuality" implies that heterosexuality remains a defining construct, even for lesbians. Consequently, lesbian feminist theory not only analyzes and deconstructs compulsory heterosexuality but works toward a true inclusion and valuing of lesbianism (Kitzinger, 1996; S. Rose, 1996).

A true inclusion of lesbian ideas requires that lesbians are made central to the discussion of women's issues and that the diversity of lesbians be addressed (e.g., race, ethnicity, and social class; Kitzinger, 1996). In keeping with their efforts to make lesbian life central, lesbian feminist theorists emphasize themes that affirm and embrace lesbian culture and life experiences. These themes include the following: the impact of growing up lesbian in a heterosexual society, the "coming out" process, lesbian culture and lesbian lifestyles, lesbian intimate partnership and parenting concerns, differences between lesbian and gay identity, and the realities of lesbians who represent diversity in terms of race, ethnicity, and social class (Calhoun, 1997). Similar to the feminisms of women of color, lesbian feminism emphasizes social activism, and the act of "coming out" represents an important form of social action that not only requires one to publicly declare one's sexual orientation but also deconstructs heterosexuality. Coming out as a political act is an integral component of lesbian feminist theory because it decentralizes heterosexuality, and thus, makes lesbian experience visible (Stein, 1997).

Lesbian feminists posit that the pressure to choose between identities is problematic, and lesbian identity politics calls for the inclusion of what it means to be lesbian as separate from being gay (Esterberg, 1997; S. Rose, 1996). Although the volume of writings and literature by and about lesbians has increased, psychology has tended to focus predominantly on gay male issues and sexuality. Simultaneously, lesbians are often portrayed as the female counterpart to gay men, which may marginalize lesbian concerns. Lesbian identity politics argues that lesbians are not the female counterpart to gay men but have an identity and culture of their own and that lesbian concerns must be addressed as legitimate in and of themselves (S. Rose, 1996). For a lesbian feminist theory to exist, lesbians need to be discussed as lesbians rather than as persons who are contrasted to heterosexual women or gay men.

As lesbian feminists have emphasized the uniqueness of lesbians, lesbians of color have critiqued White lesbian feminist theory for not attending to the diversity of lesbians and the multiple discriminations faced by lesbians of color. Beverly Greene (1997) suggested that the concerns of lesbians of color are often rendered invisible in the scholarly research of both women of color and lesbians. Lesbians of color often experience triple discrimination for being women, lesbians, and persons of color. Similarly, the "public discourse on the sexuality of particular racial and ethnic groups is shaped by processes that pathologize those groups" (Hammonds, 1997, p. 138). The discrimination faced by lesbians of racial or ethnically different groups is complicated by the fact that their sexuality is seen as perverse both within their ethnic group and by society (Hammonds, 1997). Although women-of-color feminists have stated that to understand the dual discrimination of women of color one must analyze the societal oppression of men of color (Espín, 1994), lesbians of color contend that one must understand the specific cultural factors that underpin lesbian oppression within their ethnic group (Greene, 1997; Lorde, 1984). Audre Lorde noted that Black lesbian feminists are seen as a threat to "Black nationhood" and that lesbianism is seen as a White women's problem. Thus, Black lesbians are caught "between the racism of white women and the homophobia of their sisters" (Lorde, 1984, p. 122). An inclusive lesbian feminist theory must address the concerns of lesbians of different races, ethnicities, and social classes (Espín, 1997; Greene, 1997).

In response to the multiple critiques of both traditional and lesbian feminisms, some lesbian feminists have embraced queer theory. Some lesbian feminists have characterized lesbian feminisms of the 1970s and 1980s as being "essentialist," or of overemphasizing commonalities of lesbian identity, sexuality, and community, and not attending adequately to the diversity of lesbians' lives and experiences (Garber, 2001; Rudy, 2001; Zita, 1994). In contrast, queer theory, which has its roots in postmodern and poststructuralist thought, seeks to deconstruct traditional categories of sex and sexuality, to "spoil and transgress coherent (and essential) gender configurations" (Luhmann, 1998, p. 141), and to support gender fluidity and flexibility. As noted by Kathy Rudy, queer theorists "defend a reconstruction of a multiplicity of genders as a way of disrupting the binary which keeps us locked into the hierarchical man/woman system" (2001, p. 209). Queer theorists challenge widespread assumptions about the connections between gender and sexuality and examine the perspectives of people who are marginalized or disparaged because of their sexual orientation or gendered experiences. Some queer theorists argue that the categories gay and lesbian create artificial divides between these two groups and that deconstructing these categories will also result in a collapse of other divisions, such as heterosexual and homosexual (Esterberg, 1997; Rabinowitz, 2002).

Queer theory and feminist theory share many commonalities and can be seen "as two branches of the same family tree of knowledge and politics" (Weed, 1997, p. vii). Queer theory allows for a discussion of sexuality that transcends identity categories such as gender and race and can encompass lesbian, gay, bisexual, transvestite, transsexual, and transgendered persons. It allows for an overarching, inclusive umbrella that can incorporate "queer heterosexuals" (Jagdose, 1996), and also emphasizes the possibility of experiencing a multiplicity of overlapping female sexualities. For example, to reclaim Black women's sexuality, one must make it visible (Hammonds, 1997). Queer theory increases the visibility of Black women's sexuality by allowing Black women to experience multiple female sexualities; thus, the need to compare Black and White lesbians or the expectation that Black women need to choose lesbian as a primary identity and race as a secondary identity disappears. Despite these advantages, queer theory is sometimes critiqued for ignoring oppression and experiences that are specific to women and lesbians, for privileging experiences associated with the male and public sphere, and for downplaying the role of feminism in outlining possibilities for liberation (Esterberg, 1997; Rudy, 2001). Deconstructing the notion of identity does not change the fact that a lesbian is a woman who negotiates a world that discriminates against her for both her lesbianism and her womanhood. Lesbian feminism needs to be attentive to issues of diversity and the multiplicity of identities; however, removing identities such as gender, race, or ethnicity from discussion is premature because oppression based on these factors remains pervasive (Esterberg, 1997).

In summary, lesbian feminism has played an important role in decentralizing heteronormality, whereas queer theory provides a critique of identity politics and the notion of fixed identities. Both lesbian feminism and queer theory emphasize the importance of (a) exploring multiple identities and their relationships to oppression; (b) deconstructing and decentering assumptions about normative heterosexuality as well as the subtle and not-too-subtle ways in which heterosexism permeates psychological theory and notions about normality; (c) emphasizing social action; and (d) identifying and appreciating the diversity among those with marginalized sexualities with regard to age, social class, race, culture, and ethnicity.

Lesbian Feminism, Queer Theory, and Pedagogy

Consistent with themes addressed in the previous section, lesbian feminists argue that feminist teaching must include a commitment to making the invisible visible and to educating for social change (Crumpacker & Vander Haegen, 1987). Feminist pedagogy must include the experiences of sexual minorities, analyze homophobia and the oppression that ensues from homophobia, decentralize heterosexuality, and be attentive to the diversity among sexual minority groups. Lesbian feminists believe that the inclusion of lesbian experience is the first step to transforming the classroom environment. Inclusiveness can range from including one lecture on lesbian experience to an optimal situation in which information and discussion about lesbians are integrated throughout the course (S. Rose, 1996). Through the systematic integration of literature and discussions about lesbianism, heterosexuality becomes decentralized, requiring students to specify whether they are discussing heterosexual or lesbian concerns as well as encouraging them to analyze the differences and similarities among women. To make discussion truly inclusive, feminist educators must also address diversity among both heterosexuals and lesbians with regard to age, social class, race, ethnicity, and other social locations (Esterberg, 1997; Greene, 1997).

Homophobia is often the most extreme form of oppression experienced by sexual minorities and represents "a deadly form of prejudice and discrimination, not merely a phobic reaction" (Crumpacker & Vander Haegen, 1987, p. 65). Thus, the analysis of homophobia is essential to lesbian feminist pedagogy. Educators must be willing to address their own homophobia and any resistance they have to addressing lesbian and bisexual women's concerns (S. Rose, 1996) and need to be prepared for conflict to arise when addressing homophobia (Chesler & Zuniga, 1991). A first step in addressing homophobia may involve clarifying the definitions of homophobia and heterosexism. Defining and redefining these terms, and analyzing the role these two phenomena play in the oppression of lesbians and bisexual women, helps broaden students' perceptions of "who defines what and why." This practice limits misinterpretations and thus minimizes the prejudice connected to homophobia (Crumpacker & Vander Haegen, 1987).

A discussion of lesbian feminist pedagogy is incomplete without addressing the notion of coming out. A great deal of controversy exists about who should be "out" and when, and many lesbian academics experience conflict about being out in academe. These issues are magnified, at least in part, by concerns about achieving tenure or experiencing potential discrimination from students and colleagues (Adams & Emery, 1994; P. Bennett, 1996; Davenport, 1996). Because radical lesbian feminist theory proposes that coming out is an act of social transformation that clearly decentralizes heterosexuality, the act of coming out would seem to be an essential component of feminist pedagogy. Many lesbians believe, however, that they place themselves at great risk by coming out. As a result, they may include course content about lesbians but remove personal disclosure from the equation. On the other hand, feminist heterosexual academics who teach lesbian content may be viewed as lesbian or bisexual, and thus, must make a decision about whether it is necessary for them to clarify potential misperceptions. Although theoretically, the educator's coming out may be viewed as a strong social and political act, the realities of the class environment and risk of job loss may preclude academics from making this choice.

Feminist educators share the belief that self-disclosure and personal narratives are useful tools for deconstructing the classroom hierarchy and providing alternative standpoints. Lesbian feminists suggest that educators need to be sensitive to the effects that coming out has on both students and educators. In addition to making personal choices about coming out, feminist educators must be sensitive to issues and concerns faced by students who are both in and out of the closet as well as avoid placing subtle pressure on lesbian and bisexual students to come out. Although coming out in the classroom may be a positive experience for many students, educators need to be sensitive to students' concerns and willing to address them openly.

In recent years, the literature on "queer pedagogy" has offered a shift in pedagogical emphasis (e.g., Britzman, 1995; Bryson & de Castell, 1997; Dilley, 1999; Luhmann, 1998; Quinlivan & Town, 1999; Rabinowitz, 2002). Susanne Luhmann characterized mainstream gay and lesbian pedagogical approaches as those that attempt to provide adequate and accurate representations of lesbians. The assumption behind these approaches is that "with representation comes knowledge, with learning about lesbians and gays comes the realization of the latter's normalcy, and finally a happy end to discrimination" (Luhmann, 1998, p. 143). Although the educator seeks to expand the definition of *normal*, heterosexuality is not necessarily deconstructed and often remains the implicit and *natural* standard of what is normal (Britzman, 1995). In contrast, queer theory deconstructs the very concept of normalcy, and offers a "querying pedagogy" that nurtures "pedagogic curiosity" (Luhmann, 1998, p. 148), which entails reading for difference rather than similarity, engaging in dialogue with oneself and others about how one has come to understand identity, and exploring the "infinite proliferation of new identifications" (p. 151).

In conclusion, lesbian feminists call for a pedagogy that values the diversity of lesbian and bisexual women's voices and allows for the decentralizing of heterosexuality. The classroom must be a place that analyzes societal and individual homophobia and heterosexism to provide a space for tolerance in the learning environment. Finally, the classroom needs to become a place where coming out and being out are viewed both as choices and as political statements.

GLOBAL AND TRANSNATIONAL FEMINISMS

Global and transnational feminisms have emerged out of efforts to examine women's experiences across national boundaries, analyze their interdependencies, and build linkages and coalitions with feminists around the world. To understand interconnections between women, one needs to explore the interplay between religion, colonialism, nationalism, multinational systems, and gender (Saulnier, 1996; Tong, 1998). Global feminists operate from the assumption that the circumstances, choices, and experiences of women in one part of the world have an impact on women in other regions. For example, Western women's efforts to ban harmful birth control methods may be successful in removing them as alternatives in the West, but an unanticipated consequence may be the imposition of these devices on women in other, less wealthy parts of the world. Any local feminist efforts must take into account the global implications of feminist activity (Burn, 2000; Saulnier, 1996; Tong, 1998).

Economic issues and the impact of multinational systems on women are especially important to global and transnational feminists. Many goods sold in the United States are produced in other countries, and a high proportion of factory workers who produce goods for limited remuneration are women. Multinational business practices and international monetary policies often have a significant impact on the social structure of other countries. These companies have often chosen "third-world" countries as locations for major factories because employers are able to pay workers low wages and can be less attentive to health, safety, and pollution standards. The monetary lending and repayment policies of powerful institutions such as the World Bank and the International Monetary Fund may also trigger wage reductions and cutbacks in public services (e.g., child care and health). These economic issues have very significant consequences for women, who are typically responsible for practical matters related to family survival, and represent 70% of people around the world who live at the absolute poverty level (Basu, 2000; Kirk & Okazawa-Rey, 2001). Many global feminists note that women's exploitation as inhabitants of the third world is often more virulent than their oppression as women. Like many women-of-color feminists, many women around the world prefer the label womanist instead of the label feminist, because it implies a commitment to the survival of a people and their society (Saulnier, 1996; Tong, 1998; Ward, 2002). Women throughout the world often see general economic and political issues as more critical to their oppression than issues that are traditionally defined by Westerners as gender issues (Burn, 2000; Peterson & Runyan, 1999; Saulnier, 1996).

The exploitation of women through sex trafficking, prostitution, and sexual violence is another important emphasis of global and transnational feminisms. Sex tourism is a major economic enterprise and often intersects with modernization, capitalism, and colonialism in supporting the oppression of women. A related issue is the use of rape as a weapon of war to destabilize a country, reinforce the domination of one group over another, or accomplish ethnic cleansing. Global feminists work together to provide refuge to women and challenge governments to create policies that can protect women from abuses (Anderson, 1999; Saulnier, 1996).

Global feminisms challenge Western feminists to recognize that each woman lives under unique systems of oppression and that Western feminists have sometimes promoted the intrusive, colonial, patronizing, or disrespectful treatment of women around the world (Burn, 2000; Hase, 2002; Lips, 2003; Ward, 2002). One ethnocentric practice of Western women has been the tendency to view women in other parts of the world as passive victims who need Western women's expertise and insight to overcome oppression. In reality, many successful and culturally sensitive grassroots feminist efforts are being enacted around the world, and Western feminists can learn much by observing these activist efforts, gaining information about the powerful impact of feminist efforts around the world, and forming coalitions and alliances with these women's groups (Anderson, 1999; Burn, 2000; Tong, 1998).

A major unresolved issue is the degree to which global feminists should adopt the values of cultural relativism. To what degree can one culture or group of women judge the acceptability of another culture's standards? A major challenge facing global feminists is to find some balance that allows for the transcendence of ethnocentrism but the rejection of a form of relativism that seems to condone virtually any behavior as long as it is acceptable within a specific culture. These behaviors include acts such as female circumcision, domestic violence, sexual violence, bride burning, or honor killings of women who have been "dishonored" by rape. Global and transnational feminists focus on the importance of respecting difference but are still struggling to deal effectively with cultural differences that contribute substantially to the oppression of women (Burn, 2000; Tong, 1998; Ward, 2002). Mary Maynard (1996) proposed that current postmodern arguments in feminism have contributed to overly cautious attitudes about making value judgments regarding practices that are harmful to women. She argued that our fear of operating from a "position of voyeuristic privilege" (p. 19) has often led Western feminists to romanticize the lives of women in other countries and uncritically support practices of male domination in a variety of cultures around the world. To resolve difficult questions about culture and gender, it is important to distinguish between cultural relativism and respect for other cultures. Whereas cultural relativism offers no common ground between women and implies that one must view all cultural practices as acceptable, respect for culture encourages individuals to explore and understand another culture on its own terms without necessarily condoning all practices. Also, it is useful to differentiate between advocacy and appropriation. Appropriation involves redefining and reworking women's issues in Western terms, which often results in alienating and objectifying women from non-Western traditions. In contrast, advocacy implies that women around the world will speak on their own behalf and that Western feminists can become informed, and in turn, educate others about experiences of women around the world.

Global and Transnational Feminisms and Pedagogy

The global feminisms focus on not only the needs and issues of ethnic minority groups within the United States but also the concerns of people throughout the world. Educational efforts should also attempt to impart multinational and transnational ideas in addition to multicultural ideas as typically defined by Western psychology. Also, education should emphasize the interdependency of members of the global village, the manner in which the individual decisions of persons in the West may affect persons in less privileged countries, and how certain Western practices may oppress these persons or repeat colonial practices of the past.

Third, education must challenge the ethnocentrism of our *advanced* society by listening and learning from women and men around the world. Michiko Hase (2002) observed that students often show interest in "'exotic' issues affecting third-world women while showing little interest in the ways in which the United States—its government, its corporations, and U.S.-dominated international institutions—shapes (and even dictates) the process of globalization" (p. 93). Dealing effectively with student resistance to topics such as nationalism is an especially important feature of multicultural feminist pedagogy. By becoming informed about feminisms and social activism around the world, Western feminists gain insight about the limitations of feminisms as well as information about successful international strategies that can be adapted and applied to challenges faced in the West. Fourth, training for building effective coalitions and social activism across cultures will become essential as changes related to telecommunications, transportation, international events, and economics increasingly link citizens throughout the world (Kirk & Okazawa-Rey, 2001; Marsella, 1998).

THIRD-WAVE FEMINISMS

Third-wave feminisms, which encompass the feminist belief systems of many younger women who first defined themselves as feminist between the early 1990s and the present, are built on the contributions of second-wave feminists to feminist theory and practice during the past 30 years. Although expressing gratitude to feminists of their mothers' generation, third-wave feminists have expressed disappointment that second-wave feminists have sometimes characterized their generation as postfeminist, narcissistic, self-obsessed, disorganized, consumed by trivial concerns, and as "divorced from matters of public purpose" (Bellafante, 1998, p. 60). Third-wave feminists have also been critical of some aspects of second-wave feminism, occasionally characterizing it as inflexible and dogmatic and too concerned with political correctness and as promoting "rules" about what one must believe and do to be a "real" feminist (Walker, 1995).

A major goal of young feminists has been to reclaim feminism on their own terms, to correct what they perceive as some of the inflexibilities and mistakes of the previous generation, and to replace some of the distortions of feminism that have permeated American culture in recent years. Although feminists of the second wave needed to raise awareness of sexism and other oppressions through *raising* consciousness, third-wave feminists face the challenge of *changing* consciousness by influencing the perceptions of those who have been exposed to a feminist backlash and pejorative descriptions of feminism (Siegel, 1997). They recognize the major economic opportunities available to them as daughters of the second wave and the significant social change brought about by new understandings of issues such as sexual harassment, reproductive freedom, and affirmative action. However, they have been critical of the previous generation's limited progress combating major social issues such as the AIDS epidemic, violence against women, economic crises, and ecological concerns. Young third-wave feminists have also expressed dismay about the presence of stereotypes that portray feminists as hating men or refusing to shave their legs. They also speak to the impossibility of living by the rules of second-wave feminism and express the need to define feminism in their own terms (Baumgardner & Richards, 2000; Findlen, 1995; C. M. Orr, 1997; Walker, 1995).

Third-wave feminists have sought to fight a feminist backlash in the larger culture by proposing feminisms that are flexible, expand the public's view of what it means to be feminist, and allow women to express their individuality and uniqueness. Leslie Heywood and Jennifer Drake (1997) characterized third-wave feminism as dealing with the contentious climate surrounding feminism by developing "modes of thinking that can come to terms with multiple, constantly shifting bases of oppression in relation to the multiple, interpenetrating axes of identity, and the creation of a coalition politics based on these understandings" (p. 3). Third-wave feminisms draw "strategically" (Heywood & Drake, 1997, p. 3) from a variety of feminisms, including second-wave feminisms, women-of-color feminisms, working-class feminisms, and prosex feminism. They also emphasize the variable nature of oppression and that the experiences deemed oppressive by one individual or group of women may be experienced as benign or nonoppressive by another.

Finally, Heywood and Drake pointed out that although "different strains of feminisms directly contradict each other" (p. 3), it is possible to transcend these contractions and create a hybrid feminism that is meaningful to contemporary women and men.

In keeping with their desire to endorse a feminism of action, third-wave feminists have also been involved in a wide variety of activist causes, such as voter registration, health care costs, parental laws related to abortion, sex education, violence against women, subtle forms of racism, HIV infection, equal gendered access to the Internet, global issues in feminism, child sexual abuse, eating disorders and body image, self-mutilation, and sexual health (Baumgardner & Richards, 2000). The emphasis on organizing across categories that have often divided individuals can be seen in the mission statement of Third Wave, which reads as follows: "Third Wave is a member-driven multiracial, multicultural, multisexuality national nonprofit organization devoted to feminist and youth activism for change" (cited in Heywood & Drake, 1997, p. 7).

Third-wave feminists have often emphasized the "personal" dimension of "the personal is political." Their writings have often been autobiographical, and several anthologies consist primarily of personal accounts of encountering feminism (e.g., Findlen, 1995; Walker, 1995). Many third-wave feminists believe that the political implications of feminism are often most clearly revealed in autobiographical writings, which are more accessible than academic writings to a wide audience and convey an appreciation for diversity of experience. The Internet and "zines" have become important methods for sharing ideas and theories as well as for building activist coalitions (Baumgardner & Richards, 2000; Findlen, 1995; C. M. Orr, 1997; Siegel, 1997).

In summary, third-wave feminists have highlighted the important of recognizing multiple identities and rejecting polarities or convenient dichotomies such as male–female or good–evil. Thus, they tend to express appreciation for feminisms such as global feminism and women-of-color feminisms. Third-wave feminists have aspired to be honest about the daily ambiguities, contradictions, and messy dilemmas that confront them. Many published personal narratives embrace seemingly contradictory identities such as being feminist and Christian, being male and feminist, desiring to be "treated as a lady" and being feminist, wanting to be married and devote oneself to the care of children while being a feminist, working as a model and participating in the beauty culture while also being feminist, or enjoying hip-hop music (which is often identified as antifeminist) and being feminist (Findlen, 1995; Walker, 1995).

Third-Wave Feminisms and Pedagogy

Productive conversation across feminist generations is sometimes difficult. Whereas third-wave women have been frustrated with a lack of respect accorded them by women of the previous generation, second-wave feminists have expressed concern that younger feminists have been inclined to describe the second wave's contributions in monolithic terms and to label these ideas as obsolete or irrelevant. Gloria Steinem has cautioned young feminists against "reinventing the wheel." Generational dynamics can also be replicated in the classroom and among different generations of academics. An important task for feminist educators is to identify ways of discussing generational themes and differences in a manner that conveys respect and appreciation for difference.

Younger women can sometimes feel intimidated by the erudite writings of academic feminists, and feel that it is important for young feminists to have spaces for formulating their own feminisms in informal discussion groups, focus groups, Internet chat options, and local zines (Rubin & Nemeroff, 2001). In contrast to the consciousness-raising groups of second-wave feminists, which focused on shared aspects of oppression, third-wave feminist discussions tend to emphasize the diversity of meanings and activities of feminism. In keeping with new forms of communication, chapters on feminist pedagogy now focus on topics such as meeting in cyberspace (E. C. Rose, 1998), becoming "webbed women" (Pramaggiore & Hardin, 1998), and as facilitating "cybergrrrl education and virtual feminism" (McCaughey & Burger, 1998).

Third-wave feminisms also contribute important knowledge about the complex intersection of historical events and feminisms. Second-wave feminisms emerged in the midst of strong human rights movements, including the civil rights movement, the women's movement, and peace movements. Young feminists must become engaged with social justice in a much more complex society in which opportunities for activism may sometimes seem less obvious. Whereas many blatant human rights violations related to racism and sexism have decreased, the everyday experiences of subtle racism, sexism, and heterosexism as well as the subtle and invisible benefits of privilege are woven intricately into the fabric of society. Although equally harmful, these isms and forms of privilege are often more difficult to see and challenge directly. Enacting the principles of feminist pedagogy may be even more complicated than it was 20 years ago.

Third-wave feminists have encouraged academic feminists, who are the most prolific creators of theory, to become more flexible about the manner in which they communicate their work. Open-mindedness on the part of feminist educators about a variety of issues, such as how feminism and activism should be defined, is also necessary. What appears on the surface to be a "nonfeminist" comment on the part of a student may reflect her or his struggle to come to terms with difficult human rights issues. When feminist educators can recognize why students hold specific worldviews and imagine the world as their students see it, they are most likely to be effective as mentors and teachers.

THE DIVERSITY FEMINISMS: A SUMMARY OF IMPLICATIONS

Some major implications of the diversity feminisms are that educators need to be consistently aware of how language and meaning are produced or reproduced in the classroom and how power and oppression influence knowledge, classroom dynamics, and student–teacher interactions. Of particular importance is the need for educators to scrutinize their own practices, assumptions, and beliefs about power, oppression, empowerment, and social change. In the paragraphs that follow, we summarize some of the major implications of the diversity feminisms for multicultural feminist pedagogy.

First, the diversity feminisms theorize from difference and work toward moving perspectives that have been marginalized to the center of inquiry. The diversity feminisms emphasize how power influences "canons" of knowledge and question unexamined assumptions and norms (Bell, Morrow, & Tastsoglou, 1999). Second, reality is complex and multifaceted, and an inclusive feminist pedagogy is facilitated by an analysis of a complicated matrix of oppressions and privileges. A single person may experience privilege by virtue of some identity statuses (e.g., gender or race) as well as oppression based on other statuses (e.g., class, race, or sexual orientation). Third, knowledge and identity are socially constructed. Knowledge and identity are situated in specific cultural and historical contexts and are influenced by whether one is an outsider or insider in these contexts. Exploring multiple identities and knowledge bases as well as the contexts in which specific components of identity or knowledge become salient is central to a pedagogy that is multicultural and feminist (Kirk & Okazawa-Rey, 2001).

Fourth, the diversity feminisms emphasize the importance of activism and provide a foundation for pedagogies of activism and social change. However, any one analysis of oppression is incomplete; various participants in social change may foreground or emphasize different goals. Important qualities and skills for pursuing social change include flexibility, a self-reflective attitude, a recognition that "our experiences of others will always be partial" (Hoodfar, 1997, p. 213), the ability to form alliances across difference, and the willingness to work at the borders and intersections of various groups' interests (Hoodfar, 1997; Kirk & Okazawa-Rey, 2001). Fifth, learning to speak for oneself is an empowering activity. However, given the tendency of individuals to "center" their personal experiences, learners often have difficulty listening actively and attentively to the perspectives of others, especially when the voices of others have been marginalized. Helping students develop skills for listening and weighing perspectives related to difference is an important component of the educational process (Bell et al., 1999).

Sixth, when dealing with issues of difference and oppressions that may be played out in classroom dynamics, a "safe" pedagogy may not be possible (e.g., hooks, 1994). However, a "safer pedagogy" may be supported through the development of classroom guidelines for confidentiality, conveying respect, listening, and giving effective feedback (Bryson & de Castell, 1997). Seventh, centering or foregrounding difference may be especially difficult for students from privileged backgrounds. Altering one's worldview is especially difficult if it challenges the positions of power and privilege one enjoys. Pedagogical practices that help students understand structural dynamics that facilitate privilege and oppression and challenge myths associated with individualism and meritocracy are important. However, overcoming resistance to this new learning is often complicated and requires student openness to self-reflection and self-confrontation (Bell et al., 1999). Eighth, self-reflective attitudes and activities and an exploration of the impact of one's social identities, privileges, and oppressions provide a foundation for considering the impact of multiple identities on the lives of others. Self-reflection is a never-ending process and requires ongoing openness to modifying one's frameworks.

Ninth, dialogue and critical questions that call on learners to consider underlying assumptions that give rise to specific points of view are essential catalysts for moving learners and educators beyond merely validating their subjective reactions or reinforcing the notion that "individual experiences are valid in and of themselves and do not need to be explored further" (Bell et al., 1999, p. 33). Examples of questions that facilitate critical reflection include the following: (a) What are the basic assumptions and values that give rise to this person's experience and perspectives? What are the assumptions for defining normal or typical? (b) What circumstances, cultural factors, historical events, personal experiences, privileges, and oppressions have influenced this person's or group's viewpoints? (c) Whom and what does this person or theory address? Who or what is left out? Why has this perspective become popular or why has it been excluded? Who benefits from this point of view? (d) What are the implications of this person's view, experience, or theory? Finally, pedagogies associated with the diversity feminisms call for consistent attention to the positionality of educators as well as students. The social locations and identities of the educator and the particular and (often complex) mix of students in a given classroom affect pedagogical process and outcomes, their openness to content associated with difference, and their willingness to be changed by this content.

Each of the feminist pedagogies discussed in this chapter is built on the goal of liberating learners, and thus, the content being taught needs to be inclusive and pluralistic. Theorists, researchers, and practitioners need to be careful to avoid the "add-and-stir" approaches to women of diversity (Greene & Sanchez-Hucles, 1997). As such, texts and readings need to explore the lives of women from the perspectives of people of diversity, be based on culturally sensitive definitions of constructs such as gender roles, and focus on the strengths and coping functions of behaviors rather than on behaviors that represent weaknesses or exceptional patterns when compared to dominant groups.

In summary, the feminisms discussed in this chapter are characterized by many similarities, including a focus on power and privilege and an emphasis on difference. However, each of the diversity feminisms offers specific pedagogical strategies for addressing the specific concerns of that feminist position (e.g., women-of-color feminism or lesbian feminism). It is likely that an integration of these pedagogical positions may result in students and educators broadening their understanding and awareness of diversity.

4

MULTICULTURAL EDUCATION AND CRITICAL PEDAGOGY APPROACHES

SABA RASHEED ALI AND JULIE R. ANCIS

A large and dynamic body of literature addresses the characteristics of multicultural education, and much of this literature focuses on educating elementary, secondary, and undergraduate college students about issues of diversity. In addition, a growing body of literature critiques this literature and outlines alternative teacher education approaches for preparing future professionals to work toward ending oppression and achieving social justice in educational settings (Goodman, 2000; Jennings & Smith, 2002; B. G. Wallace, 2000). In this chapter, we describe and compare major approaches to multicultural education, discuss the role of critical pedagogy approaches to multicultural and feminist education, and examine efforts to integrate multicultural training within teacher training programs. We conclude by summarizing contributions to and limitations of the multicultural education literature as well as implications for pedagogy that is multicultural and feminist.

Special thanks to Julia Phillips who participated in the original working conference on pedagogy and contributed a written description of the multicultural education approaches summarized in this chapter.

69

APPROACHES TO MULTICULTURAL EDUCATION

Contemporary multicultural education has evolved and grown through an initial phase that was influenced by the civil rights movement and involved integrating content about African Americans in the curriculum to an emphasis on multiethnic content and to recent emphases on the interactions between ethnicity, gender, and class as foundations for theory, research, and practice (Banks, 1995). Christine Sleeter's and Carl Grant's (1987, 2003) widely cited model identifies five major approaches to multicultural education: (a) education for the exceptional and culturally different, (b) human relations approaches, (c) single-group studies, (d) multicultural education, and (e) multicultural and social reconstructionist education. The following overview and Table 4.1 summarize the major characteristics of these approaches.

Education for the Exceptional and Culturally Different

The exceptional and culturally different approach seeks to help individuals from disadvantaged groups develop skills that support achievement and assimilation within mainstream American schools and society. This approach, which focuses on the needs of students with disabilities as well as culturally diverse students, is based on the human capital theory and assumes that education is an investment that allows individuals to gain skills for successful employment and that certain groups have not achieved because their home and cultural environments are different from mainstream American environments (Sleeter & Grant, 2003). Emphasis is placed on "building bridges between cultures to facilitate individual achievement and social mobility, rather than combating unequal distribution of goods and power among racial groups" (Sleeter & Grant, 1987, p. 423). A major goal involves changing persons to fit mainstream America rather than changing mainstream America to accommodate the needs and preferences of diverse groups. Most teachers using this approach typically maintain high expectations for students and believe that the traditional curriculum is useful for all students but must be adapted to the needs of various students (Sleeter, 1999). This approach has progressed over time from viewing culturally diverse students as culturally deprived to culturally different to, more recently, "at risk" (Banks, 1995).

The phrase *equity pedagogy* refers to teaching methods that support the achievement of students from diverse backgrounds (Banks, 1995). Strategies include making the curriculum personally relevant for students by building on the strengths of students, teaching content in students' native languages, identifying and filling gaps in knowledge, matching teaching styles to students' cultural preferences (e.g., cooperative learning with high degrees of interpersonal interaction), and using immediate positive reinforcement of small, successive accomplishments.

TABLE 4.1
Multicultural Approaches and Pedagogies

Approach	Goals	Pedagogy
Exceptional and culturally different	Facilitate success of diverse students in mainstream society	Teach skills for achievement and success; adapt teaching to learning styles of students
Human relations	Promote tolerance; facilitate positive feelings and relationships among members of diverse groups	Implement activities to reduce stereotyping and prejudice; teach about similarities and differences among individuals; emphasize cooperative learning; create opportunities for interaction with diverse groups
Single studies	Establish social, economic, and political power for members of the identified group; encourage social change that benefits members of the identified group	Employ critical pedagogy; integrate content about the identified group; question knowledge assumptions; teach social change skills; teach about racial and ethnic identity development; use teaching strategies preferred by members of the identified group
Multicultural education	Create structural equality and a pluralistic society in which all have equal access to power and opportunity	Teach all content multiculturally; teach bilingual skills for all; extend teaching outside the classroom; model diversity through staff values and composition
Multicultural and social reconstruction	Promote structural and personal equality by restructuring education and society	Employ critical pedagogy; provide an integrated analysis of racism, classism, sexism, and other isms; use students' experiences as tools for analyzing oppression; teach social action and empowerment skills; use democratic decision making

Human Relations Approach

The intergroup education movement arose in response to the events of World War II and racial tensions in the United States and was influenced primarily by White liberal educators who assumed that assimilation represented the best means of reducing racial tension (Banks, 1995). Emerging from the intergroup education movement, the human relations approach emphasized the importance of feeling good about oneself and diverse others and learning to relate to, respect, and communicate with those from different backgrounds (Sleeter & Grant, 2003). Teachers who adhere to this approach generally believe that American society is open and fair and that teaching people to love, respect, and communicate with others will lead to improved relationships among diverse groups of people.

Research suggests that young children's racial attitudes mirror those found in American society (e.g., Phinney & Rotheram, 1987), and thus, reducing students' prejudice and instilling democratic racial attitudes are of great importance (Banks, 1995). Students learn about problems associated with stereotyping and receive accurate information that challenges societal biases. Teaching strategies include content integration about diverse groups, prejudice reduction activities, positive reinforcement of multicultural stimuli, vicarious interracial contact, and cooperative learning experiences. Information about contributions of people from diverse groups is presented so all students, especially those who are members of marginalized groups, feel positively about themselves and their reference groups. Finally, students are also given opportunities to work with diverse others through cooperative-learning exercises, role-playing, social skills, training, and participation in community projects.

Single-Group Studies

Providing in-depth educational experiences about specific oppressed groups is a priority for single-group-studies perspectives (Sleeter, 1999; Sleeter & Grant, 2003). Catalysts for single studies approaches included (a) efforts during the first half of the 20th century to disseminate information about the African American experience in America and (b) the emergence of Black studies and ethnic studies programs (1960s and 1970s) that focused on teaching about the history, experiences, and perspectives of African Americans and members of other racial and ethnic groups (Banks, 1995).

Goals of single studies and ethnic studies programs have included (a) content integration, which involves providing information about diverse groups or illustrating ideas and concepts by using examples relevant to members of diverse groups, and (b) efforts to gain economic, social, and political power for group members. These strategies address the knowledge construction process, such as why the perspectives of a group have been excluded, why inequality exists, and how traditional education perpetuates inequality. Those who adopt this perspective assume that education is not neutral, that the unspoken assumptions underlying traditional Eurocentric educational approaches need to be revealed, and that knowledge of one's own history is a source of power (Sleeter, 1996). In recent years, material related to racial and social identity development models (e.g., Cross, 1991; Hardiman & Jackson, 1997; Tatum, 1992, 2002) has been integrated with this model to support students' positive identity within a racist society. Knowledge of racial identity development allows students to recognize, articulate, and transcend their emotional responses to learning about racism or other oppressions (Tatum, 1992).

Strategies associated with single-studies approaches include (a) examining the significance of starting points or assumptions about knowledge, (b) critiquing socially constructed "natural" or binary categories associated with identity (e.g., Black vs. White), (c) restructuring the canon of knowledge, (d) exploring the strengths and resilience of specific oppressed groups, (e) fostering a positive collective identity among members of a group, and (f) empowering and liberating group members from injustice (Sleeter, 1996). The use of critical pedagogical approaches (see chap. 1, this volume) and teaching strategies consistent with learning styles valued by many members of specific groups is embedded in this approach. For example, Afrocentric teaching strategies may be used to maximize African American students' learning, and feminist pedagogy strategies may be used to support girls' and women's learning.

Multicultural Education Approach

Advocates of this approach use the phrase *multicultural education* to describe methods that promote human rights, social justice, equal opportunity, cultural diversity, and the equitable distribution of power for oppressed groups (Gollnick, 1980; Sleeter & Grant, 2003). The multicultural education perspective, which is among the most widely discussed approaches in the educational literature, calls for education that transforms mainstream America into a culturally pluralistic society in which all people have equal opportunity for success. Curriculum content is reorganized to incorporate knowledge of diverse American racial and ethnic groups, genders, and social classes. Those who endorse this model recommend the total reform of schooling for the benefit of all students. Teaching strategies associated with the single-studies, human relations, and teaching the culturally different approaches are relevant to this model.

Information about diverse groups is integrated throughout the curriculum to ensure that all subject matter is consistently taught from a multicultural perspective (Sleeter, 1999). Educators propose that all students should become bilingual and recommend changes in evaluation criteria and the decreased use of standardized testing. School personnel provide extracurricular activities that are equally accessible to all students regardless of gender, ethnicity, ability, or class, and parents and the community are encouraged to be involved in school life. Persons from diverse groups, rather than those who reflect social hierarchies of power, are represented within the school staff and administration. This approach seeks to change school cultures and organizations so they represent and empower diverse groups of students.

Multicultural and Social Reconstructionist Education

Social reconstructionist educators not only endorse the multicultural education emphasis on changing the structure of American education but also seek to teach students about social justice and empower them as agents of change in society. The social reconstructionist approach supports a more radical restructuring of education and society than that proposed by the multicultural education perspective and deals more directly with issues of oppression, power structures, and social structural inequalities that reinforce oppression (Sleeter, 1996). Goals include (a) helping students become aware of issues and problems associated with injustice and inequality; (b) building students' commitment to expending the time and energy necessary to make a difference in the world; and (c) enhancing students' skills for enacting change through the use of communication and listening, information gathering, conflict resolution, and social action skills (Sapon-Shevin, 1999).

The ultimate goal of the social reconstructionist approach is increased democratic participation of students in a global society that is based on structural equality and cultural pluralism and is attentive to the intersections of race, gender, class, sexual orientation, and disability issues. Teaching about the knowledge construction process helps students (a) critically examine how knowledge generated by scientists is influenced by the cultural norms, biases, and worldviews of these experts and (b) challenge prevailing ideas (Banks, 1995).

Educators create learning environments in which students practice democratic principles by voicing opinions, working with others to solve problems or make decisions, and using power constructively. Also, students learn to analyze the circumstances of their lives, develop awareness about social justice and privilege, and generate adaptive responses to these circumstances. Students also develop social action skills and they learn to form coalitions among diverse groups to enact social change (Sleeter & Grant, 2003).

Comparisons Among Multicultural Education Approaches

Whereas the exceptional and culturally different approach involves helping students from underrepresented or nondominant groups to gain cognitive skills to enhance success in mainstream America, the human relations approach emphasizes the feelings and attitudes of individuals. The human relations approach helps individuals from diverse groups develop positive attitudes and skills for interacting with each other and can be referred to as an "I'm okay, you're okay" perspective (Grant & Sleeter, 2000). Both approaches focus on individual growth; neither approach focuses on exploring or challenging social power structures that support or reinforce cultural oppressions (Leistyna, 2002). Both approaches are mindful of the specific learning needs of those who have been marginalized (exceptional and culturally different) and highlight the necessity of prejudice reduction (human relations). These perspectives share many assumptions with the liberal feminist theories discussed in chapter 2. Cultural feminism, which seeks to revalue the specific learning styles of women, also resembles some aspects of these approaches.

The single-studies approach supports social change by challenging traditional knowledge bases, incorporating content that validates perspectives that are often excluded in traditional classrooms, raising the consciousness and increasing the sense of pride and empowerment of the identified group, and exposing students from dominant groups to perspectives of nondominant group members (Grant & Sleeter, 2000). The theoretical assumptions and pedagogical strategies associated with this approach resemble many of the assumptions and pedagogies of the women-of-color and lesbian and queer feminisms (see chap. 3, this volume).

The multicultural education and social reconstructionist approaches seek to transform education at all levels. Value is placed on ensuring equal opportunity as well as examining privilege and power structures that maintain the status quo and marginalize those from nondominant groups (Appelbaum, 2002; Nieto, 1999a). Both approaches are attentive to a wide range of social statuses such as race, gender, and sexual orientation. Whereas multicultural education advocates tend to consider diverse statuses as separate and overlapping social identities, social reconstructionist educators promote the examination of intersections among the multiple identities and view such exploration as crucial to understanding the complex dynamics of social identity and power. Exploring the hidden assumptions associated with the dominant statuses of Whiteness, middle-class status, and heterosexual privilege provides important information for developing positive social action alliances across groups (Leistyna, 2002).

Of the major multicultural approaches, the social reconstructionist approach is most closely aligned with the critical and liberation pedagogies discussed in chapter 1 and in the next section of this chapter. In addition, various strands within this approach are reflected in themes associated with the socialist, postmodern, and global feminisms (see chaps. 2 and 3, this volume).

CRITICAL PEDAGOGY, FEMINIST PEDAGOGY, AND MULTICULTURAL EDUCATION

We turn to a discussion of the relationships between critical and feminist pedagogies and multicultural education. As mentioned in chapter 1, critical, multicultural, and liberation pedagogies are closely related to many of the multicultural education approaches, especially the single-group studies and multicultural and social reconstructionist approaches. These pedagogies emerged out of movements that focused on liberation from oppression or inequality and have been applied at various stages of education. In the following sections, we provide recent examples of critical pedagogy approaches and research that are relevant to adult literacy education, critical antiracist feminist pedagogy, and multicultural feminist pedagogies.

Critical Pedagogy and Literacy Education

In 1987, Henry Giroux characterized the research on literacy education in the United States as almost entirely connected to preparing workers for jobs that demand functional reading and writing skills or to efforts to indoctrinate the poor, underprivileged, or minorities into a dominant Western worldview. Both of these views, he argued, were disempowering and oppressive:

> Critical theorists proposed a radical view of literacy that revolved around the need to identify and transform any existing or social conditions that served to undermine possibilities for the existence of community and public life organized around the imperatives of critical democracy. (Ball, 2000, p. 1007)

However, critics of critical pedagogy as applied to literacy argue that this approach lacks clarity in language and usefulness to educators (i.e., making links between the approach and actual teaching methods; Ellsworth, 1989; Johnston, 1999; Knight & Pearl, 2000).

More recently, attempts to increase linkages between critical theory and practice have been implemented. For example, using analysis of discourse and pedagogies, Arnetha Ball (2000) studied critical pedagogy within three literacy focused community-based classrooms taught by three African American women. The community-based classes consisted of two job-training programs that served predominantly African American students and an ethnocentric rites-of-passage program for African American females. Discourse analysis revealed that a sense of community, which is essential to implement critical pedagogy, was established via collaboration, negotiation, interactive discourse patterns, and the creation of opportunities for students to view themselves as knowledge sources and an important part of the community. Students were also exposed to multiple and diverse forms of oral and written literacy. These components are similar to aspects of social reconstructionist multicultural education approaches. Two central ideas emerged as keys to success. The first concept focused on self-perceptions of students. Teachers emphasized consciousness-raising and preparing students for the multiple roles they would play in society. Second, they assisted students in developing personal and group agency that facilitated their response to societal challenges with action. For example, one teacher encouraged students to become more conscious of the type of language used in the machinist industry and to take more control of the language they use in their everyday work situations.

Arnetha Ball (2000) contended that these teachers were able to create true multiculturally sensitive environments where dynamic constructions of knowledge occurred and students were able to consider alternative life opportunities. She also challenged teachers who seek to implement critical pedagogy in their classrooms to help students think of themselves as problem solvers and critical thinkers instead of passive recipients of knowledge. Ball's research reveals that critical pedagogy from a social reconstructionist perspective holds promise for making connections between theory and practice.

Feminist Critical and Antiracist Pedagogy

In her work, bell hooks (1994) discussed the integration of feminist pedagogy and critical pedagogy (Freire, 1970, 1994b) and emphasized the need for pedagogical practices that promote mutual participation and critical thinking among both teachers and students. Critical feminist pedagogy cannot focus only on gender but must also incorporate the experiences of racism faced by women of color. A true feminist classroom seeks to provide safety for women of color who desire to express their concerns about feminism and evaluate it critically but also helps them "deal with sexism and racism," develop "important strategies for survival and resistance" (hooks, 1994, p. 118), and share these strategies within classrooms and communities of color.

More recently, Susan Sánchez-Casal and Amie Macdonald (2002) proposed that feminist teachers have tended to use information about intersecting social identities (e.g., race, class, and sexual orientation) to explain the dynamics of oppression but not to transform feminist teaching. Their feminist antiracist model is informed by realist identity theory, which is based on the idea that students' identities are shaped by various social constructs (e.g., race, class, and sexual orientation) and that the dynamics of how these operate in the real world also manifest in the classroom.

Therefore, the feminist antiracist model assumes that through classroom sharing, students can learn that oppression is associated with real consequences and is also mediated by a variety of potentially contradictory experiences and social locations that are sometimes associated with privilege and sometimes associated with oppression. Class discussion of personal experience yields crucial information. However, it is also "misguided to maintain that an individual making a personal testimony has private, privileged, and conclusive . . . knowledge that is derived from and conferred from that experience" (Macdonald, 2002, p. 125). Thus, dialogue about difference becomes a central focus of pedagogy and leads to discussions about how realities and identities shift across situations within and outside the classroom. Strategies similar to those advocated in critical pedagogical approaches are used to meet the goals of "decentering the authority of the professor, developing and foregrounding subjugated knowledges, legitimizing personal identity and experience (especially marginalized identities and experiences), discussion-based classes, and an emphasis on student voice" (Sánchez-Casal & Macdonald, p. 4).

When feminist antiracist pedagogy is anchored in realist identity theory, educators engage students' perceptions and evaluations of power relations and construct a learning community that not only challenges reactionary thinking of students from the dominant culture but also allows students of color to discuss their experiences without "falsely imbuing them with uncontested epistemic authority" (Sánchez-Casal & Macdonald, 2002, p. 5) or expecting them to act as experts who speak for "their people." Reframing feminist teaching through realist identity theory provides "a coherent context for developing pedagogies that account for the complex networks of privilege and oppression that structure all our identities" (Sánchez-Casal & Macdonald, 2002, p. 5). Bonnie Moradi (2002) described how she encourages students to understand these complex networks of privilege and oppression by role-playing or shadowing a woman who is different from the student in terms of age, ability status, religion, race, ethnicity, sexual orientation, or pregnancy. Class members write a paper about the experience, addressing differences in privilege, status, and how women are treated because of differences. This exercise brings "the intellectual discussion of diversity home to a personal experience of power, privilege, and life experience" (Moradi, p. 8).

MULTICULTURAL EDUCATION AND TEACHER TRAINING

We now turn to the multicultural education literature on teacher training, which is an especially important topic in light of the gaps between theory and practice that have been observed. Christine Bennett's (2001) review of research on multicultural education concluded that there is little evidence that demonstrates the influence of kindergarten through Grade 12 (K–12) multicultural curriculum reform. In addition, a gap exists between the multicultural curriculum theories described earlier in this chapter and pedagogical practice. For example, studies demonstrate that K–12 teachers use bias and stereotype reduction and discuss multiple perspectives in history but do not focus on social action and curriculum transformation (C. Bennett, 2001). These findings point to the importance of preparing educators for effective multicultural teaching; thus, proponents of multicultural education have recently turned their attention from a sole focus on the multicultural education of students to the preparation of teachers who implement multicultural curricula. Specifically, numerous authors call for changes in multicultural training within colleges of education (Goodman, 2000; Grant & Wieczorek, 2000; Obidah, 2000; B. G. Wallace, 2000).

Multicultural teacher education has evolved through three distinct phases of exclusion, inclusion, and infusion (Goodwin, 1997). Colleges of education have recently implemented infusion perspectives, which focus on preparing teachers to be multicultural in both practice and perspective. Although current models of multicultural training hold promise for meeting the goal of ending oppression of all members of society (B. G. Wallace, 2000), additional improvements need to place greater emphasis on (a) linguistic diversity, (b) gay and lesbian parenting and sexual orientation issues, (c) disability issues, and (d) spirituality. Graduate programs are also advised to pursue the goal of organizational multicultural competence, a call that echoes Sue et al.'s (1998) recommendations that graduate schools of education "engage in an institutional audit of programs, policies, and practices, as part of determining whether the organization is appropriately pursuing multicultural development" (B. G. Wallace, 2000, p. 1105–1106).

Discussions about increasing teacher competency often emphasize improving the quality of teachers by attracting the "best and the brightest," or infusing subject matter knowledge into teacher training and then testing acquisition of this knowledge (Grant & Wieczorek, 2000). Training also needs to promote teachers' ability to question "the effects of social, cultural, and historical movements as well as power relationships" (Grant & Wieczorek, p. 913) that influence the nature and scope of knowledge that is considered important. Carl Grant and Kim Wieczorek advocated the practice of social mooring to facilitate critical reflection about how one's knowledge is influenced by social, cultural, institutional, and political contextual aspects and to use personal reflections to inform pedagogical practice. Social mooring calls on teachers to "'enlarge the frames' [of relevance] within which we view and discuss problems and issues" (p. 914) by moving beyond the content driven system of multicultural education to a systematic critical analysis of the construction of knowledge. The goal is to "help teacher educators and their students to see where ideas come from in terms of race, class, gender, and power relations" (Grant & Wieczorek, 2000, p. 925).

Louise Jennings and Cynthia Smith (2002) used two case studies to demonstrate how critical inquiry and problem posing can be used to "burrow into the foundations, ideologies, and deeper meanings of things otherwise taken for granted" (p. 458). Similar to social mooring, elements of critical inquiry include (a) examining existing assumptions and knowledge, (b) gaining and creating new information, (c) acquiring new perspectives, (d) engaging in critical analysis, (e) sharing one's learning with classmates, and (f) implementing multicultural and diversity plans in classrooms.

The first case study described how critical pedagogy helped 14 teachers transform their practices from "tourist" approaches to more comprehensive understandings of multicultural education. Analysis of students' writing revealed movement from viewing multicultural education as a passive information giving process to one in which students develop responsibility for their own learning. The second case study described the long-term impact of training on a teacher's multicultural practice. This teacher used critical inquiry practice to design a history unit that included antibias curriculum materials and helped students understand history in a sociopolitical context. She also critically investigated her teaching practices in a social, political, and historical context. For two years, this teacher corresponded with the former multicultural education instructor and consistently engaged in dialogue about implementing critical inquiry and multicultural practices. Jennings and Smith (2002) concluded that "multicultural teacher education needs to include but extend beyond particular courses to more expanded venues that provide opportunities for collaboration and critical reflection in action over time" (p. 456).

CONTRIBUTIONS, CHALLENGES, AND LIMITATIONS OF THE MULTICULTURAL EDUCATION LITERATURE

Multicultural Approaches and Critical Pedagogy

Our discussion of the multicultural education literature reveals a variety of important contributions. The exceptional and culturally different approach is designed to help individuals acquire skills for survival in mainstream society; the human relations approach promotes prejudice reduction by focusing on respect, communication, and improving relationships; and the single-studies group approach emphasizes education about and from the perspective of specific oppressed groups (e.g., African American). The multicultural education approach promotes cultural diversity and the equitable distribution of power within and beyond the classroom, and the social reconstructionist approach advocates social justice, the overhauling of American schools, and the empowerment of students as social change agents.

Educators who seek social transformation rather than individual empowerment alone are likely to find the single-group studies, multicultural education, and social reconstructionist approaches to be the most informative and useful. In general, the multicultural education literature offers insights about (a) changing educational systems, (b) creating more effective instructional methods, (c) improving the evaluation process, (d) ensuring that the experiences and cultures of all students are included in educational content, (e) paying attention to the process as well as content of teaching, (f) promoting an appreciation of difference through diversity training, and (g) developing methods and models that empower students.

As noted earlier in this chapter, multicultural education approaches are sometimes interpreted or applied in superficial ways and can resemble a tourist or "voyeuristic" approach to multicultural knowledge. When multicultural education is reduced to information about the "holidays and heroes" of persons from diverse cultural backgrounds, stereotypes may be reinforced or students may gain limited knowledge about contributions of these groups or the consequences of oppression in their lives. Multicultural educators also face the challenge of deciding whether to teach about aspects of multicultural experience in specific modules that focus on specific oppressions such as racism, sexism, or heterosexism or to address these "isms" in an integrative manner (Adams et al., 1997). Whereas some educators believe that speaking to these issues simultaneously may dilute attention needed to understand a specific issue or group, others believe that when efforts to integrate these issues are not present, multicultural education is interpreted narrowly as education about race and ethnicity, and concerns related to disability, sexual orientation, and class may be minimized.

Critical theory and related multicultural approaches have sometimes been criticized as providing a utopian, idealistic, and impractical perspective about the possibility that students can transcend their oppression and enact social change. In addition, theoretical perspectives are sometimes inadequately linked to the practice of teaching (Ball, 2000; C. Bennett, 2001; Grant & Wieczorek, 2000); training for implementing critical pedagogies is sometimes limited (Jennings & Smith, 2002); and assessment of the effectiveness of multicultural methods may be inadequate. Finally, multicultural content is sometimes confined to a specific course or module rather than integrated into a sequence of activities or venues over time (Jennings & Smith, 2002).

Teacher Preparation

Despite the limitations addressed previously, the multicultural education literature is increasingly attentive to the ways in which teachers and school personnel are trained. The teacher-training literature advocates reforms regarding how issues of diversity are addressed within graduate programs in education. First, this literature proposes that understanding multiple diversities is critical and supports the infusion of multiculturalism across the curriculum rather than requiring a "catch all" course on diversity. Second, colleges of education are encouraged to evaluate their organizations' programs, policies, and practices to ensure that they are promoting the multicultural competence of faculty and students as well as supporting and graduating diverse groups of students from their programs. Third, colleges of education need to help students examine the dynamic construction of knowledge and critically evaluate knowledge within a historical, political, cultural, and social context. Finally, it is important to train teachers and school personnel to carry a commitment to social advocacy throughout their careers. Therefore, it is necessary to examine whether current teaching practices support an atmosphere in which students can think critically about social justice issues and learn how to be change agents in a culturally pluralistic democratic society.

Class Issues

Although multicultural education approaches provide a solid foundation for understanding ethnic and cultural diversity, dialogue about the intersection between race and class issues has been noticeably absent from this literature. Class is often referred to as an important consideration in the dynamics of privilege and oppression, but little in-depth discussion is devoted to the subject. Furthermore, this literature rarely addresses specific ways in which teachers may introduce the subject of economic and class oppression into the curriculum.

One notable exception is Sonia Nieto's (1999a) application of Pierre Bourdieu's sociological theories to culture and learning. Pierre Bourdieu (1990) introduced the importance of social and cultural capital, noting that money or economic capital alone does not determine a person's social standing. Social structure is also influenced by acquired tastes, values, language (cultural capital), and social networks and obligations (social capital). Nieto noted the following:

> Most schools are organized to reflect the cultural capital of privileged social and cultural groups; in the United States that group is middle-class or upper class, English speaking Whites. As a result of their identity, some children arrive at the schoolhouse door with a built-in privilege because they have learned this cultural capital primarily in the same way as they have learned to walk, that is, unconsciously and effortlessly. (p. 55)

Nieto (1999a) highlighted the importance of understanding the impact of class issues on students and their learning styles as well as the inherent classism that exists in current pedagogical approaches. When schools are organized to reflect the cultural capital of upper- and middle-class individuals, educational structures automatically set up classroom environments that may limit the achievement of persons from lower-social-class backgrounds.

Contemporary socialist feminist writings have made significant contributions to the understanding of gender politics and social class, and these writings may enhance a multicultural feminist pedagogy that is attentive to class issues. As Carolyn Enns (1997) pointed out in the following:

> Contemporary socialist feminists believe that Marxist analyses are useful for articulating the material or economic ways in which women are oppressed under capitalism. The role of work and economic exploitation and its relationship to alienation and estrangement is a central emphasis. (p. 67)

Furthermore, social feminists known as dual-systems theorists have argued that capitalism, patriarchy, and other forms of oppression are "impossible to separate and must be analyzed simultaneously to understand the various ways in which the oppression of women operates in various contexts and cultures" (Enns, 1997, p. 69). The emphasis on understanding gender politics and classism is a unique contribution of the feminist literature that can be used to enhance multicultural education and critical pedagological approaches.

CONCLUSIONS AND IMPLICATIONS FOR A PEDAGOGY THAT IS FEMINIST AND MULTICULTURAL

One of the major overarching messages of the field of multicultural education and critical pedagogical approaches is the importance of paying special attention to how we teach about diversity as well as what we teach about diversity. These perspectives also remind all educators of the importance of total reform of the curriculum and the institutional structures, policies, and practices. Specifically, multicultural education advocates raise questions about how students are evaluated and propose that bilingual competence should be encouraged for all students.

Feminist theories have long acknowledged that "the personal is political," which reinforces their affinity to multicultural approaches that call for social change and the critique of institutional policies and practices. One of the major contributions of a social reconstructionist perspective is its reminder to attend to the complex intersections of race, gender, class, sexual orientation, and disability issues. Both critical pedagogy and social reconstructionist approaches highlight the importance of understanding the dynamics of privilege and oppression and empowering students to see themselves as agents of change. Similarly, the feminist pedagogy literature increasingly emphasizes the centrality of understanding privilege and power differences among women and using approaches that empower students to understand diversity issues in the context of their own experiences (Sánchez-Casal & Macdonald, 2002).

Both the multicultural education and the social reconstructionist literatures remind educators to attend to how power relationships operate in society as well as in the classroom and encourage educators to embrace a system of bidirectional learning. Similarly, one of the underlying principles of feminist scholarship and practice involves changing ways in which power is used in institutional, political, and social relationships and embracing collaborative systems of power. These approaches remind educators that collaborative relationships between teachers and students are integral aspects of multicultural and feminist pedagogy.

The multicultural education and critical pedagogy literature is vast and impressive. As stated in chapter 1, significant integration of feminist and critical perspectives on pedagogy has already occurred, and examples of this can be seen by the influence Freire's writings have had on the theories and pedagogical ideas of many feminist educators (e.g., hooks, 1994). Future multicultural feminist pedagogies will only be viable and effective if educators focus consistently on the multiple intersections of identity and sources of oppression. As stated in chapter 1, the goals of a feminist multicultural pedagogy are to explore the intersections, fluidity, borders, and boundaries among identities. Multicultural and critical pedagogical approaches can play an important role in advancing the exploration and understanding of identities within a feminist multicultural pedagogy and in moving us toward meeting this goal.

5

MULTICULTURAL COUNSELING TRAINING APPROACHES: IMPLICATIONS FOR PEDAGOGY

JULIE R. ANCIS AND SABA RASHEED ALI

A variety of approaches to multicultural counseling are described in the literature (e.g., Comas-Díaz & Greene, 1994; Helms & Cook, 1999; Myers, 1993; Sue, Ivey, & Pedersen, 1996). These approaches have been identified as essential to working with an increasingly diverse population (American Psychological Association [APA], 2002; Sue et al., 1996). Relatedly, facilitating multicultural counseling competence among trainees and clinicians is considered imperative to meeting the needs of clients who differ along such dimensions as race, ethnicity, gender, socioeconomic status, ability, age, and identity.

In this chapter, we review multicultural counseling approaches and associated conceptual frameworks for which specific training strategies have been delineated and present relevant research that links theoretical approaches to actual pedagogy. We briefly explore the linkages between these approaches and the literature on multicultural education and discuss the implications of the multicultural counselor training literature for a pedagogy that is multicultural and feminist. We do not discuss those multicultural counseling approaches and frameworks for which specific training approaches have not been developed (e.g., Gonzalez, Biever, & Gardner, 1994, a social constructionist approach; Ramirez, 1999, a multicultural model of psychotherapy). Unlike other educational approaches discussed in the first four chapters of the book, the primary recipients of multicultural counselor educational efforts are defined rather specifically: counselors and psychologists in training. However, many of the teaching tools associated with multicultural counselor training models are relevant to a broad range of courses designed to help individuals develop the attitudes, knowledge, and skills necessary to communicate effectively in a multicultural society.

Multicultural training differs along a number of dimensions. First, definitions of culture vary from a relatively broad definition that includes most demographic variables, status variables, affiliations, and ethnographic variables (Fukuyama, 1990; Pedersen, 1991), to a more specific conceptualization of culture that focuses on race, racial identity, or ethnicity (e.g., Carter, 1995; Locke, 1990). Second, multicultural counselor training approaches differ in the extent to which contextual variables in people's lives are emphasized. Third, multicultural training approaches vary in terms of the goals of training. Fourth, approaches differ in terms of the content and process of training.

APPROACHES TO MULTICULTURAL COUNSELING TRAINING

Robert Carter and Adil Qureshi (1995) have asserted that the philosophical assumptions underlying multicultural training approaches can be grouped into five types: (a) universal, (b) ubiquitous, (c) traditional, (d) race based, and (e) pan-national. Other authors (e.g. Porter, 1995; Sciarra, 1999) have presented alternative multicultural counseling philosophies that do not necessarily adhere to these typologies. The following overview, which organizes counselor training approaches into four broad categories, incorporates Carter and Qureshi's description of multicultural training models, our interpretations of the multicultural training literature, and more recent training approaches. Although we present these training models as independent and discrete entities, they overlap in terms of underlying philosophical frameworks and training methods. Approaches are summarized in Table 5.1.

Existential or Universal Approach

Proponents of this approach explicitly advocate the application of existential philosophy or existential principles to cross-cultural counseling (e.g, Ibrahim, 1985; Vontress, Johnson, & Epp, 1999). Individuals are viewed as more similar to each other than different, and problems such as loving, living, and dying are viewed as universal human problems that transcend culture (Fukuyama, 1990; Vontress et al., 1999). Moreover, many clients seek counseling for problems in living that have nothing to do with culture.

TABLE 5.1
Multicultural Counseling Training Approaches

Approach	Key concepts	Counseling process	Pedagogy
Existential or universal	Universal human problems transcend culture	Focus on clients as individuals and problems encountered in everyday living	Develop counselor qualities such as acceptance of one's own and client's worldview
Ubiquitous	Broad conception of culture; recognition that cultural salience may change with time and situation	Attend to clients' multiple cultures and identities	Develop counselor's multiple identities and internal dialogue
Focused culture specific	Focus on race and ethnicity	Use interventions that are culture specific and developed with attention to client's cultural context	Train counselors to understand client's cultural frame of reference and intervene accordingly
Race based	Emphasis on the social and political significance of visual racial characteristics	Attend to counselor's and client's racial identity and sociopolitical implications of race and culture on the therapeutic relationship	Develop counselor racial self-awareness and understanding of racism

Clemmont Vontress et al. have proposed that counselors focus on issues that are "non-culture-specific" (1999, p. 62) and recognize clients as individuals. Cultural differences are deemphasized so as not to negate the person in his or her entirety and to minimize the promotion of stereotyping (Fukuyama, 1990; Patterson, 1996). This conceptualization does not mean that cultural factors are ignored. In fact, counseling interventions may need to be modified according to the client's cultural background (Vontress et al., 1999). Existentialists propose that all cultures include individuals who present a range of cultural behaviors. Large within-group differences exist and all counseling is viewed as cross-cultural.

Farah Ibrahim (1991) has advocated the assessment of a client's worldview to process concerns and develop goals consistent with the client's cultural assumptions. Pedagogical approaches focus on facilitating counselor qualities such as understanding and accepting one's own worldview as well as the client's worldview (Ibrahim, 1985, 1991). The aim is to develop greater rapport between counselor and client by creating a climate that minimizes client stereotyping and oppressive counseling approaches that do not "fit" the client's worldview. In fact, "cultural misunderstanding or communication problems between clients and therapists" has been identified as potentially preventing racial and ethnic minority group members from "using services and receiving appropriate care" (U.S. Department of Health and Human Services, 2000/2001, p. 42). Instructors help students map their worldviews, use affective and structured techniques to confront biases and stereotypes; present information regarding ethnic and cultural groups; and finally, teach skills for effective multicultural communication (Ibrahim, 1991). As such, training targets cognitive, affective, and behavioral components. Instructors facilitate counselor self-awareness; cognitive, affective, and behavioral flexibility; and empathy and understanding. Counselors are encouraged to understand the client and to convey this understanding to the client.

Ubiquitous Approach

Paul B. Pedersen (1991, 1999) has advocated a broad definition of culture that includes demographic variables (e.g., age and gender), status variables (e.g., social and educational), affiliations (e.g., formal and informal), and ethnographic variables (e.g., nationality and ethnicity). Pedersen has asserted that all counseling is to some extent multicultural and that cultural salience may change with time and situation (Pedersen, 1991). A broad definition of culture attends to the complexity of cultural identity patterns that do not necessarily include ethnicity or nationality as well as within-group variables. Pedersen (1991) has recognized the dangers inherent in an exclusive adherence to either a specific or a general definition of culture. A narrow definition of culture may result in "the ethnocentric domination by culturally defined special interest groups" (p. 10). Similarly, a universalistic perspective may ignore the realities of power differentials in society (Lee, 1991). Pedersen has argued for a multicultural approach that emphasizes both culture-specific and culture-general characteristics.

Similarly, Derald Wing Sue et al. (1996) proposed a metatheory of multicultural counseling and therapy (MCT), which acknowledges the validity of both universal and culture-specific approaches. Culture is defined broadly to refer to any group that shares a theme or issue(s). Sue et al. have asserted that the culture-bound values of current counseling theories (e.g., individualism, linearity, and emphasis on self-disclosure) are often inconsistent with the worldview of culturally diverse clientele. They outlined a series of propositions and corollaries associated with a metatheory. Such a theory is culture centered, accounts for the representation of different worldviews, and acknowledges the person–environment interaction. A metatheoretical framework allows for the continuous acknowledgment and reclassification of new theories and the evolution of established theories.

The multicultural counseling competencies developed by Derald Wing Sue, Patricia Arredondo, and Roderick McDavis (1992) and the Professional

Standards Committee of the Association of Multicultural Counseling and Development serve as the framework of training. The three primary goals of MCT training coincide with three primary multicultural counseling competencies. The first goal consists of increasing trainees' awareness of their own values, biases, stereotypes, and assumptions about human behavior. Objectives include cultural self-awareness and awareness of the culture-bound and class-bound values of traditional therapies. Proponents assert that a lack of awareness often results in the imposition of values on culturally different clients. Training encourages students' appreciation of the validity of multiple worldviews. Pedagogical approaches may involve increasing students' self-awareness by having them develop a personal genogram (Ivey, Ivey, & Simek-Morgan, 1993) or an autobiography in which they investigate educational experiences that have historically been available or not available to members of their cultural group (Arredondo & Arciniega, 2001). Didactic instruction is used to increase students' knowledge of the culture-bound and class-bound values of traditional psychotherapies. Students may also read materials regarding identity development (Arredondo et al., 1996).

The second goal consists of increasing trainees' knowledge of culturally different clients' worldviews, including gaining specific knowledge about the life experiences, cultural heritage, and historical background of culturally different clients. Instruction may include readings about the cultural values and experiences of diverse racial and ethnic populations. The intercultural assimilator model (Fiedler, Mitchell, & Triandis, 1971) integrates the cognitive, affective, and behavioral experiences of trainees by presenting intercultural scenarios along with alternative interpretations of situations to teach students to perceive situations from the perspective of members of that culture. After participants select the attribution they believe is most likely made by persons in the target culture, culturally relevant feedback is provided. Cultural immersion experiences represent another approach in which students spend time in communities or attend events that are different than those in their own traditions (Arredondo et al., 1996).

The third goal involves the development of culturally appropriate intervention strategies, such as being able to engage in a variety of verbal and nonverbal helping responses. Pedersen's triad training model aims to foster counselors' sensitivity to clients' positive and negative internal dialogue and thus make culturally appropriate attributions relevant to clients' multiple cultures and cultural identities (Pedersen, 1994). Fieldwork placement with culturally diverse supervisors and clients represents an important training approach to skill development (Kiselica, 1991). Research has demonstrated a moderate relationship between immersion experiences such as multicultural internship training and cross-cultural interactions and multicultural competencies, particularly in the area of self-reported knowledge and skills (e.g., Díaz-Lázaro & Cohen, 2001; Manese, Wu, &, Nepomuceno, 2001; Merta, Stringham, & Ponterotto, 1988).

Focused Culture-Specific Approach

Proponents of the focused culture-specific approach (e.g., Locke, 1990; Nwachuku & Ivey, 1991; Sue, 1990), also referred to as the traditional or anthropological approach (see Carter & Qureshi, 1995), have argued that given the history of racism in North America, multicultural counseling should focus primarily on African American, Asian American, Latino, and Native American cultures or racial and ethnic minority populations. Proponents believe that an exclusively universal or general approach results in ineffective and oppressive counseling methods; in contrast, relevant theories and interventions are derived from the host culture's point of view. Examples of culture-specific counseling approaches include Carolyn Attneave's (1969) Network Therapy for Native Americans, an integration of Native American concepts of relationship and community with family therapy, and José Szapocznik's and William Kurtines's (1989) Brief Strategic Family Therapy for Hispanic adolescents and their families. Culturally responsive interventions (Ancis, 2004) consider culture as primary to assessment, diagnosis, and treatment. Many culture-based interventions emphasize the role of family and social ecology in assessment and treatment. Several studies suggest that culturally sensitive interventions may increase service use, length of treatment, client's satisfaction, and therapy outcomes (Flaskerud & Soldevilla, 1986; Rogler, Malgady, & Rodriguez, 1989; Sue, Zane, & Young, 1994; Szapocznik et al., 1989).

Possessing an accurate understanding of the various cultural groups with which one works and using culturally relevant and effective intervention strategies are considered essential components of multicultural counseling competence (Sue et al., 1992). Relatedly, the generation of training models involves starting from the target culture's frame of reference and conducting an analysis of the culture. The effectiveness of the culture-specific training is then evaluated. Training focuses on teaching culture-specific knowledge (e.g., Leong & Kim, 1991; Nwachuku & Ivey, 1991; Parker, Valley, & Geary, 1986) such as promoting knowledge of culturally sanctioned healing practices within specific communities and the recognition that helping styles and approaches may be culturally based. The clinician may need to consult with and enlist the assistance of change agents within the family and community, including community, religious, and spiritual leaders and practitioners (APA, 2002; Arredondo et al., 1996; Lewis, Lewis, Daniels, & D'Andrea, 1998). Clinicians must also be familiar with and use organizations that provide support and services in different cultural communities. Roderick McDavis and Max Parker (1977) described an ethnic minority counseling course in which students view videotapes of instructors counseling ethnic minority clients. Subsequently, students role-play a counseling interview with an ethnic minority client.

Another training tool is the Intercultural Sensitizer (IS; Leong & Kim, 1991). The IS consists of a booklet of critical incidents of cross-cultural interactions. Trainees review the narratives, describe relevant intercultural interactions and outcomes, and provide a series of possible explanations for the sequence of events and outcomes. All possible explanations, including the most preferred one, are discussed in light of the target group's cultural values. Thus, training moves beyond acquiring culture-specific knowledge to actual skill development. Behavioral flexibility is emphasized.

Race-Based Approach

The race-based approach assumes that one's racial group supersedes other experiences in the United States and cultural groups are defined by racial categories (Carter & Qureshi, 1995). Proponents of this approach emphasize the social and political significance of visual racial characteristics related to the history of racism and racial discrimination in the United States and associated with historically ingrained assumptions (Carter, 1995; Helms, 1990, 1995). Sociorace is seen as defining cultural groups in North America, and other reference group memberships are understood in the context of racial group membership. Attention is paid to intergroup power relations and its deleterious effects for people of color. Race-based theorists propose that interactions and social relations between European and American Whites and people of color influence each group member's psychosocial development or racial identity development (Carter, 1995; Cross, 1978; Hardiman, 1982; Helms, 1990). Racial identity involves one's attitudes, thoughts, affect, and behaviors toward oneself as a member of a racial group and members of the dominant racial group. Racial identity development is typically viewed as movement from an identity in which one accepts the status quo and traditional messages about one's own group and those of others to an awareness of oppression and racism to a more complex and flexible identity. The counselor's and client's levels of racial identity are seen as influencing counseling process and outcome.

Related training efforts focus on increasing racial self-awareness, understanding the effects of racism, and fostering racial identity development (e.g., Helms, 1990; Katz, 1985; Sabnani, Ponterotto, & Borodvsky, 1991). Training addresses White ethnocentrism and racism (e.g., Ancis & Szymanski, 2001; Corvin & Wiggins, 1989) and racial issues within supervision (Ancis & Ladany, 2001; Helms & Cook, 1999). Haresh B. Sabnani et al. described specific goals and training interventions associated with stages of White racial identity to facilitate counselors' White racial consciousness. For example, a student at a primary stage of racial identity may be encouraged to engage in "safe," nonthreatening contact with individuals from other cultures to expand awareness regarding their own culture and those of other ethnic groups. Similarly, Sue Ann Corvin and Fred Wiggins (1989) described a stage model of antiracism training based on characteristics of White identity development.

Robert Carter (2003) described the Racial–Cultural Counseling Laboratory as a cognitive, behavioral, and affective approach to racial–cultural competence training. Racial and cultural self-awareness is promoted through didactic, experiential, and skill-based learning. Students respond to questions about reference group memberships such as religion, social class, ethnicity, and race. The lab is competence based, and feedback regarding students' use of counseling skills and their ability to use and communicate racial–cultural knowledge is provided throughout.

Research has revealed that multicultural training with White students that incorporates education and role-playing related to White racial consciousness is positively correlated with higher levels of White racial identity development (Neville et al., 1996; Parker, Moore, & Neimeyer, 1998). Moreover, advanced levels of White racial identity are significantly associated with higher levels of self-reported multicultural competence (Ladany, Inman, Constantine, & Hofheinz, 1997; Ottavi, Pope-Davis, & Dings, 1994; Vinson & Neimeyer, 2000).

RELATIONSHIPS AMONG MULTICULTURAL COUNSELING AND EDUCATION LITERATURES

Although the multicultural education approaches discussed in chapter 4 and the multicultural counselor training literatures have developed along separate tracks, some parallel and intersecting themes are evident. The existential or universal counselor training model and the human relations approach to multicultural education share the following goals or strategies: (a) helping students understand and accept the worldviews of others, (b) challenging stereotyped thinking and replacing biased values with positive attitudes about difference, (c) promoting skills for effective communication across boundaries and cultures, and (d) emphasizing the uniqueness of students' and clients' life experiences and attitudes. Both the ubiquitous training perspective and the multicultural education and social reconstructionist approaches (a) view culture as encompassing a broad array of variables such as race, class, and gender; (b) are concerned with the intersections among the multiple and complex social identities negotiated by individuals; and (c) challenge the basic assumptions of traditional institutions or structures in which education and counseling occur (e.g., Ridley & Thompson, 1999).

The single-studies approach in multicultural education shares with the focused culture-specific approach the concern that when *culture* and *multicultural* are defined in broad terms, the unique histories, perspectives, learning styles, or culture-specific values of groups may be diluted or given inadequate attention. The single-studies approach also shares with the race-based models of counselor training an emphasis on (a) culture-specific healing and learning processes; (b) attentiveness to racism, power, and privilege in counseling, and education; and (c) the fostering of racial awareness on the part of students, educators, clients, and counselors.

As noted in chapter 4, both the single-studies and the social reconstructionist approaches to multicultural education rely on frameworks, assumptions, and strategies associated with critical pedagogy. Although critical pedagogy has received limited attention within the counselor training literature, Don Locke and Marie Faubert's (1999) use of critical pedagogy as an "innovative" approach to counselor education points to possibilities for increased cross-fertilization between the multicultural education and counselor training literatures. Efforts to integrate themes from these related literatures are likely to foster broader foundations and greater coherence to both multicultural and feminist approaches to education and counselor training.

IMPLICATIONS FOR MULTICULTURAL FEMINIST PEDAGOGY

Each of the multicultural counselor training approaches described previously contains elements that are consistent with and can be integrated with a feminist multicultural pedagogy. They may be used to increase students' self- and other-awareness as well as their behavioral flexibility. For example, the existential or universal approach emphasizes developing the ability to understand multiple perspectives (Nieto, 1999b). Consistent with feminist critical and multicultural pedagogy principles, active engagement in critical thinking and self-reflection are viewed as essential to understanding and accepting multiple worldviews. The importance of the client's as well as the counselor's frame of reference to counseling parallels the emphasis placed on the student's lived experience as central to teaching and learning in feminist classrooms.

Similarly, the emphasis on multiple dimensions of counselor competence (e.g., self-awareness, knowledge, and skills), and related attention to the emotional, cognitive, and behavioral components of learning within the ubiquitous approach are consistent with both multicultural and feminist pedagogy. Both MCT and related training as well as multicultural and feminist pedagogies emphasize a culture-centered perspective, the appreciation of diverse worldviews, and the acknowledgment of person–environment interactions. Trainers use approaches that encourage students to demonstrate flexibility and accommodate client differences. Moreover, the MCT metatheory assumes the continuous acknowledgment and reclassification of new theories as well as the evolution of established theories. This assumption parallels the emphasis on dynamism, process, and ongoing knowledge construction in both multicultural and feminist pedagogies.

Consistent with both multicultural and feminist pedagogies, the focused culture-specific approach emphasizes the impact of social group memberships and identities on lived experience. In fact, this concept is integral to this approach, which attends to the broader social context and power differences both within the family and in the larger society. The broader social context includes gendered role expectations and economic resources. Related pedagogy and training involve fostering flexibility and respect for multiple perspectives to facilitate students' ability to work effectively and competently with diverse populations. As such, training challenges the imposition of a particular theoretical orientation on all clients and considers the interplay between the client's cultural context, related experiences, and presenting problems.

Race-based approaches overlap with feminist and critical and multicultural pedagogies in their emphasis on increasing one's consciousness with regard to the effects of internalized racism on emotional, affective, and behavioral functioning (people-of-color racial identity models) or overcoming privilege (White racial identity development) through self-reflection. The process of racial identity development involves developing definitions of self and others as racial beings. As such, one is liberated from restrictive racist societal messages. Consequently, therapists' and clients' interactions may be relatively free of societal racial stereotypes. Teaching approaches and associated training goals are tailored to the student's developmental level, and thus provide the appropriate amount of challenge and support (Carney & Kahn, 1984; Corvin & Wiggins, 1989; Sabnani et al., 1991). Assessing a student's unique level of development is considered essential to effective teaching. For example, a role-playing exercise or stereotype awareness exercise may be relevant for a student at an early stage of development, whereas a more challenging cross-racial encounter may be relevant for a student at a higher level of racial awareness (Sabnani et al., 1991). Also consistent with feminist and multicultural pedagogies is an emphasis on self-reflection. In the future, the integration of racial identity models with other social identity development models that focus on feminist identity (Downing & Roush, 1985), womanist identity (Ossana, Helms, & Leonard, 1992), and lesbian identity (McCarn & Fassinger, 1996) is likely to contribute to the usefulness of identity development models as a foundation for pedagogy that is both multicultural and feminist.

In addition to the strengths of these training approaches for informing feminist and multicultural pedagogy, some limitations also exist. For example, both the existential or universal and ubiquitous approaches tend to overlook intergroup power dynamics and sociopolitical history by assuming that various group memberships are equal (Carter & Qureshi, 1995). As a result, students may not develop an understanding of social and contextual influences on individuals. An inability to conduct an accurate assessment and engage in trusting therapeutic relationships with clients, particularly those with different histories and experiences from the counselor, may result. Another limitation of the ubiquitous approach is the tendency to define culture too broadly (Nuttall, Sanchez, & Webber, 1996). Terms such as *culture, diversity, minor-*

ity, *race*, and *ethnicity* are often used interchangeably. Because these terms are not clearly defined, conversations about interactions within cultural contexts are often ambiguous. Moreover, as the word *minority* is used to refer primarily to racial and ethnic minorities, the needs of other individuals who have experienced differential and unequal treatment in society, such as women, gays, lesbians, and people with disabilities, may not be addressed.

A limitation of most of these training approaches from some feminist and multicultural pedagogical perspectives is the almost absent discussion of the interplay of individuals' race, ethnicity, gender, and other socio-identities within different contexts. Although this is an issue for most of the approaches, it is most evident within the race-based approach. Several authors have described the importance of attending to the intersections and interactions of clinicians' and clients' multiple socio-identities, situational and historical contexts, and presenting issues (e.g., Comas-Díaz & Greene, 1994; Deaux & Stewart, 2001). However, such a perspective is not necessarily clearly articulated as a training approach. Increasingly, there has been movement toward attending to the intersections of diverse social group memberships and identities (e.g., race, ethnicity, gender, religion, and sexual orientation) in multicultural counseling training approaches and toward conceptualizing individuals and communities in context (Leach & Carlton, 1997). Students seem to consider issues of race, ethnicity, and social class more readily when these factors are at the forefront of information presented in class rather than relegated as secondary issues (Ancis & Sanchez-Hucles, 2000).

FUTURE DIRECTIONS

The previously described approaches to multicultural training represent diverse philosophical frameworks for defining multicultural counseling competence, the goals of multicultural training, and the content and process of training. The availability of diverse approaches to multicultural counseling theory and training represent a rich literature. However, the lack of a unifying framework often results in confusion and the tendency for trainers and educators to use a hodgepodge approach to facilitating students' multicultural competence. The lack of agreement regarding the definition of terms is a further barrier to the advancement of multicultural training approaches. Moreover, most approaches, although using specific methods, lack a structured training focus that can be systematically followed and applied with students who differ in terms of their multicultural competence.

Empirical research on the efficacy of specific training approaches is limited. Rather, existing research has focused on the impact of multicultural counseling training in general, on self-reported multicultural counseling competence, and on knowledge about racial and ethnic minority populations. Instruments that have been developed to measure competence tend to assess awareness, knowledge, and skills and are based on the MCT approach, for example, the Multicultural Counseling Awareness Scale (MCAS; Ponterotto et al., 1996); the Multicultural Counseling Knowledge and Awareness Scale (MCKAS; Ponterotto, Gretchen, Utsey, Rieger, & Austin, 2002); the Multicultural Counseling Inventory (MCI; Sodowsky, Taffe, Gutkin, & Wise, 1994); and the Multicultural Awareness, Knowledge, and Skills Survey (D'Andrea, Daniels, & Heck, 1991). The significant and positive relationship between the self-report multicultural counseling competence inventories and social desirability attitudes (Constantine & Ladany, 2000) presents serious limitations. Nevertheless, multicultural counseling training has been found to be significantly and positively related to self-perceived multicultural counseling competence, particularly the knowledge dimension, among both undergraduate and graduate students (e.g., Constantine & Gainor, 2001; D'Andrea et al.; Estrada, Durlak, & Juarez, 2002; Sodowsky, Kuo-Jackson, Richardson, & Corey, 1998).

Although information regarding the effectiveness of specific training approaches is limited, several findings have particular implications for feminist and multicultural pedagogy. For example, empathic concern, such as feelings of concern, warmth, and sympathy toward others, significantly predicts school counselor trainees' self-perceived multicultural counseling competence (Constantine, 2001). In addition, emotional intelligence, characterized by the ability to attend to, clarify, and discriminate among feelings as well as to engage in mood-regulating strategies (Mayer & Salovey, 1993) significantly predicts self-perceived multicultural counseling knowledge among school counselors (Constantine & Gainor, 2001). These results suggest that to promote cultural competence, those using pedagogical approaches must move beyond providing information about diverse populations. Training that facilitates students' ability to understand and appropriately respond to others on an affective level is needed.

Exercises that encourage students to reflect on their own experiences of privilege and discrimination may help them to better understand the lived experiences of others. Students who have examined the privileges associated with their own multiple socio-identities related to gender, ethnicity, and class are also able to articulate an understanding of privilege and its impact on others (Ancis & Szymanski, 2001). Limited self-exploration of multiple socio-identities may hinder one's ability to acknowledge related privileges and to empathize with others (Ancis & Ladany, 2001). Moreover, White counseling students have identified personal experiences with people of color as a primary contributor to their own awareness of White privilege and its effects on people of color (Ancis & Szymanski, 2001). Exercises that facilitate such encounters, such as conducting interviews with individuals about their lived experiences or participating in events that reflect the values and practices of cultural groups, may promote understanding and empathy. Identifying which activity engages students on many levels (e.g., cognitive, affective, and behavioral) seems crucial to promoting the development of professionals who can effectively work with diverse populations.

Research has demonstrated that counseling students differ along a number of dimensions such as feminist identity, cognitive complexity, self-awareness, and racial attitudes, which influence their responses to multicultural material (Ancis & Sanchez-Hucles, 2000; Ancis & Szymanski, 2001). A pedagogy that is both feminist and multicultural acknowledges these unique and multiple perspectives and promotes increased consciousness, perspective taking, and behavioral flexibility by modifying approaches accordingly. The approaches to multicultural counseling training described in this chapter may inform such a pedagogy.

6

MULTICULTURAL AND FEMINIST LITERATURES: THEMES, DIMENSIONS, AND VARIATIONS

ADA L. SINACORE AND CAROLYN ZERBE ENNS

In this brief chapter, we summarize the parallel and divergent features of the multicultural and feminist theoretical positions discussed in chapters 2 through 5. It is our hope that this overview, along with the common principles, foundations, and converging themes discussed in chapter 1, will provide the foundation necessary for educators to articulate meaningful pedagogical models. Common to all the multicultural and feminist models discussed in previous chapters is the goal of reenvisioning pedagogy such that the voices of individuals who are marginalized in traditional education are centralized. However, the specific aims and the process by which this goal is achieved are likely to vary depending on one's theoretical entry point or standpoint. Our purpose in this brief chapter is to facilitate integration and synthesis by summarizing common dimensions as well as areas of overlap and difference among the feminist, multicultural education, and multicultural counselor training approaches.

ENTERING THE PEDAGOGICAL DIALOGUE

A fundamental area in which multicultural and feminist positions differ is the point at which they enter the pedagogical dialogue. In this section, we focus on two dimensions associated with pedagogical priorities: (a) the degree to which approaches begin with and emphasize gender or culture and ethnicity and (b) the degree to which approaches highlight social locations and embeddedness in systems or personal positionality and identity. We believe that it is important for multicultural feminist educators to integrate both gender and culture, as well as content related to both social location and identity. However, individual educators are likely to initiate their integrative efforts from a variety of perspectives, and their decisions are likely to be influenced by their own positionalities, experiences, and training.

Gender or Culture

Common to all feminist theories is the notion that sexism and misogyny are endemic to the challenges faced by women and society. Although feminist theories are characterized by varying perspectives on the specific role that sexism and misogyny play, analyses related to sex and gender are central components of all the feminist theories. However, culture, which is often defined primarily in terms of race and ethnicity, is central to multicultural discourse. Although the level of emphasis placed on particular cultures and racial and ethnic identities varies, these factors are viewed as primary entry points into discussion. Historically, feminists have critiqued multiculturalism for its inadequate attention to gender, and multiculturalists have critiqued feminism for its limited attention to racial, cultural, and ethnic diversity. As a corrective to these critiques, recent multicultural and feminist approaches have increasingly proposed goals and strategies that address the interconnections of gender, sexual orientation, culture, race, and ethnicity. The diversity feminisms and the social reconstructionist approaches to multicultural education represent examples of approaches that emphasize these intersections.

Social Location or Identity and Positionality

An important question regarding one's starting point is whether analysis should flow from the exploration of (a) the sociopolitical location of groups and their interactions within various contexts in society or (b) the individual identities and personal positionality of persons within these categories. The first alternative focuses on examining the privileges and oppression that result from experiencing various social locations in society. To understand privilege and oppression, one analyzes the contexts in which groups and individuals are situated as well as how the identity of the individual interacts and intersects with these contexts. In this case, the context and related aspects of power and privilege are as important as the individual.

The second alternative foregrounds the identities of individuals. That is, individuals have multiple identities that arise from the basic demographics of who they are (e.g., race, religion, sexual orientation, and social class), and these identities inform the kinds of oppression that individuals may or may not experience. In this case, priority is placed on identity that is situated inside the individual regardless of context. Whereas in the former approach, emphasis is placed on how individuals experience differential levels of power, privilege, and oppression in different contexts, the latter approach views oppression or privilege as relatively stable experiences of persons with particular identities. For the most part, multicultural and feminist theories support an analysis of both identity and context but tend to place greater weight on one or the other.

Feminist approaches that tend to foreground context include the global, third-wave, postmodern, and socialist feminisms. In contrast, the liberal, cultural, lesbian, and women-of-color feminisms tend to focus more specifically on identity themes. The very nature of many counseling goals, which tend to emphasize the development and well-being of individuals, supports the emphasis on identity or positionality in much of the multicultural counselor training literature. Whereas the ubiquitous, race-based, and existential universal approaches tend to highlight individual identity, the culture-specific multicultural counseling model also emphasizes the shared features and context of those persons with a specific cultural background. Some multicultural and feminist approaches emphasize both context and identity as evenly as possible. For example, the single-studies, social reconstructionist, and critical pedagogical approaches to multicultural education not only accentuate the contexts, oppressions, and privileges experienced by specific groups but also consider how individuals negotiate identity issues as outlined by various racial identity models.

DIMENSIONS OF MULTICULTURAL AND FEMINIST SOCIAL JUSTICE PEDAGOGIES

Many of the models discussed in chapters 2 through 5 tend to vary along four additional dimensions: (a) their level of emphasis on individual or social structural change, (b) the degree to which they challenge dominant ways of knowing and learning, (c) their emphasis on single or multiple intersections of oppression and privilege, and (d) their views about self-reflection and reflexivity. Table 6.1 provides exemplars of approaches that tend to stress one end of a continuum more strongly than others. It is not our intent to suggest that these dimensions represent bipolar categories, but rather, to identify some general "leanings" associated with specific approaches.

Individual Empowerment and Social Change

Approaches differ with regard to their relative emphasis on individual empowerment or social and cultural change as goals of pedagogy. Liberal

TABLE 6.1
Four Dimensions of Multicultural and Feminist Pedagogies

Dimension	Individual response	Outcome
Empowerment	Individual empowerment	Social change
	F = liberal feminism ME = human relations and cultural differences MC = most counselor training approaches, but especially the existential or universal approach	F = radical, socialist, women-of-color, global, and third-wave approaches ME = single-studies, social reconstructionist, and critical pedagogy
Knowledge and knower	Access and reform	Transform knowing
	F = liberal feminisms ME = human relations and cultural differences	F = cultural feminism, postmodern and social constructionist, antiracist, and women-of-color approaches ME = single studies, social reconstructionist, and critical pedagogy MC = most approaches
Oppression and privilege	Single, salient oppression	Multiple intersecting oppressions and privileges
	F = radical, cultural and lesbian issues ME = single-studies approaches MC = race-based and culture-specific approaches	F = socialist, global, third-wave, women-of-color issues ME = social reconstructionist approach MC = ubiquitous and existential or universal approaches
Reflexivity and self-awareness	Awareness of personal attitudes and beliefs	Power, privilege, and personal attitudes
	F = liberal feminist ME = human relations and cultural differences MC = existential or universal and culture-specific approaches	F = socialist, global, women of color, lesbian and queer, postmodern ME = social reconstructionist and critical pedagogy MC = race-based and ubiquitous approaches

Note. The approaches listed in this table represent exemplars rather than an exhaustive list of possibilities. F = feminism; ME = multicultural education; MC = multicultural training.

feminism has focused primarily on how society and social institutions can be reformed to ensure the autonomy, self-fulfillment, and equal opportunity of individual men and women. Likewise, within multicultural education, the exceptional and culturally different approach has concentrated on providing individuals with the means of succeeding in mainstream culture, and the human relations approach has emphasized the need to build positive relationships among individuals of diverse backgrounds. The existential or universal approach to multicultural counselor training shares some similarity to these approaches in that it accentuates the importance of helping individuals understand and accept another person's worldview and culture as well as recognize unique qualities and issues that transcend culture. In general, the aforementioned approaches involve valuing the individual and her or his choices and often facilitate change within individuals, dyads, small groups, and other microsystems. However, they do not call for substantial change in social structures or institutions.

Other feminist and multicultural approaches seek to transform social structures by revealing hidden norms about power and privilege, identifying the political nature of education, critiquing stereotypes and social inequities that are often perpetuated by educational institutions, providing counter discourses and pedagogies as an alternative to dominant methods, and advocating for social and structural change (Leistyna, 2002). In general, transformation values are important cornerstones of the multicultural, social reconstructionist, and single-studies approaches to multicultural education. Transformation is also a cornerstone of the women-of-color, radical, socialist, global, and lesbian and queer feminisms. Although multicultural counseling approaches are often directed toward helping individuals make changes in their lives, many of the counseling training approaches also question Western and individualistic assumptions about human experience and seek to transform trainees' views of others and their approaches to counseling. These models also emphasize consciousness-raising and critical thinking as tools for challenging educational, mental health, and other social structures that reproduce inequality. Our position is that strategies designed to address social change and social activism represent especially important components of integrated multicultural feminist pedagogies.

Knowledge and the Knower

Most reformist approaches to feminist and multicultural education, such as liberal feminism, human relations, and culturally different approaches to multicultural education, focus on increasing fairness for individuals within education as well as helping individuals gain access to educational opportunities. In general, these approaches do not challenge traditional structures of knowledge. In contrast, many approaches to multicultural and feminist pedagogy seek to value knowers and forms of knowing that have been ignored by traditional approaches to education. Postmodern, social constructionist, and antiracist feminists share the view that knowledge is fallible and that truth is socially constructed. These approaches pave the way for valuing alternative ways of knowing and learning. Similarly, cultural feminists indicate that the devaluation of women's ways of knowing and the limited appreciation for learning through relationship and connection result in the overvaluation of masculine values. Related positions are echoed within the diversity feminisms, many multicultural counseling approaches, and the single-studies and social reconstructionist approaches.

Those who endorse transformation positions argue that to combat the hegemony of dominant perspectives, one must have curricula that reflect the voices and worldviews of diverse groups as well as analyze privilege and multiple oppressions. Common to all these points of view is the notion that pedagogy must address, value, and incorporate multiple forms of knowing and diversity. These approaches not only seek to infuse knowledge about previously ignored or devalued groups within the curriculum or counseling relationship but also share a critique of traditional educational and social institutions that overemphasize rationality, separation, individualism, or Western values or reject relational, connected, holistic, and more collective forms of knowing. These feminist and multicultural approaches provide a critical analysis of oppression that has contributed to the disregard of specific ways of knowing and experiencing (e.g., classist, sexist, heterosexist, colonialist, individualistic, Eurocentric, or ethnocentric practices and thought). Forms of knowing that have been marginalized are centralized and revalued (e.g., Afrocentric, collectivist, or connected knowing), incorporated within educational systems, and used to empower those who have previously had limited or no voice.

Single or Multiple Oppressions and Privileges

Another important dimension is the degree to which specific approaches or theories emphasize the oppressions and concerns of groups of people who share a single specific identity (e.g., African Americans) or intersections of multiple social locations and positionalities (e.g., working-class African American lesbians). Approaches that tend to place primary emphasis on a specific oppression or social location, such as race, ethnicity, or sexual orientation, include the single-studies approaches in education, the race-based and culture-specific approaches to counselor training, and some of the women-of-color and lesbian feminisms. The advantage of these single-group approaches is that they ensure that knowledge about the oppressions and strengths of individuals in specific groups is not diluted by discussions that attempt to deal simultaneously with myriad and complex intersecting social identities, locations, oppressions, and privileges. For example, race-based oppressions can often be more extensive and ubiquitous than other forms of oppression because of the constant visibility of one's "minority status." Because of the salience of race and color as major categories of oppression and privilege in much of North American society, some educators and counselors believe that explicit and undivided attention needs to be devoted to those prejudices and discrimination associated with perceptions about race as well as the privileges associated with Whiteness. Without this emphasis, issues related to racism can be glossed over or minimized.

One of the limitations of theories that focus on a single aspect of identity, culture, or social location is that educators, students, and counselors may begin to see individuals from a certain "category" as a homogenous group, draw overgeneralizations or reductionist conclusions about oppressions or characteristics of group members, and ignore intragroup differences. In addition, the phrase *identity politics* is often used to characterize perspectives that tend to place one aspect of identity or social location (e.g., race, sexual orientation, or gender) at the center of analysis and as the most important foundation of oppression and empowerment. Although organization around a specific aspect of identity supports a sense of "we-ness" and common ground among identified group members, it may also contribute to competition for resources and recognition among oppressed groups. Questions about which group's oppression is most extensive or virulent can contribute to divisions and conflicts among groups that might otherwise be allies in social justice causes. Identity politics may also limit opportunities to consider complex forms of advantage and disadvantage that individuals experience because of their multiple identities and positionalities (Kirk & Okazawa-Rey, 2001). Finally, identity politics also tend to be embedded in a particular political or national system. An identity that is associated with minority status in one country may be connected to majority status in another; such nation-based differences influence how individuals experience themselves or are experienced by others. Thus, focusing on a particular identity without looking at sociocultural or national contexts may result in misunderstandings or limited perspectives about those who have multinational experiences.

In contrast to multicultural and feminist models that tend to consider a specific culture, "ism," or issue, an increasing number of approaches seek to deal simultaneously with multiple and intersecting identities, privileges, and oppressions. These approaches share an attentiveness to power structures and how experiences of privilege and oppression may vary in salience across time and situations. For example, the socialist, postmodern, and diversity feminisms speak to the complexity of truth and oppression. Within multicultural education, the multicultural, social reconstructionist, and critical pedagogy literatures emphasize most the borders between and intersections among groups and social identities and locations. Within the multicultural counseling literature, the ubiquitous approach to counselor training encourages counselor trainees to be mindful of their own and clients' multiple cultures and identities that may influence the counseling process.

Reflexivity and Self-Awareness

Reflexivity and self-awareness are viewed by all multicultural and feminist theories as important for linking personal and academic experiences.

Consciousness-raising and conscientization require that individuals understand the intersections of their personal experiences with varying systems of knowledge and education. Although each of the theories and pedagogies described in the previous chapters support self-reflection, some approaches diverge with regard to the forms of self-reflection valued and the degree to which reflection is connected to an understanding of social power, oppression, and privilege.

Approaches that tend to prioritize reform support self-reflection and are directed toward helping each educator and student enact or experience principles of individual fairness and equality. In contrast, some perspectives have pushed educators and therapists to recognize the ways in which dominant norms and "taken-for-granted" assumptions (e.g., heterosexual privilege and White privilege) influence the structure of education as well as the life experiences of both oppressed and privileged individuals. Models that accentuate the latter perspective include the single-studies, critical, and social reconstructionist perspectives; socialist, women-of-color, and lesbian feminisms; and race-based perspectives within multicultural counseling. Since the 1980s, postmodern thought has also been a particularly powerful influence within both multicultural education and feminism, challenging theorists to recognize the social construction of power and knowledge across many identities and domains.

The social construction of Whiteness as a dominant referent and organizer of Western societies has received significant attention during the past decade (e.g., Giroux, 1997; Kailin, 2002; Maher & Tetreault, 1997; Manglitz, 2003). Whereas some authors view Whiteness and other statuses associated with power as "nothing but privilege and oppression" (Manglitz, 2003, p. 123), others have called for the creation of a positive antiracist identity. This second perspective asks individuals to go beyond individual solutions that involve claiming "special status for anti-racist whites" (Scheurich, 2002, p. 33) to social activism that involves examining how statuses of power and dominance become embedded in societal and institutional systems and challenging the hegemony of these systems. Those who choose antiracist identities not only reject race-related oppressions at an individual level but also fight against structures of dominance that limit the potential of individuals and societies. These types of social change understandings are increasingly evident within the social reconstructionist approaches to education, the race-based approaches to multicultural counseling, and the diversity feminisms.

MULTIPLE ENTRY POINTS AND MULTIPLE MULTICULTURAL FEMINIST MODELS

As the first half of this book proposes, many theoretical and experiential entry points inform educators and students about social justice. We believe that multiple perspectives and entry points can form a foundation for multicultural feminist approaches. As the perspectives of individuals and educators evolve, they may also continue to incorporate new theoretical perspectives to inform their understandings. Thus, for example, lesbian and women-of-color feminists may be especially important for validating the experiences of women with specific identities as they begin to develop initial womanist, feminist, or multicultural self-concepts or worldviews. However, they may later explore and integrate additional frameworks that emphasize the multiple and intersecting nature of oppression and empowerment.

Despite their very important role, single-issue or single-identity approaches within feminism or multiculturalism may sometimes be associated with incomplete analyses, isolation, or lack of recognition of diversity within identified groups. Single-issue models may also run the risk of overlooking oppression that is culturally and nationally linked, and thereby, may limit understanding of global or multinational identities. Thus, these approaches may be most useful when they are linked or integrated with perspectives that emphasize the multiple and intersecting nature of oppression and empowerment.

Recent trends within both the multicultural and the feminist literatures reveal increased emphasis on intersections of social identity as well as the recognition that it is impossible to separate one aspect of experience (e.g., gender or ethnicity) from other aspects of the complex equation that contributes to "who I am" definitions. As noted in chapter 1, one example of recent pedagogical innovations is the appearance of "border" pedagogies that are designed to help individuals negotiate the intersections marked by culture, sexual orientation, gender, ethnicity, citizenship, class, and race. This emphasis on intersectionality provides a promising framework for integrating multicultural and feminist pedagogies, and we encourage readers to consider multiple ways of knowing, contexts, identities, and theories as they create meaningful models of pedagogy. In general, we believe that approaches that hold the most promise for comprehensive multicultural feminist pedagogies are those that are attentive to borders and intersections and are identified in Table 6.1 as associated with (a) social change perspectives; (b) transformation; (c) multiple identities and oppressions; and (d) the integrated analysis of privilege, oppression, and personal attitudes.

7

THE FEMINIST CLASSROOM: FEMINIST STRATEGIES AND STUDENT RESPONSES

ADA L. SINACORE AND KARYN J. BOATWRIGHT

Feminist pedagogy is recognized as a unique and distinct pedagogy with a defined set of principles and values, instructional techniques, and a political standpoint (Manicom, 1992; Sinacore, Healy, & Justin, 2002). Feminist educators attempt to challenge, interrupt, and change the nature of higher education (Lewis, 1993) while at the same time empowering students to make changes in their personal and social lives (Boxer, 1982). To this end, educators apply feminist theories to course content and pedagogical strategies.

Although feminist pedagogical strategies are typically linked to particular feminist theories as discussed in chapters 2 and 3, a common base of pedagogical strategies and principles (as suggested by Kimmel & Worell, 1997) is applicable to all feminist theoretical positions. The most predominant of these values is that feminist pedagogy seeks to transform and create teaching and learning experiences that do not reproduce the status quo (Forrest & Rosenberg, 1997). Feminists argue that teaching is to be transformative, bringing about social action and change (hooks, 1994; Lewis, 1990, 1993). Prin-

---

Note: Order of authorship does not indicate level of contribution.

ciples and activities that define a unified feminist pedagogy include (a) addressing power and authority, (b) establishing equality, (c) confronting and incorporating diversity, (d) emphasizing collaboration, (e) valuing personal and academic experiences, and (f) integrating cognitive and affective learning (Belenky, Clinchy, Goldberger, & Tarule, 1986; Enns, 1993b; hooks, 1994; Kimmel & Worell, 1997; Maher & Tetreault, 1996; Manicom, 1992).

Feminist educators perceive student experiences as a meaningful source of knowledge (Forrest & Rosenberg, 1997; Kennedy, Lubelska, & Walsh, 1993) and believe that "researching and theorizing our own educational practice and sharing our knowledge is one way of moving the field forward" (Kenway & Modra, 1992, p. 162). The goal of this chapter is to provide an overview of the principles, values, and strategies used by feminist educators as well as student responses to these strategies. In each section, we present an overview of the feminist principle or value and a discussion of students' responses to the principle.

The literature on student responses to feminist pedagogy is very limited. As a result, we collected anecdotal reports and empirical (qualitative and quantitative) studies by searching the psychology, education, and women's studies literatures. Linda Forrest and Freda Rosenberg (1997) observed that the feminist pedagogy literature is replete with anecdotal reports and that a paucity of empirical studies examines students' and educators' experiences in the classroom. Thus, much of the information reported here is from anecdotal accounts. Second, given the emphasis of this book on college and university level training, we focus on reports related to college or graduate students. Third, most of the literature on students' responses is located in the area of women's studies and we operated under the assumption, which is supported by the literature, that this research explores reactions to feminist pedagogical strategies (Forrest & Rosenberg, 1997; Musil, 1992; National Women's Studies Association [NWSA], 1996; Schniedewind, 1987b, 1993). Finally, most research participants were female, White, and heterosexual, which limits generalizations to students with other social identities. When the sex of student respondents was identified, females outnumbered males 10 to 1. Therefore, the term *student* refers to female students and *male* refers specifically to male students.

FEMINIST PEDAGOGY AS TRANSFORMATIONAL: THE PRINCIPLE OF SOCIAL CHANGE

Feminist pedagogy is associated with a political standpoint (Briskin, 1990) and the goals of informing and reforming both teachers' and students' "ways of acting in and on the world" (Manicom, 1992, p. 365). In 1994, bell hooks discussed the necessity of a revolutionary feminist pedagogy that seeks to transform society by eradicating patriarchy, ending sexism and sexist oppression, and challenging the politics of domination wherever they occur. In addition, feminist educators argue for the necessity of bringing about social change, facilitating personal development, and reclaiming women's histories and contributions (Forrest & Rosenberg, 1997; Lerner, 1993; Maher & Tetreault, 1996; Manicom, 1992).

In 1979, Adrienne Rich stated that given the "spoken—and unspoken—assumptions of a man-centered society, it would be naïve to imagine that the university could be a vanguard for change" (p. 127). However, many feminist educators believe that feminist pedagogy is only complete when students use their knowledge to promote social change; thus, many university classrooms have become that "vanguard" for social change (Forrest & Rosenberg, 1997; Hayes, 1989; Manicom, 1992; Scanlon, 1993; Schniedewind, 1987b, 1993; Tomlinson & Fassinger, 2002). Some instructors have reported that using feminist pedagogy is, in and of itself, a form of social action that facilitates students' developing awareness of their own power and how they can use this power for social activism (Sinacore, Healy, & Justin, 2002). In addition, some instructors have encouraged or required students to become change agents by engaging in projects such as analyzing and revising campus sexual harassment policies; writing a letter to a politician, friend, or organization about a particular social issue; conducting a needs assessment survey on reproductive health services; or creating a feminist campus newsletter (Boatwright, 2003; Drenovsky, 1999; Hawoode & Scanlon, 1987; Peet & Reed, 1999; Thompson, 1993). Others have reported that social change results from the privileging of voices that are otherwise silent (Lewis, 1990, 1993). After learning about the dynamics of power and oppression in the classroom, students apply their knowledge to bring about change outside the classroom. Although feminist educators agree that social action and social change are inextricably linked to feminist pedagogy, students' responses are mixed.

Students' Responses to Social Action Interventions

The literature, both empirical and anecdotal, indicates that students' responses to social action in the classroom are, for the most part, positive. Some anecdotal accounts have indicated that participation in educational experiences related to social change leads to continued involvement in social action after the completion of feminist courses (Hawoode & Scanlon, 1987; Wetzel, 1999). Cyntha Drenovsky (1999) reported that a small faction of her women's studies students who were new to feminism were unwilling to advocate for feminist ideals and reacted negatively to social action projects, but the majority of her students reacted positively.

Empirical evidence has supported anecdotal accounts and has indicated that feminist courses inspire students to engage in social action (Elovson & Cockroft, 1977; Musil, 1992; Stake, Roades, Rose, Ellis, & West, 1994; Wetzel,

1999). For example, students from Oberlin and Wellesley defined the very concept of empowerment as "the power to be socially responsible to a larger community," adding that although their traditional coursework "would help them function better in the world," women's studies courses "would help them change the world" (Musil, 1992, p. 203). As part of an NWSA national assessment project, Caryn Musil found that most current and former women's studies students agreed that feminism and social action were inextricably connected. These students were also more likely to engage in future activism than control students enrolled in non-women's studies courses. These findings are consistent with studies indicating that students enrolled in a women's studies course participated in more feminist-related activities and reported greater interest in continuing these activities than students enrolled in non-women's studies courses (Elovson & Cockroft, 1977; Stake et al., 1994). These findings are tempered by the findings of Jayne Stake and her colleagues that female students in non-women's studies courses demonstrated as strong an interest in social action as those enrolled in women's studies courses, suggesting that other factors such as gender role socialization may also be related to social action interests.

THE PRINCIPLE OF POWER AND AUTHORITY

Feminist theorists have stated that hierarchical and authoritarian classrooms "may replicate and perpetuate dominant knowledge systems that often neglect feminist principles" (Luchetta, 1996, p. 7). To increase the likelihood that students will acknowledge and embrace their own healthy notions of authority, theorists encourage the use of nonoppressive classroom authority, a principle that is rarely granted and practiced in traditional settings (Friedman, 1985). Many feminist instructors have transformed their teaching role from that of an all-knowing authoritative expert to that of a partner (Forrest & Rosenberg, 1997; Litner, Rossiter, & Taylor, 1992; Morgan, 1987; Ryan, 1990; Schniedewind, 1993). They attempt to construct this partnership by creating a climate that is conducive for multiple ways of learning and teaching, raising questions about the legitimacy of certain types of knowledge over others and inviting students' perspectives (e.g., Sinacore et al., 2002).

One technique designed to equalize power and authority is self-disclosure. According to hooks (1994), self-disclosure on the part of the educator brings about collaborative learning and models alternative uses of power in the classroom. By inviting, modeling, and reinforcing open discussion, feminist instructors encourage students "to know each other as people, speak honestly, take risks and support each other in the classroom" (Schniedewind, 1987a, p. 171). However, the body of feminist pedagogical literature challenges the myth "that a feminist classroom is one where power and authority have somehow disappeared" (Culley, 1985, p. 211). More typically, feminist professors attempt to redefine authority, eliminate the "crippling effects" of power (Moglen, 1983), and find a balance between "maintaining leadership while simultaneously encouraging collaboration" (Sinacore et al., 2002, p. 353).

Students' Responses to Collaborative Power and Authority

Although most students seem to respond favorably to nontraditional, egalitarian approaches to teaching, some students perceive the egalitarian instructor as overly nurturing, "impositional" (Jipson, 1995b, p. 29), or disempowering (Gardner, Dean, & McKaig, 1989). In some cases, students have demanded that the instructor "reclaim [her or his] professorial authority . . . share [her or his] expertise, or . . . act more like a teacher" (Gardner et al., 1989, p. 66). Few researchers have investigated particular students' responses to self-disclosure as a pedagogical strategy. In a comprehensive study of 1,698 students (676 male and 1,022 female) enrolled in 64 undergraduate classes, Gary Goldstein and Victor Benassi (1994) found that a professor's level of self-disclosure was positively related to student participation. In addition, Evelyn Beck (1983) found that, with the exception of "only a handful," most of the 161 female and male undergraduate and graduate students felt that when relevant to the course material, the professor's use of self-disclosure increased the openness and unity in the classroom and added to the overall "meaningfulness of the course" (p. 160). In contrast, Kelly Bignell (1996) reported that a frequent student response to intimate disclosure was discomfort.

THE PRINCIPLE OF INCORPORATING AND ATTENTING TO DIVERSITY

As indicated in chapter 3, diversity feminisms address the critique that feminism is for and about White middle-class heterosexual women. Consistent with these theories, feminist educators have reported that attending to and incorporating diversity into the feminist classroom is essential (Sasaki, 2002; Sinacore et al., 2002). Feminist educators emphasize diversity by (a) using strategies that help students understand the dynamics of privilege and oppression and challenge myths associated with meritocracy (Bell, Morrow, & Tastsoglov, 1999); (b) addressing assumptions about normalcy and decentralizing commonly held beliefs or notions about privileged and oppressed groups; (c) facilitating the analysis of how and where knowledge is situated and how it influences multiple identities (Kirk & Okazawa-Rey, 2001); and (d) making course content inclusive by incorporating texts that address a diversity of perspectives (Greene & Sanchez-Hucles, 1997). Feminist educators attempt to create a classroom that is inclusive, pluralistic, and open to multiple perspectives and ways of knowing.

Student Responses to Diversity in the Classroom

There are limited reports and studies about how students respond to articles and books with diverse content and how students respond to an inclusive classroom environment. Cultural feminist theories suggest that women's socially constructed relational interests (Miller, 1987) and subjective ways of knowing (Belenky et al., 1986) facilitate women's positive responses to strategies that use "relational conceptions of knowing" (Jipson, 1995a, p. 26) such as interactive projects and discussions (Belenky et al., 1986; Maher & Dunn, 1984; Philbin, Meier, Huffman, & Boverie, 1995). Conversely, men have been socialized to "repress everything society has identified as passive and feminine, including sensuality and emotional expressiveness" (D. J. Orr, 1993, p. 244), which includes interpersonally oriented pedagogical strategies. These theoretically based predictions indicate that female students are likely to respond more favorably than males to feminist content and strategies that involve cooperation, collaboration, interaction with peers, and sharing of personal experiences (e.g., Gawelek, Mulqueen, & Tarule, 1994; Luchetta, 1996; Maher, 1984; Surrey, 1983).

The predominant literature on diversity focuses on a single identity of the student and does not address the complexity of students' multiple identities such as religion and sexual orientation. In the next sections, we summarize anecdotal reports and research that address student responses to diversity as they relate to gender, commitment to tradition, race, and class.

Male Students' Responses

The literature on male students' responses to the feminist classroom proposes that men sometimes respond with resistance and anger, which results in the silencing of women's voices. (Note: the male students referred to in these reports were predominantly White and heterosexual, unless otherwise noted.) Resistance can take on many forms including refusing to read certain literature (Sinacore et al., 2002), suggesting that diverse course content is inappropriate (J. Nadelhaft, 1985), or using course evaluations to complain about feminist teachers (R. Nadelhaft, 1985). Some accounts indicate that mixed-gender feminist classrooms can erupt into "highly charged areas of inquiry" (Culley, 1985, p. 213) in which White male students object to their decentralized role in the class (Rakow, 1992), experience male guilt (Connell, 1993), feel threatened (D. J. Orr, 1993; Schuster & Van Dyne, 1985), resent the instructor (Culley, 1985; Eichorn et al., 1992; J. Nadelhaft, 1985; R. Nadelhaft, 1985; Rakow, 1992), "redirect the conversation away from disturbing topics" (Lewis, 1993, p. 173), marginalize other students (e.g., Bell et al., 1999), or "strike out in extreme responses" (Culley, 1985, p. 213) toward female students who disagree with their points (Lewis, 1993; Mumford, 1985; Rothenberg, 1996, 1998).

Similar to resistance, male anger in the classroom may take on many forms. For example, Margo Culley (1985) described a young male student who labeled his female colleagues as "sharks—one taste of blood and they come back and back" (p. 213) and another student who placed anonymous harassing telephone calls to women colleagues. Culley suggested that if the feminist educator "initiates a process challenging the worldview and the view of her students, she will surely—if she is doing her job—become the object of some students' unexamined anger" (p. 213). Another author described a revolt that was led by 12 male students who protested her assignment of literature that was written by a female (Baker, 1985). Over time, animosity evolved into fierce polarization: While the men overtly revolted and constructed a petition of protest against the course content, the "women seethed in silence" (p. 229). Only when the "controversial" course content was brought to the attention of the departmental chair did the female students defend the teacher.

In an anecdotal report that examined the confluence of class and gender and course content, Sandra Bell et al. (1999) reported that when asked to work closely with members of minority groups, White male students from a working-class background often expressed hostility toward the benefactors of affirmative action for threatening the careers of these men. Fueled by hostility, these students demonstrated an "unwillingness to connect their own experiences with those of other oppressed groups, [which] resulted in their adoption of dominant discourses in which 'group rights' and 'equity' [were] outlandish notions in the 'individualistic ideology' of the 'free' market" (p. 29). Throughout the course, these students continued to frame their experiences as "reality" and the experiences of others as "biased" (p. 29). In response to the professor's attempts to explain the theoretical rationale for affirmative action, a faction of the working-class White male students angrily viewed her as the "embodiment of their inability to secure career employment" (Bell et al., p. 28). These male students attempted to turn feminist strategies against the professor. They took full advantage of her efforts to encourage individual expression of voice by controlling the classroom discussion and silencing female voices.

Female Students' Responses

In response to male anger or perceived "male bashing" in the classroom, female students may "find themselves caught in the double bind of needing to speak and to remain silent at the same time in order to guarantee some measure of intellectual and emotional survival" (Lewis, 1993, p. 173). Magda Lewis stated that this bind "is often organized around [women's] historically produced nurturing capacity as a feature of [their] psychologically internalized role as caretakers," which is manifested by "hard-to-describe body language displayed as a barely perceptible 'moving' toward; a not-quite visible extending the hand or a protective stance accomplished through eye contact" (p. 160), or as more overt attempts to rescue "victimized" male colleagues. For example, one student acknowledged that she "was wondering and worrying about how the men in the room [were] feeling" (p. 157). Another student responded to a male colleague's inability to understand salient points by stating,

> I am almost embarrassed to admit that my second reaction was one of sympathy. I felt sorry for [the male student] not only because he did not understand the article, but also because he was alone in a room full of women . . . being taught by a female professor from a feminist perspective, and reading books and articles written by women. (p. 158)

Yet another female student wrote that she was "beginning to feel that we're getting a bias against men in general. . . . [I have a] growing concern about our treatment of men in these stories. . . . We seem to discuss the plight of women more" (R. Nadelhaft, 1985, p. 249). In response to women's expressed concern, some male students have felt vindicated by or supportive of their female colleagues (Lewis, 1993).

Some studies indicate that female students respond more positively to the collaborative, interactive, and cooperative principles and strategies used in the feminist classroom than their male counterparts (e.g., Boatwright & Paschiera, 2003; M. Ferguson, 1992; Nelsen, 1981). For example, an early qualitative study found that "while [female and male] students were generally willing to experiment by altering the usual classroom setting and activity, the females did so with verve—a sense of excited anticipation" (Nelsen, p. 237). The researcher attributed differences to women's socialized "expressive orientation" and men's "instrumental" orientation. Marianne Ferguson reported that compared to the male students, female students expressed stronger preferences for two strategies frequently associated with feminist teaching practices: classroom interaction and peer conversations. It is noteworthy that although gender differences were significant, most men (70%) and women (88%) expressed strong preferences for strategies associated with feminist pedagogy. Consistent with these findings, Karyn Boatwright's and Gabriella Paschiera's study found not only that female students' responses to feminist pedagogy ($n = 77$) were significantly more favorable than male responses ($n = 32$) but also that these gender differences were mediated by students' need for connection.

Although some research seems to indicate that there are sex differences with regard to a preference for certain strategies, Jayne Stake's and Margaret Gerner's (1987) study indicated that male and female students experienced similar benefits from the feminist classroom. Both male ($N = 73$) and female ($N = 313$) students showed significant improvements in performance self-esteem and job motivation. Later research conducted by Jayne

Stake and colleagues (Stake & Hoffmann, 2001; Stake & Malkin, 2003) also suggested that male and female women's studies students benefited to a similar extent. Further research regarding how men and women benefit is likely to offer further insight about proposed gender differences.

Traditional Students' Responses

Feminist scholars have suggested that students' responses to feminist pedagogy vary depending on their views toward feminism. For example, some authors report that students who identify as nonfeminists and prefer a more "traditional" style of teaching may react more negatively to classrooms that lack overt signs of professorial authority (e.g., Friedman, 1985; Gardner et al., 1989; Kaye, 1972; Mumford, 1985) and structure (Nelsen, 1981). It is possible that traditional students avoid feminist-identified teachers or courses, and thus, represent a minority of students in the feminist classroom (e.g., Ortman, 1993).

Race

Jane Kenway and Helen Modra (1992) urged feminist professors "to attend both to the sense students make of what [teachers] are doing [and] the range of factors which influence their sense-making" (p. 162), including race and ethnicity. For example, "Black women claim knowledge not only through gender, but through racial identity and relations" (Luttrell, 1989, p. 42), which would suggest that some women of color may respond differently than White students to feminist pedagogy. However, a paucity of studies examines how ethnically diverse students respond to feminist pedagogy; moreover, findings have been equivocal.

In one of the few studies to take race or ethnicity into account, Marianne Ferguson (1992) found that 88% of undergraduate women of color and 81% of men of color preferred an interactive style of teaching. Similarly, 91% of the minority women and 80% of the minority men preferred peer conversations. In contrast, a qualitative study (Nelsen, 1981) revealed that the only student in a class of 19 who experienced greater discomfort (with colleagues' attitudes and dishonesty) in a feminist-oriented class than in other courses was a female student of color. Regardless of her discomfort, she reported that the class had motivated her "to carry on discussions outside the classrooms with people at school, at work, with friends" (p. 238).

Class

We could locate only two anecdotal reports indicating that class might influence students' responses to feminist pedagogy (Atwood, 1994; Bell et al., 1999). One author described serious opposition to her feminist writing courses by first-generation college women from "solid white, lower-middle class American backgrounds" (Atwood, 1994, p. 132) who had limited experience with persons whose socioeconomic status, race, culture, or sexual orientation was different from their own. Similarly, Sandra Bell et al. reported that male working-class students were reluctant to endorse proactive attempts to reduce the oppression of those who were more disadvantaged than them.

Although researchers have cited class as an influential variable, even less research has investigated the influence of class on responses to feminist pedagogy. For example, Caryn Musil's (1992) review of a national study of seven colleges and universities noted that students from elite campuses were more likely to claim that they had experienced self-empowerment rather than "voice" in their women's studies classes. In addition, an early qualitative study (Nelsen, 1981) found that the three middle-class female students seemed to make the poorest adjustment to a less highly structured (less teacher-centered and more student-centered) class than students from the professional or working classes; however, the students did not believe that class was a significant factor in determining their response to the professor's teaching methods.

Contributors to a recent special journal issue on social class noted that class identities have received considerably less attention than race and gender-based identities in education. Furthermore, feelings of alienation, disconnection, and "not belonging" are often reported by working class or low-income students in class-dissonant (e.g., middle class or elite) academic and college settings (Fine & Burns, 2003; Ostrove, 2003; Ostrove & Cole, 2003). These findings point to the importance of studying how students with different class statuses respond to feminist pedagogy.

Students' Attitudes Toward Diversity

With the exception of studies that examine how feminist pedagogy is related to attitudes toward women, there are virtually no efforts to examine university students' responses to addressing diversity in the classroom. In his research on queer activism and antioppressive pedagogy, Kevin Kumashiro (2002) found that students thought that addressing diversity took too much time away from studying "basic classes" and that "'the true intention of school' is to teach the 'core' academic subjects of math, science, social studies, English, and so forth" (p. 80). Although his work focuses predominantly on secondary education, these attitudes may also be carried into the university.

Empirical studies that examine feminist pedagogy and students' overall attitudes toward women demonstrate that women's studies and psychology-of-women students experience more significant decreases in discriminatory and traditional attitudes toward women than do other psychology students or control group students (Bargad & Hyde, 1991; Howe, 1985; Ruble, Croke, Frieze, & Parsons, 1975; Scott, Richards, & Wade, 1977; Unger, 1983; Vedovato & Vaughter, 1980). In one of the most comprehensive empirical studies, Jayne Stake and Frances Hoffmann (2001) collected data from 789 students who were members of over 100 women's studies and non-women's studies classes. Of these students, 83% were White, 95% were undergraduates, 88% were female, and 67% were enrolled in predominantly upper-division courses. Statistically controlling for baseline differences in women's and non-women's studies student attitudes, researchers found that women's studies students reported greater increases in egalitarian attitudes and discrimination awareness than non-women's studies students. A recent study (Stake & Malkin, 2003) also found that higher levels of students' appreciation and acceptance of diversity predicted higher ratings of students' women's studies class experiences.

COLLABORATION AND VALUING PERSONAL AND ACADEMIC EXPERIENCES

An underlying principle of feminist pedagogy is the promotion of a collaborative learning environment and the valuing of students' personal and academic experiences (Sánchez-Casal & Macdonald, 2002). Feminist scholars have pointed out that women's voices are often silenced in traditional classrooms (Belenky et al., 1986; Goldberger & Tarule, 1996; Lewis, 1990, 1993; Litner et al., 1992; Luke & Gore, 1992), and this critique has inspired the development of pedagogical strategies that attempt to legitimize personal experience as an epistemological resource (Bignell, 1996) and empower women to claim (or reclaim) their voice (Maher, 1984). By claiming their "authentic voices," feminists contend that students will be better equipped to "define themselves as authors of their own world" (Ellsworth, 1989, p. 309). Feminist pedagogical strategies that give authenticity to students' voices also encourage students to understand the meaning of their personal experiences in relation to the experiences of others (e.g., Forrest & Rosenberg, 1997; Litner et al., 1992; Surrey, 1983), connect personal experiences with theory (e.g., Belenky et al., 1986; Maher, 1984), and enhance students' critical thinking (e.g., Luebke & Reilly, 1995).

Several instructional techniques are linked to these feminist principles. Reflexivity involves bringing about self-awareness and linking the personal to academic experiences (e.g., Sinacore et al., 1999). Additional techniques include the use of autobiographical accounts of women's lives that centralize women's voices (Forrest & Rosenberg, 1997), nontraditional literature, assignments that incorporate personal experience and self-awareness, group projects that promote cooperation rather than competition, and small group sharing of subjective experiences that facilitate the integration of personal experience with classroom content. Other strategies include computer-mediated discussion forums, internal reflection or reaction journals, cooperative evaluation systems, and case study analysis. All of these strategies are designed to bring about collaboration while valuing and giving voice to both personal and academic experiences (e.g., A. Ferguson, 1982; Gilbert, Holdt, & Christophersen, 1999; Howe, 1985; Lewis, 1990, 1993; Luchetta, 1996; Musil, 1992; NWSA, 1996).

Student Responses to Integrating Personal and Academic Experiences

The reports of feminist educators affirm that the previously mentioned strategies have been associated with students' increased willingness to use their voice as well as favorable evaluations from the majority of students (Baker, 1985; Bell et al., 1999; Carver, 1978; Lewis, 1993; Litner et al., 1992; Luchetta, 1996; Maher, 1984; Ortman, 1993; Roffman, 1994; Scanlon, 1993; Stevenson, 1989; Swaffield, 1996). Other educators have noted that when students are immersed in a class in which voicing personal experiences is encouraged, they may sometimes resist studying theory (Jipson, 1995a, 1995b; Simon, 1992). Dawn Currie (1992) reported that an overemphasis on subjective knowledge not only led to students' claim that all knowledge is relative but also "hindered" students' desire to share knowledge with colleagues.

Only a handful of empirical studies address the effects of integrating subjective and objective experiences in the classroom. Researchers from two national assessment research projects discovered that both women's studies and non-women's studies students believed that women's studies courses based on feminist pedagogical strategies had been more beneficial for increasing their voice in the classroom than traditional courses (Musil, 1992; NWSA, 1996). However, simply asking students to describe their feelings, thoughts, and personal experiences in a small group did "not necessarily mean that all of those participating [felt that] their perspectives were suddenly given value" (Bignell, 1996, p. 320). Musil found that although approximately 75% of women's studies students felt that they had been "heard" by their professors, many women's studies students reported feeling silenced by the anticipated negative responses or the actual responses of their peers. Indeed, some feminists have found that the increased voice of some students may come at the expense of others. In addition, researchers have found that feminist students sometimes use their experience and knowledge to dominate classroom discussions and silence students with less experience (Davis, 1981; Musil, 1992; Gardner et al., 1989). Overall, empirical studies support the anecdotal findings that demonstrate the effectiveness of feminist pedagogy in increasing students' acquisition of voice (Baker, 1985; Bell et al., 1999; Carver, 1978; Lewis, 1993; Litner et al., 1992; Luchetta, 1996; Maher, 1984; Ortman, 1993; Roffman, 1994; Scanlon, 1993; Stevenson, 1989; Swaffield, 1996) and also illustrate the challenges related to the appropriate use of voice with regard to power in the classroom.

INTEGRATING COGNITIVE AND AFFECTIVE LEARNING

Feminist educators propose that pedagogical strategies that focus on both the intellect and emotion may serve an important role in enhancing students' development. For example, bell hooks (1994) suggested that acknowledging sadness when examining the pros and cons of social policies may help students embrace their whole selves rather than compartmentalizing pieces of themselves. Karen Howe (1985) also reported that students felt that validating sadness facilitated a more complete experiencing of themselves. Other writers indirectly address the importance linking emotion and cognition by describing their students' willingness to experience and express anger as part of the learning process (e.g., Culley, 1985; Lewis, 1993).

In addition to affective components, feminist pedagogy aims to support critical thinking and "to promote teaching practices that are empowering for the students" (Weatherall, 1999, p. 211). Many feminist instructors seek to empower their students through supportive comments and strategies that demonstrate care and personal concern for their students' development. Evidence indicates that these techniques are associated with favorable student responses (e.g., Bell et al., 1999; Jipson, 1995b; Litner et al., 1992) and increased empowerment (e.g., Musil, 1992). Feminist educators help students integrate both the affective and the cognitive components of learning with the goals of developing critical thinking skills and facilitating students' understanding of both the process and the content of the classroom.

Student Responses to Critical Thinking

Several studies examined students' ability to think with "a critical eye." The American Association of Colleges' (1991) national assessment of "connected learning" in women's studies programs indicated that students increased their critical thinking skills and their ability to understand the social construction of knowledge. Several reports based on qualitative data (Elovson & Cockroft, 1977; Wetzel, 1999) noted that students viewed their women's studies courses as increasing their ability to question and rationally analyze critical issues. A study with an older student sample (Worell, Stilwell, Oakley, & Robinson, 1999) found that a group of 63 male and female psychology graduate students who had been exposed to a feminist-based curriculum scored higher on analytic abilities than a group consisting of 38 graduate students who had not been exposed to feminist-based curricula. Results from another extensive 3-year national study (Musil, 1992) suggested that women's studies courses placed greater emphasis on critical thinking than personal experience. Moreover, students felt that critical thinking was emphasized more in their women's studies courses than in non-women's studies courses.

Similar results were found in the much larger study conducted by Jayne Stake and Frances Hoffmann (2000), who collected data from 111 teachers and 789 of their students from 32 colleges and universities. They found that "teachers and students rated both the critical thinking/open-mindedness and participatory learning themes significantly higher than either personal experience/confidence or political understanding/activism, and they rated critical thinking/open-mindedness higher for Women's Studies than non-

Women's Studies classes" (p. 36). Thus, it appears that feminist educators are fairly successful at integrating critical thinking skills into the classroom.

Student Responses to Empowerment

Given the emphasis placed on empowerment, feminist educators suggest that exposure to feminist techniques should enhance students' self-esteem (e.g., Kenway & Modra, 1992). Exploring this notion, Karen Howe (1985) and Jodi Wetzel (1999) found that women's studies undergraduate students who had been exposed to feminist content and strategies reported an increase in their self-esteem. One student wrote that as a result of experiencing feminist pedagogy in her women's studies courses, she became a "competent and successful person—one who can think, express herself/himself, confidently take on a project, make decisions" (Musil, 1992, p. 183). Most reports in the literature are based on courses identified as feminist in content; in a rare account describing students' responses to a statistics course taught with a feminist pedagogical approach, students reported a decrease in "math anxiety" and an overall increase in confidence. On the basis of information gleaned from informal pre- and postclass questionnaires, the teacher reported that although most of her students reported feeling "terrified" on the first day of class, only 10% of her students reported math anxiety or a lack of confidence in their statistical skills on the last class day (Ayers-Nachamkin, 1992).

Although self-report studies indicate an increase in self-esteem, more traditional empirical studies have produced less consistent results. Results vary and are influenced by how self-esteem is measured and operationalized. Allana Elovson and Irene Cockroft (1977) found that 93% of the 136 women's studies students who were sampled reported an increase in their confidence and attributed this change to their feminist courses. Similarly, Stake and Gerner (1987) found that compared with students in non-women's studies classes, both male and female students in women's studies courses reported more pronounced increases in performance self-esteem (confidence to perform in career and educational situations). In acknowledging a critical limitation of their study, researchers noted that students' "openness to feminist ideas" (p. 282) may have mediated students' responses, but that age and class standing had not confounded the results. However, Diane Zuckerman (1983) previously found that after having been exposed to one semester of feminist pedagogy, upperclasswomen's global self-esteem increased, whereas their younger colleagues' self-esteem significantly decreased. Yet another study found that participants' global self-esteem failed to improve significantly after being exposed to feminist pedagogical strategies (Davis, Steiger, & Tennenhouse, 1989). These limited and equivocal findings underscore the need for additional studies to investigate the influence of age, class standing, precourse esteem, and feminist views on students' global and performance self-esteem.

SUMMARY AND CONCLUSIONS

As indicated by this review, feminist educators incorporate feminist principles and values into their teaching, and these principles inform the pedagogical strategies educators apply in the classroom. Educators describe the feminist classroom as collaborative, proactive, and producing change. Although educators report many positive aspects of feminist teaching, they note that feminist teaching is not without its challenges. Some of the complexities educators negotiate include students' responses that undermine feminist processes in the classroom. Despite difficulties, feminist educators' anecdotal reports and research findings have identified major benefits: increased self-esteem, the ability to think critically, and feelings of empowerment. In addition, reports demonstrate that students' interest and involvement in social action is associated with their experiences in the feminist classroom.

Despite promising findings, the literature on the correlates and effects of feminist pedagogy is extremely limited. The literature focuses predominantly on women's studies courses and includes limited discussion of the impact of feminist pedagogy on other courses. In addition, few empirical studies examine feminist educators' experiences in the classroom and the effects of these experiences on their teaching and careers. Furthermore, because studies that examine students' responses are based on a very limited pool of students who are predominantly White, heterosexual, and female, research needs to be broadened to explore more diverse student populations and classroom settings. Attention needs to be given to the multiple social locations of students and educators and how they influence interactions and the student–educator working alliance in the feminist classroom. In addition, research should explore the effectiveness of different feminist strategies and whether particular strategies are more or less effective with different types of students. Finally, research needs to assess the context in which feminist pedagogy occurs, such as the type, size, and ideology of the institution and program in which feminist educators teach. Such exploration will help us understand the broader implications of feminist pedagogy within educational institutions.

Although it is necessary for feminist educators to understand the aforementioned limitations, it is equally important to acknowledge the benefits that feminist pedagogical strategies yield in the classroom. To properly assess students' responses, feminist educators must understand the pedagogical strategies they use and the goals of these strategies. By being aware of the kinds of responses that may emerge in the feminist classroom, educators can equip themselves to assist students to understand their reactions to feminist pedagogical strategies. Finally, by developing methods that attend to power and authority, while at the same time addressing diversity and social justice, feminist educators are in a position to bring about education that challenges students' beliefs and assumptions, and results in "transformative" learning.

8

THE CHALLENGES, IMPACT, AND IMPLEMENTATION OF CRITICAL MULTICULTURAL PEDAGOGIES

ANGELA M. BYARS-WINSTON, ÖZGE AKÇALI, KAREN W. TAO, CECILIA A. NEPOMUCENO, TINA M. ANCTIL, VIANEY ACEVEDO, NAN BENALLY, AND GEORGIANA WILTON

Many authors have written about the importance of ensuring that psychology students and counseling trainees gain multicultural competence but have also expressed dismay about the slow progress or resistance of institutions, faculty, and students to implementing adequate educational programs (D'Andrea & Daniels, 1995; Gutiérrez, Fredricksen, & Soifer, 1999; Paccione, 2000; Ridley, Espelage, & Rubinstein, 1997; Vázques, 1997). Initiating and sustaining effective training programs present significant challenges despite the fact that there is general consensus about the importance of increasing students' awareness of diversity, different worldviews, racial and cultural differences, social oppression, prejudice, and racism. Progress has been hampered by a lack of curricular models for teaching about diversity issues (Butler, 2000; Russo, 1998) and the limited availability of training options for those who desire to implement multicultural and critical pedagogies (Heard, 1999). Other significant barriers include institutional or departmental resistance, educators' limited training in multicultural counseling, and students' reactions to multicultural training (Reynolds, 1995).

Although the conundrums associated with developing and sustaining diversity education experiences are sometimes daunting, hopeful signs about the outcomes of multicultural competence training are emerging. Mark Kiselica and Patricia Maben's (1999) review of the limited number of studies that have examined the impact of multicultural and diversity appreciation training concluded that students who completed such training (a) perceived themselves as experiencing decreased bias and positive changes in their attitudes about others and (b) saw themselves as undergoing cognitive and emotional changes that facilitated positive racial identity development. A recent study of precourse, midcourse, and postcourse attitudes also found increases in students' multicultural awareness, knowledge, and skills, which led authors to conclude that even a single multicultural course can spur motivation for future training (Keim, Warring, & Rau, 2001).

Though the research literature on gaining multicultural competence is scattered across a variety of disciplines and is difficult to locate, the research on developing skills for teaching about multicultural competence is even more limited. Several qualitative studies (e.g., Jennings & Smith, 2002; Moss, 2001; Paccione, 2000) have indicated that the process of developing proficiency for teaching competence is complex and is influenced by one's attitudes, personal experiences of venturing outside of one's "racial-cultural comfort zones" (Paccione, 2000, p. 991), development of a transformed cognitive map of the world, the implementation of practical strategies and action plans for building skills, and a willingness to be involved in advocacy (e.g., taking leadership roles in integrating diversity issues in teaching). Those who respond positively to multicultural teacher training programs report the following personal changes and gains: developing new thinking patterns about teaching and learning, gaining deeper awareness of the diversity of student learning styles, acquiring a deeper and more inclusive perspective about multiculturalism, becoming more conscious of social inequities and their impacts, developing more democratic teaching methods, and engaging in greater self-reflection about their practices (Heard, 1999; Moss, 2001).

Some trainees do not respond positively to instruction about teaching from a more multiculturally informed perspective. Trainees who resist developing multicultural teaching skills cite a variety of reasons for their reactions, including criticisms about the types of small-group activities associated with diversity training, fear of being verbally attacked by students, hesitancy about "invading" students' privacy, denial that Whiteness is associated with privilege, and beliefs that multicultural knowledge is irrelevant to some academic disciplines (Heard, 1999; Moss, 2001). Addressing these resistances, providing educators with adequate proficiency for teaching multicultural content, and considering ways to increase the rewards of teaching about diversity are crucial for supporting future multicultural feminist teaching efforts. A major purpose of this chapter is to discuss challenges and strategies for enhancing teaching about diversity issues.

This chapter discusses four major types of challenges and strategies for transforming the curriculum. This discussion is followed by a case illustration of the application of critical pedagogical principles in a specialized setting: a graduate seminar. Whenever possible, we weave information from relevant research into our discussion of issues, challenges, and rewards.

DEVELOPING CRITICAL MULTICULTURAL PEDAGOGIES AND TRANSFORMED CURRICULA

Our discussion is embedded in a critical pedagogical framework, which is founded on the groundbreaking work of Paulo Freire (1970), the Brazilian educator who challenged the supposed neutrality of the dominant curriculum in the United States. Freire argued that any curriculum that ignores oppressions such as exploitation, sexism, and racism serves to support the status quo (Heaney, 1995). Although critical pedagogy is more frequently associated with multicultural than feminist methods, it has also emerged as a valuable method for creating multicultural feminist pedagogies (e.g., hooks, 1994). An underlying assumption of our approach is that the intersecting principles of multicultural and feminist perspectives call attention to how privilege and oppression, as a function of social group locations and positionality (e.g., race and ethnicity, class, gender, sexual orientation, and ability status), shape teaching and learning (Taylor, Tisdell, & Hanley, 2000). These principles necessitate consideration of the sociopolitical and historical contexts of people's lives.

Traditional teaching approaches have been ineffective in addressing and facilitating the exploration of cultural diversity in psychology because they tend to focus on learning about the "other" (Espín, 1995) and often emphasize increasing dominant group members' understanding of marginalized groups. This "tourist" approach to teaching about diversity in psychology does little to change educators' practices or equip them to critically examine theories and research that inform their work. In contrast, feminist psychology and multicultural psychology offer alternative perspectives on effective teaching of psychology (Banks & Banks, 2003; Bronstein & Quina, 1988, 2003; Greene & Sanchez-Hucles, 1997). By recontextualizing the field of psychology; using pedagogical practices that provoke a critical examination of this discipline; and attending to dynamics of power, privilege, and oppression, psychology may be taught in such a way as to encourage students to transform their ways of thinking and their ways of working with others. Ultimately, the field of psychology will then become a more inclusive discipline.

Multicultural and feminist pedagogies promote shared power and mutual control over curriculum content, methods, and the coordination of learning activities, and provide a useful framework for addressing four major challenges that are often cited as inhibiting effective multicultural instruction. In this section, we consider the relevance of critical pedagogies for addressing philosophical challenges, cultural diversity challenges, pedagogical challenges, and social action challenges. Table 8.1 summarizes the challenges and strategies discussed in the following sections.

Issue 1: Philosophical Challenges

A significant challenge to transforming psychology curricula is making fundamental changes in the roles of educators and students (Chin & Russo, 1997). Higher education has primarily followed an apprenticeship model wherein the educator is the knowledge broker and students are consumers of that prescribed knowledge (Freire, 1970). Traditional classroom dynamics reinforce a passive relationship between educators and students: The student is viewed as object and power is held solely by instructors. This top-down pedagogical approach reinforces a hierarchical system that allows only certain privileged people (e.g., instructors) to create knowledge in an ahistorical, decontextualized, and depersonalized manner.

In addition to reliance on traditional communication and teaching styles, the teaching of psychology has been dominated by traditional paradigms, theoretical orientations, and curricula that have largely ignored and been unresponsive to the psychological needs and experiences of a multicultural society. Psychology is often taught from a decontextualized frame of reference that neglects to reflect on how this discipline, dedicated to the "science of the mind," operates within individual, sociocultural, and institutional systems that privilege some while disenfranchising others. Teachers of psychology often fail to examine the emergence, operation, and maintenance of psychology against the backdrops of capitalism, patriarchy, and White supremacy.

Strategies for Addressing Philosophical Challenges

Critical pedagogy, according to Paulo Freire (1970), endeavors to transform the learning context by situating the educator as a collaborative learner. The educator's role expands from being a simple purveyor of "banked" knowledge to one that involves imparting extant knowledge in such a way that learners are empowered to participate informatively and actively in critiquing the taken-for-granted knowledge of a discipline. In this collaborative model, the student moves from being a passive learner and object to an active learner and subject who actively engages in the coconstruction of knowledge. That is, students participate jointly with educators in the cocreation of knowledge in the classroom; all share the power and privilege of knowledge construction.

Consistent with this view of student constructed as subject, Johnella Butler (2000) described a *methodology of transformation* and called for a gen-

TABLE 8.1
Pedagogical Challenges, Strategies, and Curricular Implementation

Challenges	Objectives	Strategies	Curricular examples
Philosophical	Share power between students and educators Promote participatory pedagogy	Encourage students to cocreate course content and assignments Facilitate inclusive class sessions	Educators are open to negotiate course assignments; provide students opportunity to bring in supplemental readings for class discussion Students are empowered to cocreate focus and topics of discussions
Cultural diversity	Promote self-reflection Manage cultural traps (e.g., cultural appropriation and cultural camouflage)	Monitor and facilitate choices about self-disclosure by both educators and students Encourage enactive and affective learning	Facilitate structured exploration of matrix of personal cultural identities to promote self-awareness Develop here-and-now frameworks to manage feelings and reactions to course topics (e.g., anger, guilt, shame, and pride)
Pedagogical	Provide larger conceptual frameworks for critical inquiry (e.g., positionality and privilege systems) Facilitate students' critical consciousness and inquiry skills	Shift the center of knowledge base from dominant group experiences to those typically marginalized Encourage students to reconsider, reject, criticize, and accept interpretations of course content	Examine whose knowledge and research is taught from what perspective Ask different questions such as, "What do we know about the people we study and counsel? How do we know this?"
Social action	Apply students' learning beyond the classroom Find transformative work that needs to be done	Link students' daily experiences with the lives of others Stimulate student engagement vis-à-vis conscientization	Incorporate more local and community people and resources into course Connect course content to transformations needed within psychology and to local needs

erative pedagogy that "fosters students as subjects, generates knowledge and understanding through building on these interconnections among student, teacher, and context, and engages the conflictive from the strength of the multiply-centered, relational context" (p. 184). Both Butler's and Freire's pedagogical paradigms emphasize the mutual and coequal roles of educators and students. In this method, all participants teach and all participants learn (Heaney, 1995). As such, educators must be open and humble enough to receive student input on the direction and content of course discussions. For instance, educators' flexibility about course assignments can empower students to contribute to the direction of their learning and a more relevant course curriculum that meets their needs. The alteration of course content and structure may include expecting students to bring in outside readings to supplement assigned readings on the syllabus and be responsible for copresenting a lecture on a given day. Freire's (1998a) principle of transformative learning focuses on increasing students' sense of self-efficacy and empowerment to initiate and inform their own learning process. Transformation is achieved not only by redefining educator and learner roles but also by effective management of class dynamics stemming from cultural diversity factors.

Issue 2: Cultural Diversity Challenges

Dynamic challenges occur when psychology is taught from multicultural perspectives and include student resistance to exploring oppression, inevitable disagreements in classroom discussion, and intergroup conflicts around cultural experiences (Khan, 1999). The American Psychological Association (APA) Society for the Teaching of Psychology Task Force on Diversity found that many professors were unprepared or unwilling to integrate diversity integration in their curriculum, confirming the impact of the aforementioned challenges (Kowalski, 2000). The examination of culture necessarily brings diversity issues into the present, and students may be challenged to personally consider their own social group identities and locations, cultural assumptions, and prejudices. These dynamics pose further challenges to instruction management associated with structuring safe, supportive, and inclusive classroom environments that facilitate deep learning and dialogue.

Managing cultural diversity in courses also necessitates the examination of common misconceptions students have of culture: that it is exotic, arbitrary, self-explanatory, or monolithic (APA Task Force on Diversity Issues, 1998b). At the level of managing cultural dynamics, educators must reassess their approach to a culture-based pedagogy, considering how their approach facilitates students' cultural self-awareness, their preparation to deeply examine cultural issues, and their ability to learn new paradigms for understanding new insights.

Research findings indicate that students who complete self-awareness and diversity exercises may experience increased anxiety and distress when confronted with issues of cultural identity and diversity, power, and oppression (Garcia & Van Soest, 1997). These feelings may be especially apparent when students from privileged backgrounds are encouraged to place themselves in "vulnerable" situations to increase their self-awareness. However, other concerns that may contribute to students' anxiety and self-censorship in multicultural classroom discussions include "general" factors, such as not being prepared for class and shyness (Hyde & Ruth, 2002).

A study that compared the attitudes of students from a wide range of departments with attitudes of social work trainees found that a substantial number of respondents viewed multicultural awareness education to be "fine" as long as multicultural courses were not required (Swank, Asada, & Lott, 2001). Greater appreciation of multiculturalism was shown by women students, social work trainees, and students who had been involved in culturally diverse friendships. This research finding appears consistent with the observation that many people espouse cultural pluralism as long as they are not asked to make some modest alterations in their daily routines. These realities represent some of the challenges that educators face.

Approaches to Managing Cultural Diversity Challenges

Critical multicultural pedagogies encourage a purposeful and explicit examination of the specific issues educators and students are likely to confront in culture-based classrooms. First, educators need to recognize that students have varying levels of familiarity with ambiguous and complex concepts that are linked to the critical pedagogical literature. Thus, educators may begin by clarifying more familiar terms as prejudice, race, and ethnicity (APA Task Force on Diversity Issues at the Precollege and Undergraduate Levels of Education in Psychology, 1998a), building toward the incorporation of more complex terms. More complex concepts such as deconstruction, positionality, privilege, and social location will also require clarification when these constructs are introduced.

Second, students and educators exhibit individual differences and varying degrees of cultural identity development. To model multicultural competence and facilitate development, educators should be aware of and able to speak about their own intersecting cultural identities and how these inform their perspectives. They should also consider including activities that facilitate students' ability to discuss their cultural identities and make choices about the place, timing, and degree of self-disclosure in the classroom. Some of the conceptual frameworks discussed earlier in this book, such as the concept of differential consciousness (Moya, 2001) and realist identity theory (Sánchez-Casal & Macdonald, 2002), are likely to be helpful to educators and their students in managing individual cultural differences.

Third, educators should be prepared to address student resistance to exploring preconceived biases. It is important for educators to engage in constant monitoring of the interpersonal environment and to be self-aware, especially when intense emotions in reaction to course content become salient and may be directed at a specific group, other students, educators, or even the self (Butler, 2000). Intense emotions may emerge as students move from familiar knowledge to a contextualized, balanced understanding of course content. For instance, when learning about racial and ethnic identity politics and the historical construction of Whiteness through such publications as *How the Jews Became White Folk and What That Says About Race in America* (Brodkin, 1998) or *How the Irish Became White* (Ignatiev, 1995), feelings of guilt or anger may surface. In such cases, educators may use pressure-release sessions, such as those described by Johnella Butler (1985). She noted the following:

> the fear of being regarded by peers or by the professor as racist, sexist, or "politically incorrect" can polarize a classroom. If the [teacher] participates unconsciously in this fear and emotional self-protection, the classroom experience will degenerate to hopeless polarization, and even overt hostility. He or she must constantly stand outside the classroom experience and anticipate such dynamics. . . . "Pressure release" discussions work best when the teacher directly acknowledges and calls attention to the tension in the classroom. The teacher may initiate the discussion or allow it to come about in whatever way he or she feels most comfortable. (p. 236)

Johnella Butler (2000) proposed that directly addressing tensions and fears can have profound value in that this type of intervention engages students both affectively and cognitively with course content, demonstrating that paradoxes and contradictions are sometimes resolved and sometimes remain unresolved but are important to ongoing discussion.

Last, students may experience emotional incongruence between preconceived biases and new information and insights (Gloria, Rieckmann, & Rush, 2000). Strong reactions may be further complicated by pitfalls that individuals fall into when cultural issues are introduced. One pitfall includes cultural appropriation or the tendency to view a given person's or group's experience as analogous to one's own. Cultural appropriation often arises from efforts to understand another person's experience or culture's characteristics without substantially altering one's own perspective or worldview (Grillo & Wildman, 1995). Another cultural pitfall is the use of cultural camouflage wherein individuals misassign or overassign individual proclivities to cultural behavior (e.g., "That's how Black women are"). Such behavior negates the uniqueness of a person and assigns individual behavior to cultural group influences. All of these dynamics must be acknowledged, with the educator cointerpreting with students how their personal management of challenges in dealing with diversity might be manifested emotionally and interpersonally. For instance, the educator may illuminate the underlying problematic issue associated with the strategy of cultural appropriation, that being the question of authority (e.g., "who can speak"), drawing distinctions between appropriation and engagement (Weiler, 2001). Butler (2000) asserted that feelings help to clarify thinking, as both the intuitive and rational aspects of the self facilitate movement from the familiar to the unfamiliar in knowledge construction, supporting critical multicultural pedagogies' value of affective learning.

Relevant to several points made in this section is the reality that students from different racial and ethnic backgrounds may face somewhat different emotional and cognitive challenges as they are exposed to cultural diversity issues. Garcia and Van Soest's (1997) qualitative research study examined the evolution of social work students' attitudes by asking 43 first-year students to audiotape their responses to a self-administered interview at the beginning of a course on diversity issues. At the conclusion of the course, students listened to their tape recordings and wrote reflection papers on their evolving views about diversity and oppression. One category of responses was labeled as "self-critical" and included student reports of intense personal and negative emotions, such as shock or amazement, guilt or shame, and sadness, dismay, and pain. White and non-Jewish students often described emotions of "shock, amazement, guilt, and shame" (Garcia & Van Soest, p. 123), whereas multiethnic students more frequently reported feelings of dismay, sadness, and pain. Another major category of responses, labeled as "enlightened responses," encompassed students' observations about their initial lack of knowledge of discrimination or racism and barriers to and resources for confronting oppression. The study also found that 50% of the White and non-Jewish students and 71% of the multiethnic students identified White privilege as a barrier to confronting oppression. In addition, all students identified the institutionalized nature of racism as another barrier that creates an aura of "business-as-usual" (Garcia & Van Soest, p. 126). Fear of losing friends and family was another barrier reported by White and non-Jewish participants. These findings reveal that students from majority privileged cultures and from minority cultures may face somewhat different challenges in response to diversity training and that educators need to be cognizant of these realities.

Issue 3: Pedagogical Challenges

Another challenge to effective multicultural instruction in psychology is on the pedagogical level. Educators often struggle with how to integrate the vast multicultural literature into courses in an integrative manner. For example, given time constraints, what dimensions of culture (e.g., gender, race and ethnicity, sexual orientation, class, and ability status) should be addressed? Which cultural topics and cultural groups' experiences should be included? What course assignments should be given for students to demonstrate and apply acquired cultural skills in meeting psychology course objectives? How can participatory pedagogical strategies be used to stimulate critical self-reflection and inquiry? The APA Task Force on Diversity Issues at the Precollege and Undergraduate Levels of Education in Psychology (1998a, 1998b) concluded that although there is no one way to teach diversity, cultural issues should not be taught separately but incorporated within the entire curriculum. Such integration will increase the rigor and inclusiveness of psychological science.

Approaches to Managing Pedagogical Challenges

Critical pedagogical approaches urge educators to facilitate the development of critical consciousness or conscientization, building critical thinking and inquiry skills so that students can challenge the nature of knowledge and integrate it with self-knowledge (see chap. 1, this volume, for an expanded definition). Critical inquiry evolves through dialogue (e.g., Freire's dialogical approach) whereby students and educators develop metacognitive skills and examine both the content and the context of learning by asking questions such as, What factors influence the construction of psychology's knowledge base?

In managing the challenge of "what to" and "how to" teach, Margaret Andersen and Patricia Hill Collins (2001) provided a framework for reconstructing knowledge from a critical vantage point. They called for educators to "shift the center" from exclusionary thinking to centralize the knowledge and experiences of traditionally marginalized and silenced groups, such as women, racial and ethnic minorities, gay, lesbian, or bisexual persons, and people who are economically poor or working-class. From this perspective, educators ask questions differently, such as, "What do we know about the people we study and counsel?" "How do we know this?" "Who is excluded from what is known?" "Who benefits from this knowledge construction, theory, paradigm?" "What new perspectives would change the status quo to provide a more inclusive perspective of the given population?" Shifting the center of our knowledge construction illuminates the experiences of both oppressed as well as dominant groups. The integration of personal narratives enhances understanding of how social structures, identities, power, and privilege have shaped our collective experiences and, thus, social science disciplines (Andersen & Collins, 2001). In this way, educators can avoid the trap of teaching from the single-group approach that only raises consciousness about an identified cultural group (Sleeter & Grant, 2003) instead of about larger conceptual and analytic frameworks like positionality, privilege, and oppression in which specific cultural identities can be incorporated (Weber, 1998).

Judith Plaskow (2000), in her consideration of critical consciousness from a Jewish feminist perspective, argued for an engaged critical consciousness that includes willingness to wrestle with tough traditions, insist on transformation of those traditions, hear silences, and confront oppression. Thus, educators should present critical interpretations of knowledge so that students are invited to consider, reject, criticize, or accept perspectives. A level of humility is required on the part of educators to explicitly state that they do not have all of the answers. A level of trust is also required on the part of students to "trust the process" as they learn to manage the tenuous nature of understanding evolving knowledge instead of pursuing the "absolute truth."

Paulo Freire (1970) proposed that during the educational process, students tend to negotiate three phases of awareness. His three-stage model of critical consciousnesss characterizes students' experiences as they grapple with issues and develop an organic, critical view of a discipline. The changes Freire outlined bear some resemblance to the overall themes proposed by ethnic identity development models (e.g., Cross, 1991; Tatum, 1992, 2002), which describe major shifts in awareness that students encounter as they move through phases marked by limited understanding of diversity to more complex understandings of the world, themselves, and social justice. Freire's first stage of critical consciousness or "semi-intransivity" describes an initial point at which students have a very limited sense of their ability to influence their environment and learning. At the second stage of "naïve transivity," students hold an expanded worldview but may tend to oversimplify problems. During the final stage of "critical transivity," students show the ability to reflect on, test, and modify their perspectives with greater confidence. Educators can facilitate students' development and ability to critique extant knowledge by introducing discussion and assignments that challenge students to integrate personal experiences with new perspectives on psychological theory. Specifically, students may be confronted with occasions when the literature does not represent their experience, forcing collisions between personal understandings and theory. The process of reflexivity may encourage students to "use their personal experiences to critique what passes as accepted knowledge in a field, while also making sense of personal experiences through the lens of that accepted knowledge" (Sinacore, Blaisure, Justin, Healy, & Brawer, 1999, p. 267). Critical pedagogy urges educators to teach in a way that engages the whole student, helping her or him to integrate "knowledge of selves" with "knowledge that is on the shelves."

Finally, the principles in critical pedagogies also emphasize how language is used to convey knowledge in denoting power and ownership and potentially create oppression in learning. Thus, educators and students alike must be responsible and accountable in language use and particularize the use of their words to specific contexts. For instance, mindfulness about promoting inclusivity would discourage the use of the word *women* to refer to all women, and instead, would encourage specification of who is being referred to in a specific context (e.g., Latinas and Navajo women).

Issue 4: Social Action Challenges

A final challenge to transforming psychology curricula is educators' attention to the social consequences of their courses, not just the cultural consequences. What outcomes should be included in the goals of psychology teaching that integrate a multicultural focus throughout the curriculum? Thomas Heaney (1995) argued that a transformed curriculum must extend beyond the linking of problems to broader social and political dynamics to social action that emerges from critical understanding. This assertion is consistent with the eight principles in feminist curriculum development outlined by Jean Chin and Nancy Russo (1997), including diversity, egalitarianism and empowerment, and social action. Beyond facilitating students' personal insights and deep inquiry from culturally diverse perspectives, educators often struggle with how to help students translate and apply their learning to effect change within the classroom, facilitate transformations within psychology (e.g., theory, research, and practice), and address larger social issues.

Approaches to Managing Social Action Challenges

Challenging the "givenness" of the world enables students to reflect on their past and present existence, place their realities in historical context, and experience an awakening to possibilities for a transformed future. Their new visions support expectations for social change, which can then be expressed through collective social action (Mackie, 1981). Social action can be facilitated through linking course content with students' lived experiences as well as local community needs. For instance, including service learning projects as part of course requirements is likely to increase educators' and students' consciousness of the felt needs around them and stimulate them to engagement. As described in chapter 1, social action may be directed toward transformation of the personal self or the learning process as well as larger societal issues. Critical pedagogies support instructional practices that help students recontextualize their daily lives and situate themselves in relation to others locally and globally for the purpose of enacting social change. Through the process of developing conscientization, facilitated through critical and personal reflection, class members take a proactive stance toward addressing transformations to concretely enhance practice (Freire, 1998a).

Summary

Heaney (1995) stated that critical Freirean pedagogy is typified by the use of several techniques: the use of "people's knowledge" as the basis for curriculum, reflection on the political content of learners' daily experience, and the organization of "culture circles" that promote critical dialogue and peer interaction. Collectively, the principles embodied in critical multicultural pedagogies encourage more accurate and inclusive course content (what is taught) and facilitate an enactive, empowering process (how we teach and learn). They support student learning associated with three critical processes as identified by Fred Newmann and Gary Wehlage (1995): (a) attention to the construction of knowledge, (b) disciplined inquiry (critical dialogue and consciousness), and (c) the exploration of values beyond the classroom (social action). We now turn our discussion to specific application of critical multicultural pedagogy to a graduate psychology course.

AN APPLICATION OF CRITICAL MULTICULTURAL PEDAGOGY TO A GRADUATE PSYCHOLOGY COURSE

This case study describes the experiences of one educator (Byars-Winston) and her students as they negotiated some of the challenges outlined in the previous section as well as gained a deepening understanding of what a multicultural feminist approach entails. Consistent with the aforementioned recommendation that learning about the complex intersections of identity can be best accomplished by centralizing content about women of diversity, this graduate psychology course focused on the psychology of U.S. women of color. The goal of this course was to move beyond simply adding race to the female experience by uncovering the complex diversity of women of color's psychological experiences resulting from interlocking, interdependent systems of oppression and forms of resistance against such oppression. This graduate psychology course was developed and taught in the 2000 fall semester at a midwestern research institution.

Oliva Espín (1995) asserted that women of color could help to create a "true psychology for all women" as they are well suited to transform political and theoretical views as a function of their unique experiences. Johnella Butler (2000) similarly argued that teaching focused on women of color can be a transformative agent in multicultural education. Building on these perspectives, we believe that this course provides a useful example of the goals of critical multicultural pedagogy applied to psychology, namely "to provide an education that more accurately reflects the history and composition of the world, that demonstrates the relationship of what we learn to how we live, and that implicitly and explicitly reveals the relationship between knowledge and social action" (Butler, 2000, p. 185).

The course participants consisted of six doctoral students, all identifying themselves as heterosexual women from counseling and rehabilitation psychology programs. The instructor ethnically self-identified as Black and students self-identified as members of the following ethnic groups: Navajo,

Filipina, Scandinavian, Chinese, Mexican and Nicaraguan, and Greek. In contrast to undergraduate or graduate students with limited exposure to multicultural and feminist content, the graduate students who participated in this experience brought some prior knowledge of and commitment to diversity issues to the course, which enhanced thorough exploration and resolution of challenges outlined in the previous section. This in-depth learning was facilitated by the unique size and structure of this course; clearly, more examples of critical multicultural pedagogies broadly applied in diverse settings are needed.

We frame our brief discussion of course process and content within the three stages of critical consciousness described briefly in the pedagogical challenges section of this chapter (see chap. 1, this volume, for additional clarification). We use anecdotal illustrations from this class to highlight dynamics associated with these phases and to focus on two salient themes and issues observed throughout the course: intimacy and relationships and power and privilege.

Intimacy and Relationships

Participants entered the course with expectations that they would engage with each other in a supportive, nonconfrontational way. This expectation was influenced by the stereotype that women are naturally relational beings as well as perceptions about homogeneity based on the shared experience of being women. During the semi-intransivity (first) stage, we outwardly expressed acceptance of all comments made by our peers, minimizing our critical feedback to avoid disruption of a perceived "stable" collective. Paramount in the progression toward critical engagement was the instructor's consistent reminder to bring our whole selves into the room, including both the personal and the professional.

By deconstructing the myth of what is considered "authorized knowledge," group members began to participate at the level of naïve transivity. In this second stage, a roundtable discussion on multiple feminisms catalyzed an intense examination of the missing links between theory and practice, challenging students to integrate their personal voices and lived experiences with the extant literature. Inevitably, the level of engagement rose as we moved from the façade of unconditional agreement to the realization of our lack of consensus about how we defined feminism, race, or ethnicity. The interplay between White women and women of color in the group intensified, forcing us to truly examine the inconsistencies between our experiences as women. One woman of Scandinavian descent commented, "What's the role for White women in the psychology of U.S. women of color? Are we roommates, mothers, daughters, sisters, friends, acquaintances, or equals? I think I would like my role to be that of an ally, but I am not sure how to make this happen." Her question typified participants' struggle to redefine how to relate deeply and meaningfully with one another and to continue dialoguing through painful discussions.

In the final stage, critical transivity, the collective struggle that came through interpersonal dialogue to identify and challenge oppressive, noninclusive paradigms within psychology led to active reflections about how to resist such paradigms as well as to rearticulate psychological views of women that are more representative of the lives of everyday women. The theme of mothers emerged as a point of unity during this stage. We realized that we were not alone in this journey, acknowledging that our struggles for self-definition were not novel and actively reflected on the legacies of resistance to oppression that we had received from our mothers. One student of Navajo heritage expressed the following:

> We walked where our mothers have walked, where our wars were fought, where our children will travel again and again. As I have told my own daughter, you too will make this journey. You make it every time you realize the power you possess as a woman.

Another student, who identified herself as Filipina, claimed, "Our mothers already have doctorates in wisdom and survival. We are the next generation trying to deconstruct what they already know and wanted to protect us from." This collective reflection deepened the relationships among class members and provided a sense of intergenerational efficacy inherited from our foremothers that allowed us to transform our thinking and learning within traditional psychology training programs.

This set of interactions described in this section demonstrate movement from a false sense of similarity and homogeneity to conflict and increased recognition of differences among women to a greater understanding of what commonalities women do and do not experience despite their diversity. Movement was facilitated by the integration of personal experience and academic content and the willingness of participants to engage in ongoing dialogue despite experiences of discomfort and strain. The challenges and strategies related to Issues 2 and 3 (cultural diversity and pedagogical challenges) were especially relevant to the negotiation of concerns related to the theme of intimacy and relationships.

Power and Privilege

Consistent with the first stage of critical consciousness, semi-intransivity, students operated from a self-imposed, traditional framework of defending their own intellectual understanding and acquiring the existing knowledge of the literature on women of color in a detached, impersonal, and noncritical manner. In the first two meetings, the instructor invited students to cocreate the curriculum and to jointly invest in the proposed focus, process, content, and outcomes of the course. Given the fact that students are socialized to accept published scholarship and empirically validated research as the most legitimized currency for academic exchange, students' initial response was one of distrust about participating in a more collaborative approach to learning. In particular, they struggled to reconcile the focus of graduate program evaluations ("What do I need to do to get an 'A' in the class?") with the instructor's expectations, which included challenging authorized knowledge. The instructor's invitation was crucial to empowering and encouraging students to resist the tyranny of silence and monologue, and to make the transition to the second stage of consciousness, naïve transivity.

As students gained more personal agency to engage analytically with the existing literature and critiques of psychology as a field, the focus turned toward in-class dynamics regarding how power and privilege were operating amongst course members. At one point, a student identifying as Filipina expressed how she was tired of feeling pulled to educate White women about her experience as a woman of color and that she chose not to do so at that moment. One woman, who identified as Greek American, responded that she did not know how else she would come to understand the student's experience unless that student chose to share. There was a clear reversal of power in that the person usually viewed as "unknown" (Filipina) and thus voiceless and powerless, chose to take power by controlling what would be known about her and when it would be known. To move through this cultural impasse (Mobley, 1997), students were further challenged to integrate current literature with their personal experiences *and* with the experiences of others, resolving to hear each other across differences. Class members' courage to acknowledge anger, fear, and vulnerability in this process precipitated transition to the last stage of critical consciousness, critical transivity. Participants actively renegotiated the cosharing of power, privileging each others' voices, and using their personal experiences as a knowing place from which to continue critical examination of psychology as a whole, thus becoming theorists of their own lives (Weiler, 1991). The natural outgrowth of this experiential, engaged critical learning was a focus on what transformations are needed in the curriculum and training to which graduate students in psychology are exposed. Some suggestions included increasing interactions with local communities to contextualize psychology education, requiring some clinical training in a community-based mental health agency, and encouraging participatory research wherein individuals from the population studied are included in the research design and evaluation.

The interactional dynamics and content described in this section reflect many of the challenges and strategies associated with Issues 1 and 4 (philosophical and social action domains). Students gained a deeper sense of their authority and shared power holders, which contributed to their greater confidence as coconstructors of knowledge, which then led to their capacity to tie their learning to social change implications within their discipline.

CONCLUDING THOUGHTS

As the previous description of classroom interaction reveals, the principle of collaborative knowledge construction among instructors and students as colearners provides a concrete path for transformation of psychology by humanizing the people we counsel, study, educate, or train and empowering colearners to take action against social practices and conditions in psychology that marginalize individuals, groups, and their experiences. To build on this framework, it will be important for educators to provide additional examples and engage in future research about the ways in which critical pedagogy practices are best enacted with students of different ages and with a range of value systems, social identities, and knowledge and commitment to the specific subject matter being studied.

The multicultural guidelines recently adopted by the American Psychological Association (2002) advocate for psychology educators to take a culture-centered approach to education and to use multicultural constructs in their teaching. Though scant, the existing research on multicultural education in psychology and counselor training programs suggests that this educational approach produces "more competent researchers, educators, therapists, and other applied practitioners" (APA, 2002, p. 31), underscoring the enhanced value of cultural education on student learning and professional outcomes. Given the need for curricular frameworks that may facilitate multicultural competence in psychology educators and counseling trainees, we advocate for critical multicultural pedagogies that incorporate both multicultural and feminist principles as frameworks that hold great promise for providing structure to teaching about diversity issues.

Although the possibilities for curricular transformation are encouraging, the responsibilities for implementing changes are often unevenly distributed. Glenda Moss (2001) observed that the onus of training competent multicultural educators is often left to assistant or adjunct professors who have limited power to make changes in curricula, may be isolated in their efforts to challenge traditional teaching, and are sometimes expected to teach about all "minority" issues without the shared ownership of other faculty. Relatedly, a randomized national survey of the attitudes of social work faculty found that faculty members with lower status were more likely to hold critical perspectives of existing educational structures and that women faculty were more likely than men to report favorable attitudes about social equity (Gutiérrez et al., 1999). These findings remind us that teaching for social justice cannot be an individual commitment alone, but must be integrated with institutional commitments and priorities. These larger institutional issues are addressed in chapter 10.

9

MULTICULTURAL FEMINIST MENTORING AS INDIVIDUAL AND SMALL-GROUP PEDAGOGY

RUTH E. FASSINGER AND NANCY F. HENSLER-McGINNIS

Pedagogy in the form of mentoring, in which more experienced members of a community instruct, guide, and support the growth of less experienced members either individually or in small groups, likely has been in existence since human communities began. Across cultures and centuries, teacher–apprentice relationships have been central to the functioning of educational, economic, social, political, religious, and artistic institutions. Examples include the martial arts tradition of sensei (master teacher) and uschi deshi (student); mercantile and artistic guild apprenticeships; the training of priestly scribes, shamans, midwives, and herbal healers in many cultures; and current-day training models in laboratory science, law enforcement, academia, legal and health professions, sports, and the fine and performing arts.

It is primarily since the advent of industrialization that education has been compulsory and mass-produced (i.e., one teacher for many students). Although much of professional socialization now occurs within such systems, dyadic and small-group mentoring relationships catalyze a great deal of learning in educational institutions and the workplace. Particularly with the movement toward an increasingly specialized and decentralized global marketplace and with advances in Internet technology providing highly individualized e-learning opportunities, mentoring, whether provided to individuals or small groups, remains a vibrant form of pedagogy.

In this chapter, we present a discussion of mentoring in dyadic or small-group relationships and focus in particular on multicultural feminist mentoring. We review the existing literature on mentoring briefly, with a focus on scholarship that has addressed gender and race. This review is followed by a critique of the literature in the context of sweeping changes in the current workplace; multicultural feminist mentoring is described as an effective model in this context. We then consider the actual practice of multicultural feminist mentoring and conclude with suggested strategies for negotiating multicultural feminist mentoring in the patriarchal structures that characterize most educational institutions and workplaces.

THE POLITICS OF NAMING: AN ETYMOLOGY OF *MENTORING*

As is often the case when attempting to reclaim useful concepts within patriarchal cultures, linguistic conventions that encapsulate the assumptions of those cultures constrain discourse. The terms used to describe mentoring relationships are no exception. For example, the word *mentor*, now synonymous with the name of the trusted friend in Homer's *Odyssey* charged with overseeing the development of Odysseus' son, contains the masculine ending *tor* and means *man who thinks*. Inclusion of the feminine form *mentrix* remains problematic because the root itself restricts mentoring to the realm of thought (Koocher, 2002). *Protégé*, a word used to name the individual in relationship with a mentor, is derived from the Latin *protegere* (to protect) and assumes vulnerability on the part of the person being mentored. The linguistic roots of mentoring, therefore, suggest that mentoring is enacted by an older, wiser man who rationally guides a less experienced individual presumed to be in need of protection (Koocher, 2002).

It is always tempting to create more women-centered versions of terms firmly entrenched in patriarchy; for example *mom*-tor (masculine) and *mom*-trix (feminine) might better capture an interpersonal process so clearly focused on motherlike devotion to the nurturing of a largely unformed person into professional *maturity*. However, by inventing new words we run the risk of marginalizing the topic under consideration while the dominant discourse remains intact and undisturbed. Thus, in this chapter, we nod to convention and use the common terms mentor and mentee, although we note that changes in terminology form a critical venue for future scholarship.

In addition, we have attempted to be thoughtful about other language usage throughout the chapter. Believing that multicultural feminist mentoring can be enacted effectively with both male and female mentees, we use mixed-gender pronouns when referring to mentees. Although we think that profeminist men can and should provide feminist mentoring, we believe that there are unique challenges facing women in these roles, so we use feminine pronouns (she, her) to refer to mentors. Finally, because our conceptualization of feminist mentoring is inclusive of human diversity beyond gender, we use the term *multicultural* to modify the term *feminist mentoring* throughout.

BRIEF REVIEW OF THE LITERATURE ON MENTORING

Theoretical writing and empirical research on mentoring began in the late 1970s in the business arena; since then, interest in mentoring has spread to education, public health, and other fields. Most recently, critiques of existing models of mentoring have resulted in new theoretical models that consider the contributions of minority status, power relations, and political consciousness to the mentoring process (Benishek, Bieschke, Park, & Slattery, in press; Fassinger, 1997; Kalbfleish & Keyton, 1995). Although many of the models of mentoring have not been subjected to empirical testing in their entirety, important aspects of mentoring have been clarified.

Definitions and Models of Mentoring

Kathy Kram (1985) provided a foundational definition of mentoring, describing it as an interpersonal process in which a more experienced colleague provides professional guidance, instruction, and support to a less experienced individual. Mentoring relationships are characterized by an active and personal investment from both parties; ideally, these relationships are mutually beneficial, enhancing the growth of both participants.

Kram's (1985) model, based on data from an in-depth study in a large business organization, outlined two categories of mentoring activities: career-related functions and psychosocial functions. Career-related functions assist the mentee in learning skills and strategies that enhance career advancement, for example, facilitating exposure and visibility, coaching, and providing challenging assignments. Psychosocial functions include aspects of the relationship that enhance the mentee's sense of competence and professional effectiveness, for example, role modeling, counseling, and friendship. Career functions arise from the senior person's experience, status, and influence; psychosocial functions stem from a relationship that fosters mutual trust and intimacy. Recent scholars have emphasized the importance of including both of these functions in a clear, universally applied definition of mentoring (Benishek et al., in press). Kram's model also has had considerable scholarly influence in inspiring empirical research and instrument development (Hollingsworth, 2000).

Two other mentoring models (Burke, McKeen, & McKenna, 1993; Hunt & Michael, 1983) represent attempts to explicate a mentor's use of particular mentoring functions and the antecedents, process, and outcomes of mentoring. Empirical testing of the first (Burke et al., 1993) model indicated that mentors' use of career-related and psychosocial functions was associated with such factors as age, gender, organizational tenure, and perceived similarity to mentees. The authors of the second model (Hunt & Michael, 1983) postulated organizational environment, mentor and mentee organizational power, mentoring stages, and outcomes of mentoring (e.g., promotions and work satisfaction) as important factors in understanding mentoring. However, the former model is marred by sampling limitations and exclusive focus on mentors, and the latter has not been tested empirically (Hollingsworth, 2000).

Merris Hollingsworth and Ruth Fassinger (2002) adapted and expanded the existing antecedent–process–outcome mentoring models for their study on student–faculty mentoring relationships in counseling psychology research training. They found that students' mentoring experiences mediated the relationship between the research training environment and subsequent research productivity, thus providing support for a connection between research-related mentoring relationships and doctoral students' research attitudes and behaviors.

Pamela Kalbfleish and Joann Keyton (1995) advocated a mentoring model that acknowledged both the variety of career paths taken by individuals and the impact of the work environment on those with minority status in specific professional contexts. These authors emphasized the benefits of an interpersonal model, including mutually enhancing relationships characterized by authentic involvement on the part of both mentors and mentees. Citing the many challenges associated with cross-gender mentoring, they predicated their model on the assumption that only women should mentor women. This assumption has limited the utility of the model, given the general lack of senior women in many workplaces (Benishek et al., in press).

Types of Mentoring Relationships

Mentoring occurs in both formal and informal contexts. Although *formal* mentoring programs (assignment of mentors by a third party) have been implemented in numerous educational and occupational settings with some degree of success (Ragins, Cotton, & Miller, 2000), data indicate that *informal* mentorship (spontaneously developed) is correlated with more frequent mentoring (Scandura, 2001), better compensation, and higher levels of career development and psychosocial support (Ragins & Cotton, 1999). However, Belle Ragins, John Cotton, and Janice Miller have cautioned that comparisons between informal and formal mentoring may be misleading if they do not control for the quality of or satisfaction with the mentoring relationship, which account for more variance in job and career attitudes than type of mentor or presence of a mentoring relationship. *Facilitated* mentorships represent an effective compromise that acknowledges both the success of informal mentoring and the reality that not all individuals have access to informal mentoring networks. In facilitated mentoring, the organization establishes expectations, training, structures, and supports for mentoring but allows mentors and mentees to select each other (Ragins & Cotton, 1999).

Although the traditional dyadic conceptualization of mentoring is the focus of much of the *decentralized* research literature, organizations adjusting to marketplace changes are attempting new decentralized approaches to mentorship in which the principles of mentoring are applied to small groups or teams. In team mentoring, mentees are assigned to experts from various areas of an organization and rotate through different mentors, acquiring knowledge in a variety of content areas (Messmer, 2003). Mentoring circles consist of several senior organization members acting as mentors to a group of new or junior colleagues, who receive networking opportunities and psychosocial support (see Knouse, 2001). Vertical teams, increasingly being used in academic professional training programs, are structured with a faculty mentor supervising small teams of mentees; these teams foster peer interaction as well as modeling by the faculty mentor (Hughes et al., 1993). Peer mentoring, the sharing of career and psychosocial tasks between individuals at the same career stage, offers a collaborative model for navigating potentially alienating hierarchical systems (Gram, 1992).

Mentor and Mentee Characteristics

Research on mentoring suggests that its success depends on the quality of the interpersonal relationship between mentor and mentee, but the precise elements of a successful mentoring relationship have not been explicated definitively. Studies of the qualities of effective mentors have revealed a wide variety of personality characteristics, such as emotional intelligence (Bennetts, 2002), flexibility, empathy, patience, humor, encouragement, and support as well as being ethical and psychologically well adjusted (see Johnson, 2002). The scant research on the qualities that mentees bring to the mentoring relationship has highlighted personality features and problem behaviors of mentees (e.g., excessive dependence and faked enthusiasm) that contribute to dysfunctional mentoring relationships (Johnson & Huwe, 2002).

The individuals involved in a mentoring relationship may be similar or different on any number of demographic criteria associated with power in organizations such as race, ethnicity, gender, sexual orientation, (dis)ability, and socioeconomic status. Although there is some evidence that demographic matching produces favorable mentoring results (e.g., matched ethnicity, Santos & Reigadas, 2002; matched gender, Scandura, 2001), matching may not be possible in many educational and occupational settings where the majority of individuals at senior levels are White (presumably heterosexual and able-bodied) men. For example, Belle Ragins and John Cotton indicated in 1991 that, in spite of female professionals' reported need for mentors, they (compared with men) faced more barriers in obtaining mentors, including limited access to potential mentors, unwillingness on the part of senior male colleagues to mentor them, and the risk of having mentoring relationships misconstrued as sexual. Almost 10 years later, in the academic arena, Catherine Hackney and Marianne Bock (2000) identified the lack of adequate numbers of women in established positions as a chilling environment that affects the retention and promotion of female faculty members. In studies of the career development of high-achieving Black women, White women, Latinas, lesbians, Asian American women, and women with disabilities (see Fassinger, in press), many participants reported having made their way in their early careers without the help of traditional mentors, accessing support and information primarily by networking with colleagues, friends, and within social movements and women's or minority-focused professional organizations.

Whether demographically matched or not, most effective mentoring relationships are based on shared interests and cognitive style (Armstrong, Allinson, & Hayes, 2002), attitudinal and values similarity (Ensher, Grant-Vallone, & Marelich, 2002), frequency of contact, enjoyment of interactions (Armstrong et al., 2002), and shared expectations about how the relationship will work (Johnson, 2002; Messmer, 2003). In some cases, these markers of relational attraction have contributed more to mentoring satisfaction and effectiveness than demographic factors, for example, race and gender similarity (Ensher et al., 2002). However, as the following section suggests, gender as well as race, class, and other cultural identities interacts with relational factors such as personal interests, values, and expectations to create considerable complexity in the mentoring process.

The Mentoring Process

Research has demonstrated differences in the process and function of mentoring for men and women. Female mentees more frequently cited experiencing the psychosocial functions of mentoring (e.g., receiving advice regarding personal development and balancing multiple roles), whereas male mentees more frequently cited vocational functions (e.g., receiving coaching for publication and career path decisions; Paludi & DeFour, 1992). Female managers, however, were more likely than their male peers to engage in both psychosocial and career-related functions (Burke et al., 1993).

In addition, women more often reported problems in their mentoring relationships (especially with men), including interpersonal discomfort in conversations, sexual harassment, and exclusion from the mentor's professional networks (Paludi & DeFour, 1992). Documenting gender socialization patterns in the mentoring process, Lucia Gilbert and Karen Rossman (1992) found that male mentors were more likely than female mentors to define the needs of and assert power over their mentees. Mary Nelson and Elizabeth Holloway (1990) reported male supervisor–female trainee interactions characterized by a traditional hierarchical pattern in contrast to female supervisor–female trainee interactions, which involved genuine sharing manifested by power shifts in the conversation.

Mentoring Outcomes

Research in mentoring outcomes typically compares mentored organization members with their nonmentored peers. Having a mentor has consistently been associated with such benefits as higher incomes and more promotions (Dreher & Cox, 1996); greater job satisfaction (Dreher & Cox, 1996; Wallace, 2001) and career commitment (Ulku-Steiner, Kurtz-Costes, & Kinlaw, 2000); and higher levels of personal identity, self-esteem, and creativity (Atkinson, Casas, & Neville, 1994). In graduate students, mentoring outcomes reported include development of professional skills, attitudes, and identity; enhanced productivity and academic and career success; satisfaction with one's program or career; greater income and faster promotion; and willingness to mentor others (see Johnson & Huwe, 2002).

In the case of ethnic minority students, participation in mentoring programs has been associated with higher grades and attendance rates for African Americans (Linnehan, 2002), and American Indian undergraduate students who perceived that they had mentors were less likely to report wanting to drop out of school (Gloria & Robinson-Kurpius, 2001). In youth, the supportive influence of a mentor also has been correlated with lower drug use and nonviolent delinquency rates and more positive attitudes toward school (Zimmerman, Bingenheimer, & Notaro, 2002), suggesting that mentoring can be effective at any age.

The sexes of the mentor and mentee appear to affect outcomes differentially. In Jean Wallace's (2001) study of female lawyers, female mentees with male mentors had significantly higher earnings than those with female mentors; however, having a female mentor was correlated with mentees' reports of greater career satisfaction, greater career commitment, higher achievement of professional goals, and less work–nonwork conflict. In female graduate students, perceived support from mentors was associated with higher academic self-concept, departmental sensitivity to family issues, and less stress, whereas mentor support was correlated only with academic self-concept in male graduate students (Ulku-Steiner et al., 2000). Other research findings have indicated that unmentored males report better outcomes than females with mentors, suggesting that although mentoring relationships can foster women's equity in the workplace, they may not always be enough to compensate for other gender-based barriers (Bahuniuk, Dobos, & Kogler-Hill, 1990).

Multicultural Feminist Mentoring Models

Despite increased scientific attention to professional mentoring, the literature remains inadequate in addressing the experiences of women, persons of color, and other cultural minorities. Theoretical models are few and testing of the existing models has been inconsistent at best, thus providing little guidance in articulating the mentoring needs of the highly diverse populations that increasingly characterize workplaces and educational institutions.

Ruth Fassinger (1997), citing the research on mentoring that highlights challenges faced by women, persons of color, and other marginalized groups in obtaining productive mentoring relationships, identified issues of power as a central theme in the research literature. Traditionally, the mentor, who is presumed to have power in a particular organization, integrates the mentee into those networks of power. However, Fassinger argued, because current gendered distributions of power in organizations and professional fields favoring men are likely to change slowly, new conceptualizations of mentoring are needed to address the systemic power issues implicit in the mentoring literature. She differentiated between external and internal sources of power, that is, between traditional notions of mentoring as conferring power based on demographic or positional status and a feminist model of mentoring founded on empowering others to recognize their own authority and potential.

Fassinger (1997) derived her feminist mentoring model from feminist pedagogy theory, and it thus includes six elements commonly cited as core tenets of feminist pedagogy: (a) re-thinking power (shared power based on mutuality, equality, and respect; addressing power issues directly and openly), (b) emphasis on the relational (congruent sharing of self, mutual feedback, connections encouraged with other potential mentors, and valuing of mentee's personal life and relationships), (c) valuing collaboration (joint projects with mentees and bringing mentees into professional networks), (d) commitment to diversity (proactive stance in valuing marginalized voices in one's organization and field and challenging isms in oneself and others), (e) integration of dichotomies (congruent sense of self and one's knowledge, linking of abstract knowledge to personal experience, and recognition of contextual construction of knowledge), and (f) incorporation of political analysis (acknowledging and teaching that the personal is political and actively challenging patriarchal values in individuals and institutions).

Characteristic of a feminist, collaborative model, each element is associated with benefits to both the mentor and the mentee. For the mentor, benefits include gaining a colleague or friend, obtaining task assistance, experiencing increased productivity, acquiring broadened perspectives, experiencing reempowerment of the self, receiving the satisfactions of generativity, attaining enhanced professional recognition, and challenging the patriarchal status quo. For the mentee, benefits include an increased sense of competency and self-respect, support, direct experience, networking, the development of a self-image as a professional, role modeling, self-congruence, and personal empowerment to work for social change (Fassinger, 1997).

Lois Benishek and her colleagues (in press) proposed a modification of Fassinger's (1997) model to highlight more clearly the inclusion of a multicultural sensibility in the model. Additional foci included explicit examination of privilege within the mentoring relationship, the responsibility of the mentor to raise multicultural issues with all mentees, participation in projects not prescribed by the majority culture, and overt valuing of experiences gained in a nonmajority culture. Multicultural feminist mentoring is described as an interactive process in which differences are identified and explored as they affect the mentoring relationship and the professional development of each individual. This requires a continued willingness to address the tensions that may exist between feminism and multiculturalism to foster more satisfying and productive mentoring relationships.

THE ROLE OF MULTICULTURAL FEMINIST MENTORING IN A CHANGING MARKETPLACE

Development of new kinds of mentoring arrangements is increasingly important as educational institutions and workplaces adjust to a changing marketplace characterized by globalization, technological advances, flattened organizational structures, decreased predictability in occupational security and reward, and a need for a new kind of worker, emotionally intelligent and information savvy, who can process and interpret a variety of data, satisfy diverse and sometimes competing demands, operate within cross-functional and self-directed teams, navigate broad organizational networks, deal sensitively with diverse others, and actively manage her or his own career (see Fassinger, in press). Thus, new approaches to mentoring theory and research must rest on broader definitions of mentoring, based not on traditional hierarchical relationships but on diffuse, decentered networks of support, for example, multiple mentors; combined formal and informal mentoring networks; team and peer mentoring; small working groups; Internet mentoring; and collaborations among professional, academic, and community organizations (Hackney & Bock, 2000; Knouse, 2001; Messmer, 2003).

The multicultural feminist mentoring model offered by Ruth Fassinger (1997) and expanded by Lois Benishek et al. (in press) is responsive to the demands of diverse educational and occupational settings. Compared with traditional hierarchical mentoring models, multicultural feminist approaches can be used more democratically to develop the skills and productivity of individuals at all levels of organizations because power and privilege are consciously acknowledged, shared, and used to empower mentees. Moreover, the multicultural feminist expansion of mentoring relationships beyond dyadic, hierarchical approaches to shared mentoring in networks of connection is easily enacted with the use of Internet technologies, allowing individuals to have direct access to demographically similar mentors in other organizations; contemporary examples include career-coaching Web sites for African American entrepreneurs (Knouse, 2001), structured e-mentoring relationships for women in engineering and sciences established through university–industry partnerships (e.g., http://www.mentornet.net), and mentoring electronic mailing lists for women returning to the workforce (Knouse). It is possible that such strategies may help to mitigate the effects of unequal power and privilege in contemporary patriarchal organizations.

The acknowledgment of a mentee's potential need for multiple developmental relationships rather than an exclusive relationship with one mentor recognizes that individuals may define themselves through several identities (some or all of which may be nonmajority identities), and also that it can be extremely difficult to find mentors who match even one, let alone all, of their identities. Multicultural feminist perspectives value demographic and cultural diversity and promote personal and institutional flexibility encompassing a developed facility for moving, thinking, and understanding across disciplines, communities, and paradigms and a tolerance for ambiguity. Mentors overseeing the development of individuals expected to thrive in a globally interconnected society must nurture an ability to embrace interdisciplinary, multilingual, multicultural approaches to human opportunities and challenges, and mentoring arrangements themselves must model this complexity in approach. A current example is a peer-mentoring network for women scientists at an academic research institution described by Kathleen Davis (2001). These women, with limited access to established science career networks, developed their own resource network that was inclusive of diverse members, encouraging of alternative career pathways, consciously critical of the masculinized culture of science, and affirming of the legitimacy of each woman's place in the scientific community.

This latter example emphasizes another distinct contribution of a multicultural feminist context: the incorporation of political analysis and social advocacy. Mentoring, because it involves intergenerational exchange of knowledge and thus supports the continuous progress of human activity, can be a significant tool for change. The integration of multicultural feminist methodologies and epistemology into traditional systems challenges the assumption that education, work, science, and relationships are value free; identifies the importance of context in human lives and institutions; strives to eliminate oppression of marginalized groups; and demands that science be used in the service of social change (Benishek et al., in press; Fassinger, 1997). The mentoring relationship that attends to these issues of power and oppression at the interpersonal level also participates in a highly charged politics of change at group, institutional, and societal levels.

ISSUES IN THE PRACTICE OF
MULTICULTURAL FEMINIST MENTORING

In this section, we discuss some of the issues and challenges that arise in the actual practice of multicultural feminist mentoring. First we discuss the politics of power in mentoring, with a focus on the interpersonal relationship between mentor and mentee. We then ask whether multicultural feminist mentoring is possible within patriarchy, with brief highlighting of organizational and systemic challenges. We conclude with suggested strategies for remaining true to multicultural feminist principles while functioning within environments that often are antithetical to them.

Politics of Power in Mentoring

Mentoring relationships typically have been viewed as top-down, with the emphasis on what is gained from the mentor by the mentee. Multicultural feminist mentoring relationships, however, focus explicitly on the reciprocal nature of the mentoring relationship and the impact of that relationship on both mentor and mentee. This profound and deliberate disruption of traditional power hierarchies is not without interpersonal difficulties for both members in the mentoring relationship.

Mentor Issues

For the mentor, expectations of reciprocity from the mentee may position the mentor for disappointment if expectations are not met and may exacerbate doubts in her own mentoring skills should anticipated outcomes not be accomplished. In an academic setting, for example, a dissertation advisor may struggle to get a coauthored article written when a mentee's goals and energy change or become redirected, whereas in a business setting, promises of commitment to a collegial project may be forgotten as a mentee is directed to undertake new assignments.

In addition, female mentors often are burdened by the psychosocial aspects of mentoring, which mentees (both men and women) tend not to expect or demand as much from men. Women's gender socialization primes them for holistic, connection-oriented mentoring, which not only is more emotionally demanding than traditional task–function mentoring but also is being done in addition to task-oriented activities. For example, aiding an inexperienced mentee in editing a poorly written academic paper or workplace report becomes even more difficult when the mentee shares his or her fears about the writing process or the personal crisis that left insufficient time for task completion.

Challenges also can arise for mentors related to additional minority statuses that they or their mentees may hold in organizations. The burden of token or lower status of mentors may lead to excessive involvement in *shadow jobs* (e.g., committees and collegial and environmental caretaking) that are necessary to the organization but provide little or no reward as well as the assignment or acceptance of more mentees than the mentor can handle comfortably. Multicultural feminist mentors also are more likely than their male peers to mentor marginalized individuals (e.g., women, people of color, sexual minorities, persons with disabilities, and individuals from low socioeconomic backgrounds), who, in turn, can be expected to have more extensive needs for guidance and help if they are encountering an oppressive environment or emerging from an environment in which their skills and competencies were not fully developed. Moreover, the mentor may be accused of defending a "weak" mentee when she attempts to contextualize that mentee's difficulties within an oppressive system, and she may lose professional credibility with her own colleagues. Finally, marginalized status within an organization may force a mentor to depend excessively on her mentees to meet her own personal and professional needs, creating potential difficulties for all concerned.

A final challenge that multicultural feminist mentors face is that few have been adequately prepared to offer a model of shared power in mentoring relationships because most have been mentored (if at all) in more traditional, hierarchical arrangements. The absence of opportunities for observational learning, coupled with the predominance of patriarchal ideologies, means that each mentor must create from scratch the norms, rules, and boundaries within which she will operate. Moreover, because she is sharing power, she will necessarily involve mentees in this process. This can be an ongoing, exhausting, and sometimes confusing process for everyone and may lead some to question the competence of the mentor.

Despite its challenges, however, multicultural feminist mentoring offers highly empowering possibilities for the mentor. Holding a model of reciprocity in mentoring relationships can make it easier to seek out and establish peer-mentoring relationships with colleagues. These peer relationships not only are healthy for the mentor but also model important self-care activities for the mentee. There also is powerful personal transformation in knowing that one has contributed to the growth and positive development of another, and a mentor can take pride in empowering an individual to engage her or his own possibilities. A mentor also can derive satisfaction from the knowledge that she is enacting social change by giving voice, strength, and centrality to those previously marginalized and powerless. Thus, sharing power and empowering others are the means by which a mentor makes the personal political and ultimately contributes to social transformation.

Mentee Issues

For the mentee, the obvious benefits of being empowered through a multicultural feminist mentoring relationship also bring challenges. Mentees must develop skills in acquiring mentors: determining where and how to find mentors and seeking them out, making themselves appealing to potential mentors, assessing whether a particular mentoring relationship will be helpful in the way they expect, living up to implicit and explicit norms and agreements in the relationship, and disengaging from mentoring relationships when they are ineffective or have run their course. Particularly difficult are mentoring relationships in which mentors jealously protect mentees from other helpful experiences and place mentees in the position of deciding whether the costs outweigh the benefits of the relationship. As in feminist classrooms, the level of accountability demanded of mentees for attending to their own individual development is high, as shared power also brings shared responsibility.

The implicit or explicit expectation of reciprocity in the mentoring relationship may be perceived as a burden by the mentee, particularly one very new to the organizational environment, who may experience much trepidation about his or her capacity to give something back (What? When? How?). This may contribute to dysfunctional behavior, such as trying to please the mentor by faking enthusiasm over the mentor's goals and expectations but passive-aggressively enacting her or his own plans and desires. Alternatively, it simply may be difficult for a mentee to develop and articulate her or his own vision under conditions of relationship reciprocity, or it may be exceedingly painful to admit to a respected mentor that previously shared goals have changed for the mentee. In an academic setting, for example, a graduate student may shift to professional goals not highly prized by her or his mentor and fear that disclosure of the new goals will lead to loss of support by the mentor.

However, mentees who welcome a reciprocal relationship can be disappointed in the level of reciprocity they experience. Given that vertical mentoring arrangements are expected by many institutions and individuals, even a mentor who identifies as multicultural and feminist may be perceived by an older or more experienced mentee as only selectively reciprocal, for example, not acknowledging the comparatively greater knowledge of the mentee; thus, intergenerational mentoring that does not conform to expected roles based on age or experience may present special challenges.

Interactions with multicultural feminist mentors also can be confusing for nonfeminist (or not-yet-feminist) mentees, who are likely to anticipate more traditional, hierarchical relationships. Mentees may not know how to react when a more egalitarian, collegial interaction is offered, and much like the problems that occur in feminist classrooms, they may misinterpret the mentor's attempts to help them find their own voice as an abnegation of responsibility or lack of competence. For example, in an academic setting, a mentee may interpret the mentor's refusal to assign a paper or thesis topic as the mentor's lack of knowledge or direction. Mentees also may misread power-sharing cues from the mentor (e.g., disclosures about her personal life) as invitations to a level of friendship not mutually desired, and misunderstandings and feelings of rejection may occur. Finally, the egalitarianism of a multicultural feminist mentoring relationship often is viewed negatively by others, who may judge it to be an unethical dual relationship, particularly if social interactions occur. Mentees may exacerbate this problem as they describe or even unwittingly exaggerate particular aspects of the relationship to their peers, leading to jealousy and accusations of preferential treatment, particularly in environments in which mentoring is generally scarce or enacted in dysfunctional ways. This latter point highlights the salience of context in the implementation and perceptions of multicultural feminist mentoring relationships. Thus, the next section briefly addresses organizational and systemic challenges to this model.

Is Multicultural Feminist Mentoring Possible in a Patriarchal Society?

It is our position that much of the struggle and pain that occurs in feminist mentoring (as with feminist pedagogy more generally) is due to the fact that it is embedded in a patriarchal structure that is inimical to its assumptions, processes, and effectiveness. Successful nonfeminist mentoring rests largely on the successful use of power differentials between mentor and mentee and the mentor's wielding of that power to help the mentee. The power differential is thus assumed and respected for what it offers, and although mentors may enjoy the generative rewards of mentoring less experienced colleagues, there is not an expectation of reciprocity in the relationship. Boundaries thus are clear and professional distance is relatively easy to maintain because of the power and status differences between the individuals in the mentoring relationship.

In multicultural feminist mentoring, however, there is a deliberate dismantling of the traditional power structure and hierarchy, and relationships are judged successful at least in part on the basis of the equality between or among the people participating in that relationship. This complicates mentoring considerably not only because of the added demands of a great deal of psychosocial focus but also because, to assist the mentee, the multicultural feminist mentor is relying more on the relationship than on her external power and status in the organization (which, in fact, may not be very strong). Thus, she is attempting to build with feminist tools an edifice that will survive the demands of patriarchy. Ultimately, the mentee's professional success (or lack of success) is shared, and it is shaped within the functioning of the mentoring relationship itself.

Assumptions may be made about the mentoring relationship by others in the organization, and it is likely that external judgments will be formed on the basis of patriarchal notions of what is normative and appropriate. The mentor will be assumed to be in traditional, professionally detached relationships when she is not. She will be presumed to know (or care) little about the particular personal problems of her mentees, but in fact, she is likely to know much about their contextual barriers and challenges. The kinds of growth the mentor is fostering in her mentees also may diverge from accepted organizational practices. Helping mentees to articulate and enact their own goals may take longer than the demands of a particular workplace allow, for example, a graduate student choosing to have a baby while writing her dissertation instead of finishing quickly. The faculty mentor in this situation is likely to feel caught between two sets of demands, those of the patriarchy on the one hand and the needs of the mentee on the other. Further, if the mentor is approaching tenure, she needs mentees to complete work they are doing with her in a timely way so that she can survive the academic reward system and keep her job. This will make it difficult for her to support her mentee fully when months or years of writing time are lost in the throes of new motherhood.

In addition, the mentoring relationship itself is likely to be misunderstood and criticized because its boundaries differ from those in traditional patriarchal systems. Such boundaries are especially difficult to maintain in dyads or very small groups. In larger groups, such as classrooms, implicit or explicit group norms help to prevent excessive violation of accepted agreements; for example, it may be easier to deny extra time for a student in a large class to complete an assignment because there is responsibility to many other individuals and some degree of fairness may be called on as justification. However, in dyadic or very small group interactions, there are few external constraints imposed on decision making, and the dynamics of the relationship itself establish the rules. Thus, when a mentee fails to meet expectations for very understandable reasons, it may be difficult for the mentor to justify adhering to arbitrary agreements that could be renegotiated easily. A more fluid boundary arrangement in dyadic and small-group mentoring clearly makes it possible to honor individual differences in developmental trajectories, but it also may create challenges for the mentor in knowing where and when to exert the authority she holds by virtue of her position.

It also is worth noting that mentoring is much like parenting or therapy in that the overarching goal of the mentor is to ensure enough personal empowerment of the mentee that eventually she will no longer be needed in quite the same way (although, like parenting, and sometimes after therapy, relationships can endure under different rules and roles). In multicultural feminist mentoring, this transition can be quite complicated for both mentor and mentee. On the one hand, because the relationship is predicated on shared power and equality, the transition to less dependence on the part of the mentee ought to result in satisfactory collegial relationships for all concerned. However, organizations are plagued by hierarchical assumptions that render them insensitive to relationships that do not fit the norm, and humans are emotional beings, so the transition out of the formality of a mentoring relationship may feel like acute loss to either or both parties. The mentor may feel betrayed by a newly empowered mentee who shifts her or his allegiance to another mentor or project, or a mentee may feel abandoned by a mentor before she or he is ready, particularly if the relational transition is due to external forces such as graduation or transfer to another company. Fortunately, some of the multicultural feminist tools that likely contributed to the success of the mentoring relationship itself (e.g., open self-disclosure, shared responsibility, and mutual respect) can help both mentor and mentee as they together face this inevitable transition. Additional mentoring strategies are suggested in the following section.

Strategies for Practicing Multicultural Feminist Mentoring in Patriarchy

For feminist mentors attempting to negotiate the oft-competing demands of mentoring in a multicultural feminist manner while surviving in patriarchal organizations and institutions, a number of specific strategies may be helpful. A distinct advantage to dyadic or small-group mentoring is that one can borrow from both effective pedagogical and therapeutic practices in determining how best to negotiate some of the difficulties inherent in this form of interpersonal intimacy. Thus, novice multicultural feminist mentors attempting mentoring for the first time as well as experienced mentors negotiating problematic interactions can call on a wide repertoire of skills and behaviors.

Process and Relationship Strategies

As in multicultural feminist classroom pedagogy and therapeutic practice, the most important reality to consider is that there are power differentials that cannot (and perhaps should not) be fully dismantled, and the best one can do is strategically manage them to the best ends for all concerned. Given that so much of the effectiveness of multicultural feminist mentoring rests on the successful internal dynamics of the relationship, expectations of both parties must be clear and nothing should be left to assumptions. Constant, clear communication, perhaps embodied in written contractual agreements, may be helpful in specifying important boundaries and expectations that both mentor and mentee wish to establish and honor. Similar to new clients in therapy or new students in a classroom, new mentees may need a great deal of help in articulating what they need, and the mentor can use this opportunity to set personal limits and ensure her own needs are met.

Multicultural feminist mentors also need to consider their own personal and professional resources (e.g., time, energy, financial support, and special skills) in accepting or initiating mentoring relationships, and some selectivity may be required. Being too busy and overextended to attend adequately to mentees to whom one has made commitments can be seen as a form of abandonment (Johnson & Huwe, 2002). Although many multicultural feminist mentors become overworked out of a genuine desire to help those who need their particular gifts, the mentoring relationships established under these circumstances are compromised because mentoring attention is fragmented. Moreover, eventual burnout, failure to meet the other professional demands of the institution, and even exit from the organization become alarming possibilities when mentoring obligations are excessive. Multicultural feminist mentors who wish to participate in the radical transformation of patriarchal institutions must preserve their presence in those institutions through some degree of self-care.

Multicultural feminist mentors also might note that reciprocity is ideal but often impractical in relationships in which the gaps in experience are particularly wide or the mentee is especially inexperienced, with little obvious to offer initially. Remembering that the mentoring relationship exists for the benefit of the mentee, mentors may need to adjust their expectations according to the developmental needs of their mentees. Frequent check-ins about the interpersonal process (much as one would do in therapy with a client or in periodic classroom evaluations) can be helpful in keeping the mentee open about her or his reactions, in monitoring shifting goals, and in keeping the relationship functioning effectively. Mentors need to accept that they will be readjusting their demands frequently on the basis of unfolding knowledge about the mentee, including understanding the complexities of the many identity statuses (e.g., gender, racial, and sexual) a mentee may hold. Moreover, mentors should not expect their mentees to shore up their own professional commitments or output (despite the fact that this is widely practiced in academe and in many work settings). Viewing the contributions of mentees as an unexpected but delightful outgrowth of the mentoring process may help mentors to avoid exploitation in this regard. In graduate academic mentoring, for example, different kinds of scholarly expectations for research- versus practice-oriented doctoral advisees might be negotiated, with permission to exert strong pressure regarding publication for those who plan research careers.

Finally, it is important for the mentor to be honest with mentees about the conflicting demands in which she operates, so that they can better understand the inevitable compromises she will make in their dealings together. Because the mentoring relationship inherently involves multiple and sometimes competing roles (e.g., advocating for a mentee experiencing difficulty but also having to maintain professional or workplace performance standards), the mentor should openly discuss her commitments to the various roles she will occupy in relation to the mentee. She needs to be clear about her boundaries in dealing with personal issues and refer mentees for therapeutic or other community resources if needed. She can share the burden of mentoring by connecting mentees with others who can serve this function, and she needs to ensure that she has sufficient professional support in the workplace so that she is not tempted to rely on mentees to meet all of her collegial and social needs. At the very least, she should have professional colleagues who can advise her regarding mentoring problems that may arise.

It is worth noting that mentees also bear responsibility for the effectiveness of the mentoring relationship, and they too need to remain vigilant in addressing the issues noted here (e.g., initiating discussions about interpersonal dynamics, seeking peer mentoring and support, being sensitive to a mentor's needs and conflicts, and terminating an unhelpful mentoring relationship). Moreover, for both mentee and mentor, it may be helpful to view mentoring relationships as an issue of appropriate match (vs. competence), so that ineffective relationships can be terminated and referrals made with minimal self-recrimination or blame from either member of the relationship.

Organizational and Systemic Strategies

In their recent (2002) article on mentoring in graduate education, Brad Johnson and Jennifer Huwe outlined a number of institutional strategies for promoting more effective mentoring relationships: establishing the importance of mentoring in hiring criteria, developing organizational structures for addressing mentoring problems, rewarding mentoring activities, training and supervising members who are new to the organization (e.g., new faculty), and creating a culture of mentoring in which mentoring beliefs and practices are discussed openly. We support these general recommendations and note some additional considerations.

Deliberate training in multiculturalism, feminism, and mentoring are critical to the development of effective mentors in this arena. Understanding the complexities of diverse cultural identities and locations; acknowledging the inextricable, gendered links between personal issues and choices and political realities; and striving for relationships characterized by equality, respect, and shared power seem to us to be minimum requirements for engaging in any kind of effective mentoring relationship, particularly one that is avowedly multicultural and feminist in intent. It also should be noted that such training does not have to be at the expense of other curricular requirements. The first author (Fassinger), for example, using a multicultural feminist approach to vertical team mentoring, requests that each of her doctoral advisees lead a research team of diverse undergraduate students for at least a year to learn to mentor others, and the activities must include attention to the personal and professional development of the undergraduates (e.g., meetings that focus on applying to graduate school or obtaining clinical experience) as well as tasks related to completing the research project. The faculty advisor supervises the mentoring activities, participates in the research training to model skills, and offers support and resources to all of the students involved in the team.

Another arena in which training can occur is in mentoring new members of an organization. Some teacher education programs, for example, use professional development or instructional consultation models in which expert or peer assistance are provided collaboratively through in-school support for classroom teachers. In academe, periodic performance evaluations of progress toward tenure for new faculty, which typically involve observation of classroom teaching, can and should focus attention on mentoring skills and activities as well. Simply engaging in discussion of mentoring issues and problems can be helpful, but peer mentoring by more experienced faculty also can include observation, providing resources, guest teaching in the classroom, modeling of skills, and direct coaching. In addition, peer mentoring should address issues related to gender and cultural identities and differences in the mentee's own mentoring relationships.

Finally, we highlight the importance in organizations and systems of focusing deliberate and public attention to mentoring practices. The multicultural feminist assumption that mentoring relationships and processes should be transparent and open to examination can provide a healthy model for the development of an organizational culture of mentoring (Johnson & Huwe, 2002). This model also can provide useful tools (e.g., mutual respect, self-disclosure, and honoring of diversity) for initiating dialogue among organizational members about their mentoring experiences.

In conclusion, it seems clear that multicultural feminist mentoring in dyads and small groups offers unprecedented opportunities for mentees to develop the kinds of skills and attitudes they will need in rapidly changing educational institutions and workplaces. Moreover, with its emphasis on mutuality, personal empowerment, respect for human diversity, and impetus for societal change, multicultural feminist mentoring emboldens mentors and mentees to become true allies in the struggle toward equity, social justice, and a healthier world.

10

THE INSTITUTION, THE EDUCATOR, AND THE STUDENT

MICHELE C. BOYER AND HEIDI A. LARSON

Although feminist approaches to teaching and learning can be observed in a variety of educational settings, the practice of feminist pedagogy is most often associated with colleges and universities. No discussion of multicultural feminist pedagogies would be complete without examining the impact of the institutional context of higher education on multicultural feminist educators and the students they teach. Professional literature in this area of inquiry is very limited. Accounts describing the interface between institutions of higher education and feminist educators or students typically focus on anecdotal individual reports of negative personal experiences with policies or individuals within a particular institution. In this chapter we examine institutions of higher education as particular contexts that have identifiable structures and climates that have an impact on the work of educators whose pedagogy is characterized by multicultural and feminist approaches. We first provide a brief overview of the history and mission of higher education institutions in the United States. Although this overview emphasizes U.S. history, many parallel themes have been observed in commentaries on Canadian higher education (e.g., Boatswain et al., 2001; Elabor-Idemudia, 2001; Harris, 1976; Sheffield, 2003; Stark, 2001). Following the historical overview, we examine the impact of the institutional context on multicultural feminist educators and their students. Last, we discuss actions to foster an institutional climate that more consistently and equitably supports the professional and developmental needs of educators and students in higher education settings today.

THE INSTITUTION: A BRIEF HISTORY OF CHANGING MISSIONS

Today, many participants and observers of higher education assume that the primary mission of contemporary universities, particularly those identified as research institutions, is to develop new knowledge. Higher education has not always been seen this way (Boyer, 1990; Park, 2000), and knowledge of institutional shifts in mission is crucial for understanding current challenges and potential solutions.

In the 17th and 18th centuries, American colleges were developed in accordance with British collegiate educational goals of developing character and preparing well-rounded individuals for leadership roles in civic or religious settings. Student-centered roles of teaching and mentoring were highly respected as primary faculty activities. In the 19th and early 20th centuries, the purpose of higher education shifted to providing individuals with the practical and economic skills necessary to build a developing nation in the midst of the industrial revolution. Faculty members were expected to help students learn existing knowledge so that they could apply it effectively in their communities and work settings (Boyer, 1990).

In the mid- to late-19th century, research and theory development emerged as important aspects of the university mission. This transition coincided with the development of several doctoral programs based on German research university curricula that required students to produce original research in the form of a dissertation. The now familiar professorial hierarchy of instructor, assistant professor, associate professor, and professor developed and the competition for academic rank was initiated (Rudolph, 1962). By the start of the 20th century, evaluations of faculty at these research-oriented institutions included research productivity and clear distinctions developed among the three primary professorial roles of research, teaching, and community service (Boyer, 1990). Increasing levels of emphasis and prestige were associated with the research aspect of a professor's role.

Most American institutions of higher education maintained a focus on undergraduate education and practical service until World War II, when large amounts of federal funding became available to support university-based scientific research that supported national security interests. Over time, financial support from central government increased, and the emphasis on research that was held by only a few institutions spread throughout the American university system. Graduate education and the associated emphasis on scientific research became the norm for many four-year universities and colleges, and the teaching and service aspects of faculty work lost value. Loyalty to the campus and local community, previously demonstrated through a wide range of service activities and an emphasis on quality teaching and active mentoring, gave way to loyalty to the faculty member's individual discipline and research agenda (Boyer, 1990).

During the late 20th and early 21st centuries, members of the public, local legislators, and commissions on higher education began questioning the accountability of academic faculty members who seemed to spend less time in either the classroom with students or the community with members of the local citizenry and more time on narrowly focused individual research projects. This decline in public support for the relatively recent research mission in higher education, combined with increasing costs of conducting research, changes in enrollment patterns, and changes in the characteristics of the student body, all contributed to the contemporary multifaceted challenges faced by higher education contexts. A related issue is associated with recent observations that some members of the professoriate, primarily women and minorities, have been identified as carrying a disproportionate amount of the teaching and service load, which is associated with fewer rewards and recognition, than colleagues who focus their efforts on research activities (Park, 2000).

Ernest Boyer's (1990) proposed restructuring of the faculty roles of teaching, service, and scholarly research included an expanded definition of scholarship and more balanced recognition of each of the primary professorial roles. Since that time, academic institutions have struggled with the question of adjusting missions, administrative structures, and professorial reward structures that were built on the primacy of individual research (e.g., Diamond & Adams, 1995; Halpern et al., 1998; Krahenbuhl, 1998; Peterson & Trierweiler, 1999; Rice, 1991). Current educational, societal, and political contexts call for a reallocation of faculty effort that reflects more balance among these three professorial roles.

THE INSTITUTION: CHANGING PARTICIPANTS

The mission shift in higher education occurred in a context of political, social, cultural, and demographic change that has slowly but consistently contributed to a more diverse student body in higher education. Historically, access to higher education was most available to male individuals whose social and cultural heritage reflected the values, attitudes, and experiences of their European immigrant ancestors. As recent as the turn of the 20th century, approximately 85% of the U.S. population claimed European heritage. This heritage laid the groundwork for values that became uniquely descriptive of citizens of the United States: rugged individualism, competition, capitalism, reliance on the positivistic scientific method, democracy, written history, belief in the Protestant ethic, and direct verbal communication (Katz, 1985).

The first American colleges (Harvard, 1636; William and Mary, 1693; Yale, 1701), were based on the British model of higher education, and only men of social status were eligible to attend these schools. Collegiate study was deemed appropriate for men who planned to hold positions of influence in the community (e.g., ministers, physicians, lawyers, and politicians). Women were summarily excluded from collegiate study because of their gender and the lack of need for such training given their role as caretakers of the home (Solomon, 1985). Following the Revolutionary War, reading and writing skills were identified as necessary for all men to conduct business. In addition, reading was viewed as important for both men and women to support their reading of the Bible and participation in religious activities. Women's perceived role as educators of male citizens led to a more favorable evaluation of formal education for women among members of the new republic. The first half of the 19th century saw great growth in educational opportunities for women, which culminated later in the century in the establishment of colleges for women (e.g., Vassar, 1865; Wellesley & Smith, 1875; Bryn Mawr, 1884). Although coeducation became the norm by the end of the 19th century, the climate for women provided the consistent message that "society attached greater importance to men's achievements . . . no woman could forget that she was in a man's world" (Solomon, 1985, p. xix).

The post-Civil War era, which included the granting of citizenship and suffrage for African American men, brought more opportunities for expanding and diversifying educational opportunities for women and minority men. The Morrill Land Grant Acts provided public support for higher education and specified that funds be "fairly divided between Negroes and Whites" (Solomon, 1985, p. 44). Many of the institutions that are now identified as HBCUs (Historically Black Colleges and Universities) were supported by this funding. Over time, enrollments in public universities reflected the ethnic and cultural composition of their local areas, and some private colleges created selection policies designed to maintain what they saw as their traditional population to "preserve the so-called Anglo-Saxon superiority of their colleges" (p. 143). During the early part of the 20th century, ethnic and religious diversity grew in mainstream colleges, but their populations remained predominately White and Protestant. Students from ethnic and religious minority groups reported feeling significant pressure to assimilate or conform to majority standards. They often felt like outsiders and struggled with issues of personal identity development. During the second half of the 20th century, post-World War II GI Bill benefits supported the pursuit of a college education for many working-class and minority veterans. The desegregation and gender equity activities of the 1960s and 1970s led to greater diversity of students seeking higher education (Goldenberg & Stout, 2000).

Despite increasing diversity, the culture of colleges and universities themselves, with the possible exception of some aspects of women's colleges and HBCUs, reflects a climate that supports values associated with the early Western European inspired colleges. Higher education contexts continue to be characterized by competition, individual achievement, and hierarchical organization. Colleges and universities remain highly instrumental, individual, and justice-oriented environments, even though the expanding diversity in the student population includes individuals whose personal and cultural values include more expressive, communal, and care-oriented ways of knowing and being. Although women and ethnic minority individuals are present at all levels of the contemporary college and university, the social and educational environment remains most comfortable for male, Euro-American-identified students and faculty members. The characteristics, attitudes, and values of these persons most closely match those of the pioneers who founded and developed our system of higher education and who benefited from the federally funded emphasis on university research roles during the post-World War II period of expansion in higher education. The meaning of these institutional characteristics for the educators and students who work within them are explored in the next section.

THE EDUCATOR AND THE STUDENT: PARTICIPANTS IN CONTEXTUAL CHANGE

Prior to the establishment of the American republic, few women or people of non-European descent were able to attend colleges or universities; they were not deemed dispositionally or intellectually suited to higher education. The needs of a developing republic, changing demographics, and the success of women and people of color all contributed, over time, to greater college participation of these individuals and to their presence on collegiate faculties. Although women and African Americans were present on selected college campuses early in American collegiate history, they were exceptions to the rule, and their involvement in social interactions or campus activities was limited. Dramatic changes have occurred during the past 100 years. Although women represented only 21% of college students in 1870 (Solomon, 1985), they now receive half to two thirds of all associate's, bachelor's, and master's degrees (Bensimon & Marshall, 2000). By 1993, women received 45% of all doctorates conferred in the United States (Hawkesworth, 2000). Women have a strong presence in the student body but are far outnumbered by men in positions of power and leadership. Men constitute 88% of presidents, provosts, and chancellors and 77% of university trustees. Women hold 37% of all full-time instructional faculty positions (professors through instructors) in degree-granting institutions and constitute 21% of the professors, 35% of the associate professors, 45% of the assistant professors, and 51% of the instructors (Bensimon & Marshall, 2000).

Ethnic minority student participation in higher education has also shown a slow but steady increase since the first enrollments and degree conferrals occurred during the early to mid-1800s. The American Council on Education (2002) reported that during the 1990s, college enrollment by students of color increased 48.3%. At present, students of color account for approximately 30% of all undergraduates and receive 21.8% of all bachelor's degrees awarded. The percentage of faculty of color also increased during the 1990s, actually outpacing the increases for faculty overall as reported by the American Council on Education. According to the National Center for Education Statistics (2002), on the basis of data reported in 1999, minority faculty (both men and women) constitute 14% of all full-time faculty members.

Although the number of women and culturally diverse individuals participating in higher education has clearly increased over the years, aspects of institutional structure, functioning, and climate have changed very little. As a result, women and culturally diverse individuals often encounter a pedagogical environment that is different from (at best) or hostile to (at worst) their ways of knowing, learning, and being. The majority of American institutions of higher education remain most comfortable for White, male, middle-income, able-bodied, heterosexual individuals who speak English as their primary language and who are familiar with pedagogical approaches characterized by hierarchical, linear, independently oriented, competitive approaches to learning. Institutional structure, function, and climate are consistent with and support these ways of knowing and learning. Students and faculty members whose sociodemographic backgrounds and pedagogical approaches are different from this standard may experience marginalization or exclusion in higher education.

MULTICULTURAL FEMINIST PEDAGOGY AND "THE SYSTEM"

Although institutions of higher education identify themselves as centers of learning and leaders in innovation, college and university systems themselves can be slow to change. Hard-earned tenure and promotion achievements are often accompanied by attitudes of entitlement, superiority, and exclusivity that may not ease the path of those who follow. Similarly, educators may notice the changing demographics in their classrooms but cling to familiar modes of instruction even in the face of evaluative feedback indicating that students may need something different from the standpoint of pedagogy.

Several scholars and participants in higher education have observed the existence of a "hidden curriculum" that contains informal and implicit guidelines for success at both faculty and student levels in the contemporary college or university (Golombisky, 2002; Margolis & Romero, 1998). This hidden curriculum often includes subtle, and not so subtle, messages about the value of individuals considered to be "others" in the university setting. Regardless of their numerical presence on today's campuses, the needs and contributions of women and people of color are frequently seen as less important and less significant than those of the White men in the system. This sort of institutionalized monocultural androcentrism supports the expectation that women and people of color are the ones who must make the necessary attitudinal, behavioral, philosophical, and value shifts to fit into existing college and university structures and climates. Such requirements can strip individuals of their uniqueness, deny their essential humanity, and make the path to success exceedingly lonely and challenging. Even when women and people of color make the shifts they understand to be necessary, they may still be denied access to the rewards that their majority male colleagues receive on a much more routine basis.

The path to rectifying these all-too-frequent mismatches between the efforts and accomplishments of diverse groups of faculty and students is likely multifaceted. Feminist multicultural approaches to pedagogy and a reexamination of faculty work are two approaches that we believe have great potential for creating a more inclusive, comfortable, and responsive institutional climate in our colleges and universities. Faculty members who incorporate feminist multicultural pedagogies into their work or who ask questions about the changing nature or distribution of faculty work may encounter a frustrating institutional dynamic. On the one hand, leaders in the academy speak about the goals of diversifying the faculty and student body and making curricula more accessible and inclusive. On the other hand, aspects of the institutional structure and culture resist or impede progress toward these stated goals through overt and covert efforts to conduct business as usual. Navigating these conflicting messages can be difficult.

Traditional faculty reward systems include an examination of the faculty member's accomplishments in the areas of research, teaching, and service. The weight and value accorded each of these roles varies across, and sometimes within, institutions. Some roles tend to be engaged in more frequently by certain faculty members who seem to receive differential recognition and support for those activities (American Psychological Association [APA] Committee on Women in Psychology and Commission on Ethnic Minority Recruitment, Retention, and Training in Psychology, 1998; APA Task Force on Women in Academe, 2000; Benokraitis, 1998; Park, 2000; Sandler & Hall, 1986). Park observed a gendered division of labor in the academy that identified men's work as research and women's work as teaching and service. She also noted that in many institutions research work is explicitly valued and made visible, whereas teaching and service work are explicitly devalued and rarely showcased. Women in the academy are significantly more likely to spend time in teaching and related activities (Park,

2000), and women and minority faculty members tend to report high teaching loads as a source of stress (Benokraitis, 1998). Women and minority men are also more likely to identify and work to correct biases in traditional curricula (Park, 2000).

These institutional realities have valence for female and minority male faculty members who bring feminist and multicultural approaches to their pedagogy. It is likely that they will spend more time than majority male faculty members on matters related to instruction and curriculum development and receive fewer rewards and less recognition for their efforts. In environments where research is heavily weighted in tenure and promotion decisions, excellent teachers (who based on these data are likely to be women and people of color) may not survive. Their departure from the institution may be understood by some as validation of the belief that women and people of color lack the skills for success in the academic environment. The reality may be that they chose to put their energy into the aspects of faculty work (teaching and service) that attracted them to the profession in the first place. Teaching and service activities may be seen as most immediately valuable to the community of students. The interpersonal nature of teaching and service activities may yield more immediate and genuine expressions of appreciation from the recipients of the faculty member's services than do research activities.

Women and male faculty of color may also have heard and taken at face value the various statements made by administrators or written in university publications that quality teaching is valued and rewarded by the institution. The reality of promotion and tenure decisions in many institutions is that scholarship, often narrowly defined as quantitative experimental research, receives much more weight than teaching or service, regardless of rhetoric to the contrary (Halpern et al., 1998). Faculty members can spend several years at an institution laboring under the misperception that in their case stellar teaching efforts and wide-ranging local, regional, and national service efforts will receive greater recognition than is realistic. Some faculty members may engage in wishful thinking, and others may not receive the information, mentoring, or assistance necessary to develop a program of scholarship, teaching, and service appropriately tailored to the reward system in their university environment. Worse yet, women and faculty of color may be encouraged by senior members of the faculty and by faculty administrators to engage in more teaching and service activities than their majority male peers. Service, teaching, and research expectations are often not equitably distributed across faculty members (APA Committee on Women in Psychology and Commission on Ethnic Minority Recruitment, Retention, and Training in Psychology, 1998).

Even when faculty members create a work plan that maximizes the likelihood of success in the three primary areas of faculty work, those who engage in alternate pedagogies may find evaluations of their classroom performance to be negatively influenced by evaluator preconceptions. Teaching evaluations, particularly for pretenure faculty members, may include peer observations, student surveys, and teaching portfolios. Some senior faculty members and academic administrators who conduct or participate in the evaluation process may have expectations, based on their personal experiences with traditional pedagogies, about the appropriate nature of instruction in the classroom. Traditional pedagogy relies on a paternal or expert model of instruction in which objective knowledge about a single reality is passed from the veteran teacher to the passive novice (Tomlinson & Fassinger, 2002). Feminist multicultural educators, whose class sessions include participatory, process-oriented learning activities, have sometimes received negative evaluations when the observer perceived the absence of a lecture to be indicative of poor teaching. In one situation, a junior faculty member was told to invite the evaluator back when she was planning to really teach.

Similarly, many of the standardized multiple-choice, written teaching-evaluation forms completed by students consist of questions that focus primarily on didactic methods of instruction. The feminist multicultural educator who uses a wider variety of instructional methods than those included on the evaluation form may receive evaluations of limited validity or usefulness. Mindful of the limitations of the standardized forms used by their universities, some educators supplement the evaluation form with a set of narrative open-ended questions that they develop to gather information about specific pedagogical techniques. These narrative summaries require additional time for the educator to prepare and assess. They also require evaluators to take extra time and attention when reviewing the educator's teaching documentation. When teaching is seen as a less important aspect of a professor's role, evaluation committees may choose to spend their time on the "more important" aspects of the faculty member's dossier.

Teaching portfolios are relatively new educator assessment tools in some institutions. Faculty members serving on tenure and promotion committees may not be familiar with this form of documentation and may discount the material as not presenting "real (quantifiable) data" about the candidate's teaching. During a recent promotion and tenure review, a senior faculty member wondered aloud why the applicant was spending so much time on "that narrative stuff." The bias against portfolio assessment may be associated with some senior faculty members' strident belief in the preeminence of quantitative data in such evaluations. Such perceptions may also be related to the belief that the portfolio is simply a collection of syllabi and course evaluations. A thoughtfully prepared, up-to-date teaching portfolio is more than a simple collection of teaching artifacts. The portfolio allows an educator to present a rich and reflected-on picture of her or his work with students. The portfolio may also be a particularly effective presentation strategy for capturing the salient features of an educator's personal feminist multicultural pedagogy.

The instructional roles influenced by a feminist multicultural approach to pedagogy include more than an educator's classroom interactions with students. Mentoring, advising, research supervision, clinical supervision, and serving as a faculty sponsor for student organizations can all provide opportunities to put feminist multicultural values into action. In each of these settings, feminist multicultural educators take care to foster respectful relationships with students that honor and validate the multiple perspectives and experiences each participant brings to the interaction. These "high touch" and personalized approaches to learning take time. How these time expenditures are accounted for in a faculty member's workload can vary from setting to setting. Many of these professorial duties could be considered routine housekeeping activities that must be completed but are not reflected clearly in various indices of faculty effort. It is often women or faculty of color who carry a significant proportion of these duties but receive little recognition or compensation.

The importance of these nonclassroom interactions to students' sense of comfort, belonging, and ultimate academic success was demonstrated in the following interaction. The only nontraditional student in class, an African American woman, approached the instructor after class one day. The instructor took the time to speak with the student about her concerns as a nontraditional student, her sense of accomplishment in her studies, and the challenges she had experienced. After about a 90-minute discussion, the student stated that the instructor was the first one who had taken time to discuss her experiences at the university and who seemed interested in some of her personal struggles. Often, instructors feel as if there is not enough time for such discussions. This particular incident highlighted the importance of instructor–student interaction. It was a rare occurrence in this student's experience but a very powerful and affirming one for both the student and the instructor.

REEVALUATING FACULTY WORK:
THE GROUNDWORK FOR INSTITUTIONAL CHANGE

Faculty work has changed over time to include a demanding tapestry of effort across a range of shifting faculty roles and responsibilities. Diane Halpern and colleagues (1998) have observed that "a wide gap exists between the myth and the reality of academic life" (p. 1292). The reasons for the gap are multifaceted, and as outlined earlier in this chapter, include changes in student and faculty populations, changes in public expectations, and shifts in funding bases. Ernest Boyer's (1990) call for an expanded definition of scholarship and a more balanced recognition of various professorial roles is consistent with a feminist multicultural redefinition of faculty work. The inclusion of innovative, nontraditional teaching methods can help close the gap between the myths and realities of faculty life, particularly in the area of instruction and instructionally related duties.

Boyer's initial proposal suggested that members of the university community needed to redefine their thinking about research (narrowly seen as published books and articles) to include a broader understanding of scholarship that reflects four foci: discovery, integration, application, and teaching. The scholarship of discovery is most closely related to traditional definitions of research. It addresses the generation of new knowledge but includes both product and process elements of the research. The scholarship of integration involves conducting research at the intersection of disciplines, contexts, theories, and methodologies. It calls for synthesizing results, identifying patterns, and reinterpreting information. The scholarship of application connects research and service by asking researchers to use knowledge to address social challenges. It recognizes the dynamic interaction between personal, political, theoretical, and practical aspects of scholarship. Thus, service can be seen as scholarly work that produces and applies knowledge. The scholarship of teaching connects research to teaching by noting that good teachers are also learners who engage students in active, critical, creative, personalized, and reciprocal interactions with the subject matter. This sort of scholarship requires the educator to organize, synthesize, and present material in ways that are meaningful to students. It requires understanding the perspectives and histories that students bring to the academy. Effective teaching is a collaborative, transformative, and reflective experience that happens in various learning communities.

Although Boyer may not have seen his expanded definition of scholarship as an explicitly feminist revisioning of faculty roles, his ideas reflected an inclusivity that was not present in traditional thinking about research. Including integration, application, and teaching in the definition of scholarship also paved the way for recognizing and legitimizing, within accepted academic evaluative structures, the large amount of service and teaching done by women and faculty of color. Boyer's identification of the scholarship of teaching locates these activities well within the responsibility of all faculty members.

The traditional reward structure, built on the primacy of individual research designed to generate new knowledge as a prime directive, no longer seems to fit the realities of today's academy. The participants, observers, and critics of higher education want to see engaged faculty members who meet the educational needs of their students and contribute to the welfare of the community in collaborative ways. Current educational, societal, and political trends call for a reallocation of faculty effort that reflects more balance and accountability across faculty roles. These trends are actually good news for inclusive approaches to learning, such as feminist and feminist multicultural pedagogies, that provide a model for instruction in the academy that includes and speaks to all voices.

STRATEGIES TO FACILITATE CHANGE OF THE SYSTEM

A growing number of participants in higher education (students, faculty, staff, and administrators) are becoming aware of the need to be more responsive to changing sociodemographics among student and faculty populations. Recognizing the need to change the way we interact with students in educational settings and implementing change are two different tasks. Colleges and universities are massive, hierarchical, institutional systems characterized by many structural and procedural conventions that have been in place for long periods of time. Initiating change in such systems can be a long, slow, and sometimes painful process.

Recent trends within the academy pave the way to examine methods of teaching and learning. Many colleges and universities have developed campuswide Centers for Teaching and Learning (CTL) that are designed to assist teaching assistants, faculty members, and prospective faculty members in developing their skills as educators. Examples of CTL programming include using today's technology in the classroom (Internet resources, Smart Board use, streaming video, teleconferencing, etc.), incorporating service-learning activities into the curriculum, creating an inclusive learning environment, using collaborative learning in the classroom, modeling servant–leadership, developing a teaching portfolio, communicating across cultures, supporting the engaged learner, evaluating the engaged faculty member, and learning about the changing demographics and trends in higher education. Although many of these topics are familiar to feminist multicultural educators, they may be new to many colleagues. It appears that aspects of feminist and multicultural instructional approaches are being infused into traditional environments without explicit acknowledgment! If our long-term goal is to influence the system, we can forgo the acknowledgment and redirect our energies to support, promote, and attend these programs, for example, by taking a colleague to sessions we find important or interesting. The existence of topics like these within university-sanctioned in-service training programs that are well attended by faculty members portends well for eventual recognition of such activities in formal teaching evaluations. If one of our goals is to have feminist multicultural pedagogies accepted in the university, a developmental stop along the way may be to help our colleagues learn about the values, attitudes, beliefs, and techniques associated with inclusive environments.

The peer teaching-evaluation process should be informed by research on the validity of teaching evaluations (McKeachie, 1997, 2002). Teaching colleagues and administrators who participate in and vote on faculty tenure and promotion must be educated on the contributions that role expectation may make to student evaluations. There is evidence, for example, that gender and ethnicity can negatively influence student evaluations of teaching performance (APA Committee on Women in Psychology and Commission on Ethnic Minority Recruitment, Retention, and Training in Psychology, 1998). The ethnic composition of a faculty member's class in combination with knowledge about the teaching strategies provided can provide important contextual information about student evaluations. Providing training about a variety of pedagogies to faculty members who observe the classroom performance of their peers would also enhance the helpfulness of peer observation reports.

Even though the service loads of feminist multicultural educators tend to be high, it is crucial that we participate in department, school, college, and all-university committees that review faculty performance. Serving on these committees can enhance the likelihood that inclusive teaching strategies receive appropriate attention during the review process. Such service can also ensure that nonclassroom instructional work (advisement, mentoring, clinical and research supervision) is included in instructional reviews as a valuable contribution to the educational effort. Whenever possible, it is helpful to include pretenure, junior, and adjunct faculty on committees that develop policies about instructional matters. Faculty members who are in the pre- or nontenure trenches can bring insights to the evaluation of teaching that some senior faculty members may have forgotten. Inviting such inclusive involvement demonstrates a desire for all voices to be heard.

Feminist multicultural educators are well positioned to operationalize Boyer's (1990) call for a scholarship of teaching. Writing and reflecting on the impact that inclusive pedagogy has on student personal and professional growth is an important contribution to the field of higher education. Critics of higher education are looking for evidence that faculty members interact with students in meaningful ways. Feminist multicultural approaches to teaching and learning provide some of that evidence. Institutions are embracing alternative, more inclusive approaches to teaching. The pioneering and sometimes painful efforts of feminist and multicultural educators have contributed to this developing reality. The traditional university structures, expectations, and policies about teaching are changing, but the journey has just begun.

11

INTEGRATING MULTICULTURAL AND FEMINIST PEDAGOGIES: PERSONAL PERSPECTIVES ON POSITIONALITY, CHALLENGES, AND BENEFITS

CAROLYN ZERBE ENNS, ADA L. SINACORE, VIANEY ACEVEDO, ÖZGE AKÇALI, SABA RASHEED ALI, JULIE R. ANCIS, TINA M. ANCTIL, KARYN J. BOATWRIGHT, MICHELE C. BOYER, ANGELA M. BYARS-WINSTON, RUTH E. FASSINGER, LINDA M. FORREST, NANCY F. HENSLER-McGINNIS, HEIDI A. LARSON, CECILIA A. NEPOMUCENO, AND KAREN W. TAO

The authors of this book share the belief that integrating multicultural and feminist perspectives is challenging but rewarding and that our positionalities as educators have a significant impact on how we make connections among wide-ranging approaches to diversity. In this final chapter, we contribute personal reflections about the complex task of teaching from a multicultural and feminist perspective. This chapter is based on authors' responses to the following questions: (a) How does your positionality (e.g., worldview, multicultural and feminist theoretical perspectives, social identities, and roles) influence your pedagogy? and (b) What are the challenges and benefits of integrating multicultural and feminist perspectives? Because of space limitations, this summary provides only brief responses to the complex questions that authors have considered. Nevertheless, our hope is that the themes emerging from authors' statements provide a useful glimpse of the issues educators face as they teach about and for social justice.

As a group of authors, we bring a wide range of realities, identities, and life experiences to the pedagogical process. All of us identify ourselves as psychologists or psychologists in training. Beyond this common link, we identify ourselves as clinicians and academics, women who are lesbian and heterosexual, mentors and mentees, women of color and White women, women of different religious faiths and nationalities, graduate students and professors, administrators and teachers, women of different generations, women of middle-class and working-class origins, teachers from small undergraduate liberal arts institutions and educators from larger research-oriented university systems, and early- and midcareer professionals. Some of us have integrated multicultural and feminist perspectives through the organizing lens of race or culture, and others have used the lens offered by diversity feminisms. The "shorthand" we use to describe ourselves includes different terms and orderings of words such as *multicultural feminist*, *multicultural womanist*, *antiracist feminist*, *feminist multiculturalist*, and *egalitarian teachers*.

PERSONAL REFLECTIONS ABOUT POSITIONALITY AND PEDAGOGY

The reflections summarized in this section address the many different identities, themes, and experiences that contribute to our positionalities as educators, such as race and ethnicity, gender, sexual orientation, class status, nationality, multicultural and feminist theoretical orientations, religion, past and present educational roles, and educational training.

The following statement summarizes the views of many of us:

> My personal experiences and perceptions have been greatly influenced by the intersecting dimensions of my gender, race, ethnicity, religion, sexual orientation, socioeconomic status, physical ability, and geographic background. Examining these dimensions in my own life allows me to better understand these influences in other people's lives.

This narrator also noted that the fundamental principle that individuals hold multiple perspectives about events has taken her time to fully understand and has encouraged her to be more sensitive and less frustrated with students who seem defensive and unwilling to self-explore or who hold viewpoints different than her own. Multiple authors reported modifying their teaching interventions according to students' needs, developmental level, and positionalities, believing that in order for students to view issues from multiple perspectives they must be encouraged to challenge existing and ingrained assumptions. Others noted the importance of helping students understand how unexamined assumptions can negatively influence their work with diverse clientele, and thus, they have encouraged students and counselor trainees to develop flexible perspectives and skills.

Multiple Identities: Visible and Invisible, Imposed and Chosen, Stable and Changeable

Each of the authors spoke about the complexity of negotiating multiple identities, many of which vary in salience across time and situation. In this section we summarize some of the many ways in which our multiple identities are associated with self-definitions and how others respond to us.

Several authors commented on the ways in which their identities are sometimes influenced by the representations of others, who often focus on "what others see first when interacting with me." One person addressed the dialectics and contradictions between how she chooses to represent herself and the representations imposed on her. Her multiple identities include self-identification as an Asian American woman, born in Hawaii, educated in Western thought, influenced by American media, and raised by Chinese immigrant parents. She stated,

> I vacillate, sometimes not by my own volition, between identities and categories that fit particular contexts. In these multiple spheres, I am often asked to explain my position. Sometimes tacitly, but often explicitly, someone inquires, "Do you consider yourself a woman of color, Asian American, Chinese–Hawaiian American or American?" My usual reply is, "It depends." The process of reconciling the forces impinging on how I understand my position or whom I *should* represent invariably influences how I choose to engage in conversations and with whom.

Another author, whose colleague described her as a "slim, intense woman of color," noted that the "intense" part varies with the context, and the "woman of color" aspect remains ever present and is the most visible to others. She describes her identity as a blend of nonslave African American, French, Spanish, Native American, and Euro-American influences that have contributed to her preference for woman of color as an identifier. She has also been influenced by more invisible cultural aspects that involve being raised Catholic in a middle-class, upwardly mobile, intact family that valued education as a path to security and success. Although she sees herself as African American, her personal racial and ethnic heritage presents an uncertain visible ethnicity, which frequently results in the "What are you anyway?" question. She comments,

> From an ethnic and cultural standpoint I have always felt "in the margin"—not visibly distinct enough to clearly belong to one ethnic group or another but different enough to be seen as "other" in many of the social, interpersonal, and political contexts in which I participate.

Authors who identify themselves as women of color hold a range of perspectives about the degree to which race, ethnicity, or culture influence their positionalities as educators. For example, some women of color view race, culture, and ethnicity as crucial to their positionalities as educators, whereas others describe education, religion, class, or immigrant status as major influences. One author, who identifies herself as Latina, noted, "Sharing my positive and negative cultural experiences both educationally and professionally provides the catalyst in a classroom for open dialogue on issues such as class, gender, and race." Another contributor noted that as a Filipina American woman from the inner city, her multiple identities related to class, ethnicity, gender, spirituality, and sexuality, shift and take on salience in different contexts. She also describes the personal challenge of interacting with those who do not recognize this complexity, stating the following:

> In academia, I have found that class, race, and gender merge and I become "a woman of color or a student of color," and stereotypes abound that often confine me and deconstruct me into simplistic categories. Or I am just unseen and silenced. Because I am of Asian ancestry but my Spanish visage is due to colonialism, I am often allowed to experience both the model minority myth and the stereotypes placed on Chicanas/Latinas depending on what I elicit from others or what they decide I am.

Another variation on the theme of salience is offered by an author who noted how ethnic or racial group identification can offer solidarity and a protective function for stigmatized individuals but can also stifle individuality or be experienced as oppressive. She has found that joining with sisters of color is sometimes the easy path, noting that in groups largely made up of women of color, she is both an insider and an outsider. She comments as follows:

> The hard part is saying that I don't agree. This is where multiculturalism and feminism are faced with a daunting task—to acknowledge that we are not all talking about the same thing. For example, an Asian American colleague of mine was recently incensed by a classroom interaction in which another Asian American female disagreed with her statement in front of five White students and a White professor. She said, "How could she embarrass me like that? I thought she'd be on my side because she is an Asian woman too." This comment and the larger meaning associated with it have meaning for how we teach and engage within the classroom. Outcomes of situations such as these in which group identification becomes most salient and may thwart intellectual debate have serious implications for how we learn.

Although the multiple identities described in this section pose complex interpersonal challenges, several educators spoke of ways in which they use their experiences, both negative and positive, to increase their knowledge of diversity and enhance their ability to interact sensitively with students. One author summarized a view shared by multiple individuals: Her positionality allows her to bring multiple perspectives to interactions with others and provides the opportunity to help other people realize that the beliefs they hold about racial, ethnic, cultural, and sexual orientation groups may need expansion. Being able to understand a wide range of differences provides these educators with crucial coping skills, which become assets as they help others develop tools for interacting in a truly responsive and respectful multicultural society.

Multiple Identities Associated With Privilege and Oppression

Some authors discussed their experiences of privilege and how this reality intersects with their other social locations marked by limited power and status. Some authors see their roots in working-class or blue-collar families and as first-generation college students as important contributors to their perspectives. One of these authors, who also identifies herself as a White woman, wife, and mother, stated the following:

> As a White woman I know I am extremely privileged in society, yet my newness to the academy also gives me some sense of what it feels like to be an outsider. Given my blue-collar roots, I am not entirely comfortable in formal settings or in highly academic settings. I relate to the concept of "multiple selves" in that I now find I have an academic self but still must relate to my larger family who continue to live and work in a small logging community in Southern Oregon. I often experience the sense of having to work very hard to find "appropriate" pieces of myself to share with the different groups.

The same author noted that White privilege follows her into every setting and like many other White persons, she is sometimes guilty of not recognizing the race and ethnicity of others, thinking "Oh, I don't even pay any attention to that." However, her colleagues and students of color do not experience the luxury of forgetting their ethnicity and need to be constantly aware of themselves and their environments. She concluded, "I have to challenge myself to be aware of the complex social identities that we all bring to the classroom."

Another contributor has seen herself as influenced by her identification as a woman, her sexual orientation as a lesbian, and her White ethnicity. As a woman, she has encountered many of her female students' experiences with regard to silencing and devaluing and is especially cognizant of the deleterious effects that a traditional classroom can have on students' voices. As a lesbian, her students often see her as residing outside their sphere, which is marked by heterosexuality. Her identities as a woman and lesbian have made her more sensitive to the needs of historically marginalized and oppressed students, but she also noted that she has not experienced the effects of racism on an experiential level. She added the following:

> Recognizing my position of privilege with regard to ethnicity is often difficult and something I am constantly working on; I find that I am often so focused on gender or sexual orientation issues that I fail to recognize the impact of race and ethnicity.

Because of her awareness about how her identities influence her role as educator, she has made conscious efforts to recognize how various influences also intersect in students' lives.

One of the contributors has identified herself as a White, middle-class, heterosexual woman who spends most days as an administrator, but who also makes occasional forays into the classroom. Speaking of her role, which is associated with significant influence in her program, she stated the following:

> I proclaim my commitments to feminism and multiculturalism often, so faculty and students know that it means I will make transparent the policies, procedures, rules, and process of the university as well as who has what power in decision making and how they might challenge decisions. I teach tools that work in the academy while also challenging the hegemony of those rules.

This author has also been conscious of how her institutional roles interact with her other identities. She has observed that her interactions with students vary tremendously, depending on students' awareness of her roles within the institution's hierarchy as well as students' positionality in society and the university, and the stature of their program within the university, with the faculty, and within their cohort of students. As a consequence of moving up the university hierarchy, she has seen greater differences and diversity in interactions with students, which she has attributed to the multiple understandings of power and the intersections of power, privilege, and oppression that exist within groups of individuals. She commented as follows:

> White heterosexual feminist women are extremely curious about who I am and ask many personal questions that are mostly focused on my femaleness rather than skin color (e.g., How do you handle these situations?). Students of color appear to appreciate my efforts to raise questions of privilege with White students. I say "appear to appreciate" because I think they may initially mistrust my motives, are uncertain if I am safe. Some students have said directly to me, "Your words are easy; it is your behavior over time that counts." These words tell me that they are watching, observing, and will make their own judgment over time about my commitments.

This educator–administrator also indicated that some students of color, especially those who are at early phases in their identity development as persons of color, communicate that she is making a bigger deal of privilege and oppression than is necessary, and express nervousness about highlighting these issues. In contrast, White male students and students from upper-class backgrounds are typically the most at home in the classroom and know educational routines the best, so she often both directly and indirectly shifts power dynamics away from their issues, trying to pull out other positions. She concluded, "I like modeling a discourse that acknowledges the strengths and limitations of any perspective. 'Who benefits?' and 'Who is harmed by this way of organizing whatever we are talking about?' are favorite questions of mine."

The contributors whose experiences were summarized in this section have been conscious of the ways in which their statuses and those of their students are associated with privilege and influence that appear in some contexts but disappear in others. These educators have spoken about the importance of being vigilant regarding privilege and how it may shape their perspectives. Those in administrative roles have also used their access to institutional and personal power to inform their work as they influence the preparation of future psychologists and faculty members, implement evaluations of teaching performance that are attentive to social justice issues and feminist issues, and question institutionalized forms of discrimination.

Life Transitions, Changing Priorities, and Shifting Positionalities

Several writers remarked that their positionalities as educators have shifted numerous times as different aspects of their identities have come to the foreground and as the politics of negotiating these identities have shifted. One contributor elaborated that although her self-definitions have been altered, none of her identities have become stagnant as she renegotiates the role they play in her life, her teaching, and her sociopolitical positions. The remainder of this section illustrates how life transitions and new roles and locations may facilitate awareness of new issues, oppressions, privileges, and one's educational roles.

One educator described being raised and trained in the United States and developing an initial teaching identity in the United States before moving to Canada. After 9 years of living and working in Canada, she has looked at American psychology as both an insider and an outsider and has believed that her expatriate status is the predominant identity that influences her current pedagogical stance. She has become very aware that dominant definitions of feminism and multiculturalism are based on U.S. formulations and do not necessarily apply cross-nationally. For example, race dominates U.S. multicultural discussions, whereas language, ethnicity, and social class are emphasized in Canadian circles. Canadian legal rights and services, which include socialized medicine, $5-a-day day care, same-sex benefits, same-sex marital rights, and protections related to sexual orientation, highlight the dramatic differences in the day-to-day realities faced by Canadian and U.S. citizens.

She stated, "American multiculturalism and feminism are just that: American. I work hard to avoid imposing an American positionality on my students." As a teacher of many multinational students, she has encouraged her students to consider how their countries of origin negotiate multicultural and feminist issues as well as how political and multinational realities influence their personal identities and sociopolitical identities.

Another person spoke of the change in status and perspective she experienced when she left her position as a university honors program administrator to seek her doctorate. She describes this change as follows: "I found myself a student again, stripped of my institutional power and identity and struggling to identify and nurture what personal power and identity I possessed." She found that the collaboration and shared power that are at the heart of feminist approaches are often incompatible with the traditional academic hierarchy and that the rich life experiences and talents of students are often promptly submerged. She commented as follows:

> I struggle mightily with the weight of norms, spoken and unspoken, and externally and internally imposed by me, my student colleagues, my advisors, my departmental faculty, my graduate program, my educational institution, and my chosen professional field of counseling psychology. I struggle because on many days, these norms seem monolithic, inflexible, and unwelcoming. I watch myself making adjustments, contorting myself into someone's image of the perfect graduate student. According to schedule, I assume the feelings of shame, resentment, and denial.

Because of the support of faculty and student colleagues who remind her of other possibilities, this author has continued to question and challenge the norms and assumptions, accepting and staying open to the complexity and contradictions in her own life and in the lives of those with whom she interacts.

A third writer provided insights about transitions that led her to emphasize feminism and multiculturalism in different ways. Before arriving in Canada from Turkey, she had developed a feminist consciousness and fought limitations placed on her as a woman. As a member of Turkish majority culture, she was not aware of many minority groups and their experiences, in large part because many minority groups concealed their minority status to avoid less favorable treatment associated with governmental policies. However, as a member of a new culture, she stated, "My feminist consciousness took a secondary place because I was trying to make sense of what I was going through as an 'other' in dominant Canadian culture." She learned about multiculturalism, discrimination, oppression, racism, individualism, and forms of "political correctness" that can also perpetuate subtle discrimination and maintenance of the status quo. Through a multicultural lens, she returned to feminist literature and explored multiple ways of being feminist. Elaborating on a challenge that is described in related ways by other authors, she added the following:

> I have a firm understanding of other worldviews and I want to respect them. But when it comes to applying this understanding in practice, I still catch myself being entrapped in my earlier notions of what it means to be a feminist, a notion that was heavily influenced by European feminist scholars.

Consistent with the previous examples, other authors noted that transitions in the roles they play and the contexts they occupy can play a significant role in supporting a continuous cycle of self-reflection and adjustment of their worldviews.

Radical Perspectives and Positionality

Blending together thoughts about her institutional roles, lesbian identity, and the radicalness of her perspective, one author stated as follows:

> I think the most salient determinants of my positionality are my identification as a radical, multicultural feminist and out lesbian who also happens to be fairly well accepted (as far as I know!) by the professional (patriarchal) establishment in my university and in my discipline more generally.

This is an awkward place: She is grudgingly accepted in spite of her radical sensibilities because she displays enough of the trappings of traditional respectability (e.g., reputable researcher and teacher and dedicated servant to her institution and profession) for her more conservative colleagues (and students) to overlook her very public politics, ideologies, and life experiences and because she deliberately uses heavy doses of humor to keep fragile relationships intact! She added the following:

> Yet I am not really fully acceptable because I refuse to be "closeted" about who I am, and I'm sure many of my colleagues and students think I am "in their faces" just because I am not silent. I used to believe passionately that this straddling of two different worlds was a gift given to me by the Goddess so that I could build bridges for others—and I do try. But I sometimes become weary of the constant need for translation, negotiation, and intervention in environments that may appear on the surface to be hospitable but are fundamentally incapable of permitting real paradigmatic change.

Of particular concern to this activist teacher is the recent rising tide of political and religious conservatism, and she struggles most with both colleagues and students over intolerance in the guise of religious beliefs. This experience is especially painful because this seemingly unbridgeable chasm occurs in connections with many of her colleagues and students of color. "What I always regarded in the past as a seamless and unquestionable compatibility of feminist lesbianism and multiculturalism has, more recently, become more complicated and less clear to me. I struggle with it both in and out of the classroom." To summarize, this author's comments indicate that radical perspectives and marginalized identities can be translated into positions of respect and influence, but the personal costs of this work are often substantial.

She concluded with a comment about the importance of interpersonal support: "I am absolutely certain that I would not survive—professionally, personally, pedagogically—if I could not rely on my feminist colleagues to keep me grounded and striving." Of significant importance is being in contact with those who speak her language, are consciously feminist, deliberately incorporate feminism into their work, and understand the challenge of trying to live a radical life.

Religious Influences, Contradictions, and Positionality

Although religious conservatism can support narrow thinking and oppression of others, and thus, present a barrier to the integration of multiculturalism and feminism, several authors identified religious values as central to their multicultural feminist commitments. One individual described her ethnic and religious Mennonite heritage, with its emphasis on peacemaking, social justice, and service, as contributing significantly to her vision of multicultural feminist pedagogy. Another important aspect of her positionality includes her experiences as a White American growing up in Asia as well as her more recent interactions with feminists from Japan and Korea. These experiences not only have informed her about diversity but also have made her aware of the complexity of negotiating seeming contradictions and paradoxes associated with her social identities and beliefs:

> My experience as a member of a religious tradition that emphasizes service, simplicity, social justice, and pacifism has often been difficult to integrate with my experience as a member of a capitalistic, nationalistic, individualistic North American society that enjoys overwhelming wealth and privilege.

Another person made the following comments about religious foundations: "Ironically enough, I credit my Catholic education with providing the foundation for my feminist multicultural worldview. This is awkward to admit, due to the Catholic Church's long entanglement with (indeed, for some, embodiment of) patriarchy." What she gained from a Catholic education was an uninhibited values-centered approach to the world and its challenges. She likened the revolutionary teachings of Jesus to transformed understandings of humanity that are offered by radical and postmodern feminist and

186   ENNS ET AL.

multicultural practice. The prophet Jesus decentered the foundational assumptions of the most powerful institutions of his day, reclaimed the poor and marginalized as sacred, embraced women as equals, acted as a healer of physical and psychological "demons," brought a message of radical love and acceptance, and rejected simplistic, binary approaches to divinity, human relationships, and institutions. She commented,

> My feminist multicultural perspective provides me with a home for holding both my deep sense of moral outrage and my equally passionate belief that we must embrace differences and oppressors. With a moral righteousness familiar to me, I reject abuse of power, misogyny, racism, heterosexism, classism, ableism, and all other forms of evil in the world.

Educational Training and Positionality

The educational experiences of the contributors to this book have also influenced their self-identifications. One author enrolled in two influential courses at early stages of her doctoral studies: one that emphasized multicultural issues in psychology and another that introduced her to feminist therapy and theory. This exposure initiated a long-term journey marked by efforts to integrate these perspectives within writing, research, and teaching activities. Another contributor notes that she was trained in a scientist–practitioner program that was influenced heavily by an "ecological training model." She stated as follows:

> Each of my training experiences was infused with an understanding that human behavior and development occur within complex cultural, social, historical, and political contexts. In addition, every course attended to social advocacy, social justice, and the role of counseling psychologists as change agents in schools, agencies, and communities.

This contributor has worked toward empowering students to think of themselves as social justice and change agents. In keeping with an ecological model and a pedagogy of critical consciousness, she has focused on the development of students as people, scholars, teachers, and professionals. She also has sought to balance instruction and collaboration so that students feel empowered to participate in active learning. Third, she has promoted a learning environment that not only attends to understanding people in context but also locates psychological theory, intervention, and research design within historical, religious, political, and gendered contexts and supports social justice activities in psychology. A final goal involves accommodating different learning styles by incorporating a variety of activities, lectures, movies, and examples from her service and scholarship experience. She concluded the following:

> In discussing my own service and scholarship (which I believe to be steeped in a social justice agenda), I not only share my successes but also

occasions when I was not successful, and thus, allow students to provide input about how I might have proceeded differently. I reflect frequently on my own teaching and seek to improve the ways that I engage students in understanding diversity and multiculturalism in psychology.

One person spoke of the ways in which her current roles as both an educator and a student are informing her evolving self-understanding as an educator. As someone who has made regular transitions between student and teacher roles, she has been able to learn from the different teaching styles and perspectives of her teachers and also to implement the tools that she has experienced as effective. To enrich the educational experiences of her students, she also has incorporated teaching styles that have enabled her to learn, discover, and reflect. In summary, the reflections of these authors reveal that when educational training is attentive to multicultural and feminist themes, it provides a solid foundation for teaching about and for social justice.

Theory, Role Models, and Positionality

Educational identities are also influenced by various multicultural and feminist theoretical orientations. Some authors tend to foreground multicultural perspectives and see gender issues through the lens of culture; some have found feminism to be the entry point for considering multicultural perspectives; and still others see multicultural and feminist perspectives as inseparable. Several contributors described their dissatisfaction with dominant interpretations of feminism, and one person noted that many feminist readings to which she has been exposed implicitly devalue or pathologize ethnic minority values and traditions. She stated, "I believe that feminism focuses primarily on cultural limitations without observing traditions that actually empower and value women in different cultural contexts." Another person noted the inadequacy of much feminist theory for explaining the complexity of relationships in many indigenous cultures, including complementary gender roles that are built on respect for the different strengths that women and men may exhibit. She commented, "Some practices are stereotyped or misunderstood as mechanisms of control that take away women's identity when, in fact, they may offer interconnections that bring a richer commitment to one's family and community." In addition to ethnocentrism, she noted that White women still tend to ignore their race when they "identify" or "analogize" their oppressive experiences with those of women of color. To summarize, authors agreed that feminisms that hold the possibility of real change and genuine communication acknowledge the differences among women as they relate to intersections of race, class, gender, and sexuality.

Other authors have identified a variety of feminist and multicultural theories, role models, and goals as informing their educational identities.

Theories that inform contributors' pedagogies include multicultural counseling theories; social reconstructionist and critical approaches to multicultural education; and radical, women-of-color, postmodern, global, multicultural, and lesbian feminist theories. Some authors have drawn less from theory and more from the practical goal of "giving each student in my class a voice." As one author noted, "I think that all individuals have the right to be free and treated equally. I am committed to providing quality education to all students and actively engage them in the process." Although authors identified many different role models, theories, and experiences as influential, all contributors share the belief that it is essential to integrate multicultural and feminist perspectives inside and outside of the classroom.

THE CHALLENGES OF TEACHING FROM A MULTICULTURAL FEMINIST PERSPECTIVE

In the following section, we discuss complexities and issues associated with teaching from a multicultural feminist framework. These challenges include teaching effectively about multiple intersecting identities, responding appropriately to student resistance, teaching in traditional educational institutions, and defining diversity in useful and flexible ways.

The Complexity of Teaching About Multiple Social Locations

Many of the challenges of teaching from a multicultural feminist perspective arise from the complexity of addressing the many social locations, oppressions, and privileges of educators and students. One contributor disclosed feeling somewhat overwhelmed by the seeming impossibility of teaching about the huge range of diversity that exists within these multicultural perspectives. Another person noted the complexity of highlighting connections between multiple manifestations of advantage and disadvantage while also conveying the uniqueness of particular identities. A third contributor observed that if we do not offer multifaceted and multidimensional models for conceptualizing diversity, we shortchange our students by presenting, at worst, unidimensional models or at best, two-dimensional or additive models. For example, "one cannot effectively understand sexual orientation issues without understanding them from a multicultural level, which for me means grasping and appreciating the confluence of myriad variables."

Another author spoke of the challenges of integrating perspectives when conflicts appear between multiculturalism and feminism. She asked, "What do you do when being culturally sensitive is in direct conflict with feminist principles?" Closely related to this question is the necessity of responding to students' personal queries about coming to terms with contradictory aspects of their own multiple identities. These types of issues emerge repeatedly in gender and multiculturalism courses, and this professor also has observed the absence of easy answers. Knowing the importance of these concerns, she has analyzed these conflicts with students and encourages them to own the struggle and find personally meaningful ways of resolving contradictions.

One promising method for maintaining awareness and critical thinking about complex social identities is to constantly ask, "What voices are included here, and who is left out?" One author echoed the thoughts and emotions of multiple contributors with the following words:

> What I find most challenging is the incredible complexity of the layers of positionality in any group interaction in the classroom and my responsibility as an instructor to manage this complexity in some manner that makes it conscious and allows it to be part of the discourse. Some days it is exhilarating; other days it is exhausting.

In addition to the emotional impact of this work, educators also face the limitations of personal time and energy. One educator elaborated that in today's fast-paced society, it is a constant challenge to take (or make) the time necessary to understand students' and colleagues' positionality and to use information about their complex social identities to influence educational and systemic change efforts. She summarized, "Maintaining the energy to do this kind of contextually informed reflective work in environments that are most comfortable with an impersonal approach to learning is difficult."

Dealing With Student Differences and Resistance

Several individuals spoke about the challenge of teaching students who resist efforts to integrate multicultural and feminist perspectives. A major frustration involves working with students who are sensitive to the impact of one identity (e.g., race, class, or gender) but resist exploring the potential impact of other social identities. In addition, it is difficult to evaluate student work when students score high on exams but show limited sensitivity to multicultural issues. At an emotional level, students reveal multiple reactions to multicultural material, including exhilaration, excitement, numbness, guilt, or anger. Anger is a particularly challenging emotion because anger about reading material or previously unexplored issues is frequently directed toward the instructor. Creating safe spaces in which students feel comfortable expressing their true feelings without fear of reprisal is a complex process. In addition to acknowledging its importance, one contributor also observed that because didactic and experiential content have become so bifurcated within educational systems, students tend to become confused or angry with the instructor when emotions emerge. Conversations can be painful and even enraging because the content is not about distant knowledge to be acquired, but content that is lived. "In a diverse classroom, the hardest part is cultivating an inclusive environment without denying that the experience itself can feel exclusive."

Of significant concern to one educator is the resistance she has encountered from male students who feel excluded when she has emphasized women's experiences (e.g., in psychology-of-women courses). These students may also react with anger or use defensive nonverbal and verbal language when topics related to oppression are addressed. She commented, "Two of the most difficult dilemmas I face include encouraging White male students to assume a phenomenological perspective and understand issues from a different lens and ensuring that their defensive tactics do not silence other voices, including my own."

Building on these themes, one writer spoke of the frustration of needing to "teach to the middle." She added the following,

> It pains me the most when it is basic consciousness-raising around diversity and gender that I am trying to do, and my students of color or my feminist students who already "get it" don't experience catalysts for further growth because they are simply waiting for others to catch up.

At times, student resistance may be directed at the educator, especially if she holds any type of minority status. Speaking of the resistance to efforts to infuse multicultural and feminist issues throughout her teaching, one author stated as follows:

> Some students reject topics about diversity forthrightly, questioning its "relevance" in a class on interviewing techniques and communication. In addition, I must acknowledge frustration about being labeled "that Asian woman TA who pushes that multicultural thing only because she's a woman of color and this is her issue."

One author observed that her social identity as a member of a sexual minority has given her first-hand knowledge of alienation, which allows her to introduce some topics and social problems with acute sensitivity. However, student discomfort and resistance increases when they see her as residing outside their sphere, which is typically defined by heterosexuality. She added, "If my sexual orientation is fully known by European American female students, they occasionally view me as attempting to pull them away from the center and into the margins."

Although educators expressed some frustration with student resistance, they also disclosed empathy for and patience with students who are working toward expanding their worldviews. Knowledge of their own internal struggles to understand diverse experiences of marginalization augments their interpersonal sensitivity. One educator identified a sense of timing and perceptiveness about a learner's ability to hear new information as crucial to multicultural feminist pedagogy, and elaborated, "Knowing how and when to communicate requires careful awareness of the contexts within which we work and the attributes of those with whom we work."

Teaching and Learning in Traditional Institutions

Implementing liberation, feminist, and multicultural pedagogies in traditional educational institutions is often complicated. One person observed the following:

> Research is conducted in a certain way; educators who want tenure educate in specific ways; and students who want to survive graduate school decide to follow the paved road rather than question the engineering of the road or think about how to build bridges to other disciplines.

Another person noted that the multicultural feminist principle of honoring students' individual differences (e.g., abilities and learning styles) calls for the possibility of individually tailored goals and learning trajectories, with differing end points and timelines for achieving competencies. However, traditional evaluation systems (grading schemes and progress criteria) implicitly expect all students to reach some minimal level of performance within an artificial time period (e.g., a 15-week semester) regardless of where they start. Thus, some students experience inequitable advantage, because some students (by nature of demographic location, cultivated abilities, etc.) begin at less advanced places on the developmental continuum and have to work much harder to get only half as far as more advantaged students. She commented as follows:

> All of my multiculturally sensitive, feminist honoring of diversity cannot compensate for this structural inequity, and I am feeling like I have betrayed my deepest beliefs about what teaching ought to be in order to fulfill the requirements laid on me by the institution.

Practicing feminist multicultural perspectives, promoting critical consciousness, and supporting collaborative learning are also challenging when one's university system supports a traditional approach to teaching or when students and colleagues expect a banking approach to learning and teaching. In addition, students' familiarity and comfort level with traditional teaching strategies contribute to their discomfort with or rejection of feminist multicultural pedagogical approaches. To deal with this difficulty, one educator gives students the opportunity to reflect on and provide feedback about new strategies. These "teaching moments" lead to greater introspection and openness on the part of all participants in the classroom.

An additional reality is that some faculty colleagues do not view multiculturalism and feminism as legitimate areas of study but only as political ideologies. As a result, one contributor has discovered the importance of finding political allies on campus and of nominating herself for roles that support both scholarly and political aspects of being an educator who integrates multicultural and feminist scholarship. For example, her participation in committees that make curricular decisions (e.g., developing a gender and sexual diversity minor) allows her to work toward political and social change in the university.

As noted by a contributor with significant administrative responsibility, it is also important to be aware that institutional structures can limit the vision of any faculty member, and the greater one's institutional power, the more one may be vulnerable to this problem. As a result, she makes efforts to observe other faculty closely, paying particular attention to their positionality, what they can see or cannot see because of their position in their interactions with students, other faculty, and her. She articulated the following struggle:

> I see all of us who work as faculty as having a tough time remembering how much power we hold and how it has such incredible influence on our interactions with others, both students and faculty in lesser positions of power. Faculty deeply committed to feminism and multiculturalism (including me) still struggle to observe themselves from the perspectives of others, and perhaps this difficulty increases as we hold more power in the academy.

To summarize, institutional challenges are multiple and include (a) grading and course structures that do not allow for individualized progress or feedback that supports growth; (b) institutional sluggishness, inertia, and "red tape" that limit possibilities for real change; (c) student reactions to innovation that come from their accommodation to "comfortable" teaching styles; (d) the devaluation of "diversity" topics or the characterization of multicultural and feminist content as "fluff"; (e) the blank spots that individuals may acquire as they gain more power in institutions; and (f) the personal paralysis or burnout that affects individuals who have tired of trying to influence intractable bureaucratic structures.

Expanding the Concepts About What Constitutes Diversity

One author indicated that her institution highlights diversity as an important area of focus in the educational process. In reality, however, issues such as race (particularly issues of African Americans) tend to receive the extensive attention, and other kinds of diversity receive less attention. She stated, "Although frustrating, I have been able to use the institution's stated agenda of tolerance and commitment to diversity to place sexual orientation, gender, and disability issues on the table as well."

Another contributor has found that faculty seem to do rather well when teaching and learning about the influences of race, ethnicity, gender, and sexual orientation on social interactions, social structures, and institutions.

"However, we struggle still to mention, attend to, and analyze social class issues. Class has a powerful impact on class[room] interactions, and I see awareness of class as the growing edge for faculty." These observations point to the importance of defining diversity in inclusive ways.

THE BENEFITS OF INTEGRATING MULTICULTURAL AND FEMINIST PERSPECTIVES

Authors spoke personally and eloquently about the benefits of integrating multicultural and feminist perspectives. In this section we identify salient themes.

Appreciation of Difference and Multiple Perspectives

Several individuals commented that multicultural feminist frameworks expand our ability to appreciate the diverse cultural roots of women as well as what it means to be an "empowered woman" and a "feminist." Furthermore, "knowledge of the wealth of every culture enables women to be more empowered and creative with respect to fighting their battle with many forms of 'isms.'" Other contributors highlighted the ways in which these perspectives encourage open dialogue and communication about differences. "By embracing our different histories and not 'melting' them together into one generalized view of oppression, we can understand our multiple selves more deeply, and we become less invisible to ourselves and to one another." Mindfulness of our privileges in North American society and our limited global awareness is also important. When we acknowledge the limitations of our perspectives, we experience greater freedom to learn and develop skills that allow us to be more responsive to our diverse world.

New Ways of Seeing and Learning

Feminist multicultural perspectives provide catalysts for transformation that is about "experiencing those moments of discomfort, those ruptures of one's assumptions, that permit growth and learning." Educators and therapists are invited to give up their privileged expert statuses and learn, as feminist multicultural theorist Clara Sandoval describes it, "how to see from below." This writer added the following:

> This place of rawness and confusion is what makes possible new ways of seeing. We value and learn from those voices in ourselves and in our world that have been marginalized; we embrace rather than deny and pathologize our permanently partial identities and the ambiguity in our lives and theories and institutions.

Teaching from a multicultural feminist perspective provides opportunities for continuous growth and renewed vitality: "Over the years, I have had the privilege of being able to analyze my multiple identities, how they intersect with each other and in the world, as well as develop an in-depth and ever-evolving understanding of my sociopolitical position."

New ways of knowing also lead to greater opportunities and fairness for students. One educator asserted, "Many have been shut out of participation, and we are obligated to provide a fairer playing field because the consequences of not doing so are so huge in our society (poverty, violence, further erosion of democracy, to name a few)."

The Opportunity to Act on Personal Priorities

Because efforts to integrate multicultural and feminist perspectives are central to the daily activities and life priorities of many contributors, applying these personal priorities to pedagogy is especially meaningful. One person stated, "Bringing this perspective to my work with others allows me to remain centered and to value my own intersecting social identities." Several other contributors commented that it gives them permission to be whole people, to be true to themselves both personally and professionally, and to engage in dialogue that continues to challenge all of those who participate in it (students and professors). One person concluded that by bringing all of who she is to the classroom and by using this holistic knowledge to discuss complex issues, she is able to challenge students to experience "transformative education."

Growth of Students and Colleagues

Many contributors spoke of benefits to students, and the following sentences summarize their various responses. As stated by several individuals, students develop tools to evaluate concepts and psychotherapy practices critically, learn to express their voices and opinions, and gain feminist and multicultural tools that prepare them to work with people more effectively. Students and colleagues develop the skills necessary to act as educated citizens and health care professionals who are able to function effectively in increasingly diverse interpersonal and sociopolitical environments. One author summarized this growth as follows: "Students live what they learn and learn what they live."

An integrated approach also supports a collaborative pedagogy that emphasizes lifelong learning. Both students and instructors can share relevant and insightful thoughts and beliefs that add to the richness of learning. By hearing many voices that offer a wide range of views, instructors as well as students have opportunities to learn from each other as they negotiate lifelong journeys of learning.

Changes Within Institutions

According to one contributor, the effective implementation of feminist and multicultural pedagogical strategies leads to changes among colleagues, departments, divisions, and institutions, in large part because egalitarian educators have the capacity to lead in politically sensitive, collaborative, and supportive ways. Another author noted that multicultural feminist perspectives enrich institutions by providing the motivation, means, and opportunities to be truly responsive to their clientele.

CONCLUDING THOUGHTS

The experiences of these authors point to the complexity, challenges, and rewards of teaching for social justice. Their observations reinforce many of the themes addressed throughout this book. First, the positionality, multiple identities, and social locations of each educator contribute to their unique perspectives, the perceptions that students and colleagues hold toward them, and myriad and complex dynamics that result from the interactions among these factors. Educators' awareness and reflexivity about their multiple identities also contribute to their flexibility, openness, and sensitivity to differences within and beyond the classroom. Second, some of the most significant challenges that book contributors identified included (a) teaching effectively about complex multiple perspectives, identities, and oppressions; (b) responding appropriately to diverse student identities, developmental issues, and reactions; and (c) maintaining vitality while working with traditional colleagues and within traditional institutions. Finally, the benefits include opportunities for (a) engaging in ongoing personal and professional challenge and growth; (b) participating actively in the lives and development of students, colleagues, and institutions; (c) educating in ways that are true to oneself and consistent with social justice values; and (d) appreciating difference and developing useful roadmaps for integrating multicultural and feminist perspectives.

REFERENCES

Acker, S. (1994). Feminist theory and the study of gender and education. In S. Acker (Ed.), *Gendered education: Sociological reflections on women, teaching and feminism* (pp. 43–54). Buckingham, England: Open University Press.

Adams, K., & Emery, K. (1994). Classroom coming out stories: Practical strategies for productive self-disclosure. In L. Garber (Ed.), *Tilting the tower* (pp. 25–34). New York: Routledge.

Adams, M. (1997). Pedagogical frameworks for social justice education. In M. Adams, L. A. Bell, & P. Griffin (Eds.), *Teaching for diversity and social justice: A sourcebook* (pp. 30–43). New York: Routledge.

Adams, M., Bell, L. A., & Griffin, P. (Eds.). (1997). *Teaching for diversity and social justice: A sourcebook.* New York: Routledge.

Alcoff, L. (1988). Cultural feminism versus post-structuralism: The identity crisis in feminist theory. *Signs: Journal of Women in Culture and Society, 13,* 405–436.

Allen, K. R., & Farnsworth, E. B. (1993). Reflexivity in teaching about families. *Family Relations, 37,* 29–35.

American Association of Colleges. (1991). *The challenge of connected learning* (Report No. 16). Washington, DC: Author.

American Council on Education. (2002, September). *Students of color make enrollment and graduation gains in postsecondary education according to ACE's annual status report.* Retrieved June 30, 2003, from http://www.acenet.edu/news/press_release/2002/09september/OMHE.report.html

American Psychological Association. (2002). *Guidelines on multicultural education, training, research, practice, and organizational change for psychologists.* Washington, DC: Author.

American Psychological Association, Committee on Women in Psychology and Commission on Ethnic Minority Recruitment, Retention, and Training in Psychology. (1998). *Surviving and thriving in academia: A guide for women and ethnic minorities.* Washington, DC: Author.

American Psychological Association, Task Force on Diversity Issues at the Precollege and Undergraduate Levels of Education in Psychology. (1998a, March). Enriching the focus on ethnicity and race. *APA Monitor,* p. 43.

American Psychological Association, Task Force on Diversity Issues at the Precollege and Undergraduate Levels of Education in Psychology. (1998b, May). Tips for incorporating culture in class: Be aware of some common, interrelated misconceptions about culture. *APA Monitor,* p. 39.

American Psychological Association, Task Force on Women in Academe. (2000). *Women in academe: Two steps forward, one step back.* Washington, DC: Author.

Ancis, J. R. (Ed.). (2004). *Culturally-responsive interventions: Innovative approaches to working with diverse populations.* New York: Brunner-Routledge.

Ancis, J. R., & Ladany, N. (2001). A multicultural framework for counselor supervision. In L. J. Bradley & N. Ladany (Eds.), *Counselor supervision: Principles, process, and practice* (3rd ed., pp. 63–90). Philadelphia: Brunner-Routledge.

Ancis, J. R., & Sanchez-Hucles, J. (2000). A preliminary analysis of counseling students' attitudes toward counseling women and women of color: Implications for cultural competency training. *Journal of Multicultural Counseling and Development, 28,* 16–31.

Ancis, J. R., & Szymanski, D. M. (2001). Awareness of White privilege among White counseling trainees. *The Counseling Psychologist, 29,* 548–569.

Andersen, M. L., & Collins, P. H. (2001). Shifting the center and reconstructing knowledge. In M. Andersen & P. Collins (Eds.), *Race, class, and gender: An anthology* (4th ed., pp. 13–21). Belmont, CA: Wadsworth.

Anderson, A. (1999). Feminist psychology and global issues: An action agenda. *Women and Therapy, 22*(1), 7–21.

Anzaldúa, G. (1987). *Borderlands, la frontera: The new mestiza.* San Francisco: Aunt Lute Books.

Anzaldúa, G. (Ed.). (1990). *Making face, making soul, haciendo caras: Creative and critical perspectives by feminists of color.* San Francisco: Aunt Lute Books.

Appelbaum, P. (2002). *Multicultural and diversity education: A reference handbook.* Santa Barbara, CA: ABC-CLIO.

Armstrong, S. J., Allinson, C. W., & Hayes, J. (2002). Formal mentoring systems: An examination of the effects of mentor/protégé cognitive styles on the mentoring process. *Journal of Management Studies, 39,* 1111–1137.

Arredondo, P., & Arciniega, G. M. (2001). Strategies and techniques for counselor training based on the multicultural counseling competencies. *Journal of Multicultural Counseling and Development, 29,* 263–273.

Arredondo, P., Toporek, R., Brown, S. P., Jones, J., Locke, D. C., Sanchez, J., & Stadler, H. (1996). Operationalization of the multicultural counseling competencies. *Journal of Multicultural Counseling and Development, 24,* 42–78.

Atkinson, D. R., Casas, A., & Neville, H. (1994). Ethnic minority psychologists: Whom they mentor and benefits they derive from the process. *Journal of Multicultural Counseling and Development, 22,* 37–48.

Attneave, C. (1969). Therapy in tribal settings and urban network interventions. *Family Process, 8,* 192–210.

Atwood, J. (1994). Good intentions, dangerous territory: Student resistance in feminist writing classes. *Journal of Teaching Writing, 12,* 124–143.

Ayers-Nachamkin, B. (1992). A feminist approach to the introductory statistics course. *Women's Studies Quarterly, 20*(1/2), 86–94.

Bahuniuk, M. H., Dobos, J., & Kogler-Hill, S. E. (1990). The impact of mentoring, collegial support, and informational adequacy on career success: A replication. *Journal of Social Behavior and Personality, 5,* 431–451.

Baker, C. (1985). Through the eye of the storm: Feminist in the classroom. In J. Fritsch (Ed.), *Toward excellence and equity* (pp. 224–233). Orono: University of Maine.

Ball, A. F. (2000). Empowering pedagogies that enhance the learning of multicultural students. *Teachers College Record, 102,* 1006–1034.

Ballard, M. E. (1995). The politics of prejudice in psychology: A syllabus and bibliography. *Feminist Teacher, 9,* 16–21.

Banks, J. A. (1995). Multicultural education: Historical development, dimensions, and practice. In J. A. Banks & C. A. M. Banks (Eds.), *Handbook of research on multicultural education* (pp. 3–24). New York: Simon & Schuster/Macmillan.

Banks, J. A. (2000). Multicultural education: Characteristics and goals. In J. A. Banks & C. A. M. Banks (Eds.), *Multicultural education: Issues and perspectives* (4th ed., pp. 3–30). New York: Wiley.

Banks, J. A., & Banks, C. A. M. (Eds.). (2003). *Multicultural education: Issues and perspectives* (5th ed.). New York: Wiley.

Bargad, A., & Hyde, J. S. (1991). Women's studies: A study of feminist identity development in women. *Psychology of Women Quarterly, 15,* 181–201.

Basu, A. (2000). Globalization of the local/localization of the global: Mapping transnational women's movements. *Meridians, 1*(1), 68–84.

Bauer, D. M. (1990). The other "f" word: The feminist in the classroom. *College English, 52,* 385–396.

Baumgardner, J., & Richards, A. (2000). *Manifesta: Young women, feminism, and the future.* New York: Farrar, Straus & Giroux.

Beck, E. T. (1983). Self-disclosure and the commitment to social change. *Women's Studies International Forum, 6,* 159–163.

Belenky, M. J., Clinchy, B. M., Goldberger, N. R., & Tarule, J. M. (1986). *Women's ways of knowing.* New York: Basic Books.

Bell, S., Morrow, M., & Tastsoglou, E. (1999). Teaching in environments of resistance: Toward a critical, feminist, and antiracist pedagogy. In M. Mayberry & E. C. Rose (Eds.), *Meeting the challenge: Innovative feminist pedagogies in action* (pp. 23–46). New York: Routledge.

Bellafante, G. (1998, June 29). Feminism: It's all about me. *Time, 151,* 54–60.

Benishek, L. A., Bieschke, K. J., Park, J., & Slattery, S. M. (in press). A multicultural feminist model of mentoring. *Journal of Multicultural Counseling and Development.*

Bennett, C. (2001). Genres of research in multicultural education. *Review of Education Research, 71,* 171–217.

Bennett, P. (1996). Dyke in academe. In B. Zimmerman & T. McNaron (Eds.), *The new lesbian studies: Into the twenty-first century* (2nd ed., pp. 3–8). New York: The Feminist Press.

Bennetts, C. (2002). Traditional mentor relationships, intimacy and emotional intelligence. *International Journal of Qualitative Studies in Education, 15*(2), 155–170.

Benokraitis, N. V. (1998). Working in the ivory basement: Subtle sex discrimination in higher education. In L. H. Collins, J. C. Chrisler, & K. Quina (Eds.),

Career strategies for women in academe: Arming Athena (pp. 3–43). Thousand Oaks, CA: Sage.

Bensimon, E. M., & Marshall, C. (2000). Policy analysis for postsecondary education: Feminist and cultural perspectives. In J. Glazer-Raymo, B. K. Townsend, & B. Ropers-Huilman (Eds.), *Women in American higher education: A feminist perspective* (2nd ed., pp. 133–147). Boston: Pearson Custom Publishing.

Berkeley, K. C. (1999). *The women's liberation movement in America.* Westport, CT: Greenwood Press.

Bernal, D. D. (1998). Using a Chicana feminist epistemology in educational research. *Harvard Educational Review, 68,* 555–579.

Berry, E., & Black, E. (1987). The integrative learning journal (or, getting beyond "true confessions" and "cold knowledge"). *Women's Studies Quarterly, 15*(3/4), 59–64.

Betz, N. E. (1989). Implications of the null environment hypothesis for women's career development and for counseling psychology. *The Counseling Psychologist, 17,* 136–144.

Betz, N. E. (2002). Women's career development: Weaving personal themes and theoretical constructs. *The Counseling Psychologist, 30,* 467–481.

Bezucha, R. J. (1985). Feminist pedagogy as a subversive activity. In M. Culley & C. Portuges (Eds.), *Gendered subjects: The dynamics of feminist teaching* (pp. 81–95). Boston: Routledge & Kegan Paul.

Bignell, K. C. (1996). Building feminist praxis out of feminist pedagogy: The importance of students' perspectives. *Women's Studies International Forum, 19,* 315–325.

Boatswain, S., Brown, N., Fiksenbaum, L., Goldstein, L., Greenglass, E., Nadler, E., et al. (2001). Canadian feminist psychology: Where are we now? *Canadian Psychology, 42,* 276–285.

Boatwright, K. J. (2003, January). *Social action projects in a feminist psychology of women course.* Paper presented at the National Institute of Teaching of Psychology Annual Conference, St. Petersburg, FL.

Boatwright, K. J., & Paschiera, G. (2003, April). *Relationship among connectedness needs, gender role and college students' responses to feminist pedagogical strategies.* Paper presented at the American Psychological Association Great Lakes Annual Conference, Western Michigan University, Kalamazoo.

Bohan, J. S. (2002). Sex differences and/in the self: Classic themes, feminist variations, postmodern challenges. *Psychology of Women Quarterly, 26,* 74–88.

Boler, M. (1999). *Feeling power: Emotions and education.* New York: Routledge.

Bourdieu, P. (1990). *Reproduction in education, society, and culture.* Thousand Oaks, CA: Sage.

Bowleg, L. (1998). "When I look at you, I don't see race" and other diverse takes from the introduction to women's studies classroom. In B. S. Winkler & C. DiPalma (Eds.), *Teaching introduction to women's studies: Expectation and strategies* (pp. 111–122). Westport, CT: Bergin & Garvey.

Boxer, M. (1982). For and about women: The theory and practice of women's studies in the United States. *Signs: Journal of Women in Culture and Society, 7,* 661–695.

Boyer, E. L. (1990). *Scholarship reconsidered: Priorities of the professorate.* Princeton, NJ: Carnegie Foundation for the Advancement of Teaching.

Briskin, L. (1990). *Feminist pedagogy: Teaching and learning liberation.* Ottawa, Canada: CRIAW/ICREF.

Britzman, D. (1995). Is there a queer pedagogy? Or, stop reading straight! *Educational Theory, 45,* 151–165.

Brodkin, K. (1998). *How the Jews became White folk and what that says about race in America.* New Brunswick, NJ: Rutgers University Press.

Brokes, A. J., & Twine, F. W. (1998). Inter-racial teaching teams, antiracism, and the politics of white resistance: Teaching introduction to women studies at a predominantly white research institution. In B. S. Winkler & C. DiPalma (Eds.), *Teaching introduction to women's studies: Expectation and strategies* (pp. 123–136). Westport, CT: Bergin & Garvey.

Bronstein, P., & Quina, K. (Eds.). (1988). *Teaching a psychology of people: Resources for gender and sociocultural awareness.* Washington, DC: American Psychological Association.

Bronstein, P., & Quina, K. (Eds.). (2003). *Teaching gender and multicultural awareness: Resources for the psychology classroom.* Washington, DC: American Psychological Association.

Brown, K. H., & Gillespie, D. (1997). "We become brave by doing brave acts": Teaching moral courage through the theater of the oppressed. *Literature and Medicine, 16,* 108–120.

Brunner, D. D. (1992). Dislocating boundaries in our classroom. *Feminist Teacher, 6,* 18–24.

Bryson, M., & de Castell, S. (1997). Queer pedagogy?!: Praxis makes im/perfect. In S. de Castell & M. Bryson (Eds.), *Radical in(ter)ventions: Identity, politics, and difference/s in educational praxis* (pp. 269–293). Albany: State University of New York Press.

Burbules, N. C., & Berk, R. (1999). Critical thinking and critical pedagogy: Relations, differences, and limits. In R. S. Popkewitz & L. Fendler (Eds.), *Critical theories in education: Changing terrains of knowledge and politics* (pp. 45–65). New York: Routledge.

Burke, R. J., McKeen, C. A., & McKenna, C. (1993). Correlates of mentoring in organizations: The mentor's perspective. *Psychological Reports, 72,* 883–896.

Burn, S. M. (2000). *Women across cultures: A global perspective.* Mountain View, CA: Mayfield.

Butler, J. E. (1985). Toward a pedagogy of Everywoman's Studies. In M. Culley & C. Portuges (Eds.), *Gendered subjects: The dynamics of feminist teaching* (pp. 230–239). Boston: Routledge & Kegan Paul.

Butler, J. E. (2000). Transforming the curriculum: Teaching about women of color. In J. A. Banks & C. A. M. Banks (Eds.), *Multicultural education: Issues and perspectives* (4th ed., pp. 174–193). New York: Wiley.

Cacoullos, A. R. (2001). American feminist theory. *American Studies International, 39*(1), 72–117.

Calhoun, C. (1997). Separating lesbian theory from feminist theory. In D. T. Meyers (Ed.), *Feminist social thought: A reader* (pp. 200–218). New York: Routledge.

Calliste, A. M., Dei, G. J. S., & Agular, M. (Eds.). (2000). *Anti-racist feminism: Critical race and gender studies*. Halifax, Nova Scotia, Canada: Fernwood Publishing.

Carney, C. G., & Kahn, K. B. (1984). Building competencies for effective cross-cultural counseling: A developmental view. *The Counseling Psychologist, 12,* 111–119.

Carter, R. T. (1995). *The influence of race and racial identity in psychotherapy: Toward a racially inclusive model*. New York: Wiley.

Carter, R. T. (2003). Becoming racially and culturally competent: The racial-cultural counseling laboratory. *Journal of Multicultural Counseling and Development, 31,* 20–30.

Carter, R. T., & Qureshi, A. (1995). A typology of philosophical assumptions in multicultural counseling and training. In J. G. Ponterotto, J. M Casas, L. A. Suzuki, & C. M. Alexander (Eds.), *Handbook of multicultural counseling* (pp. 239–262). Thousand Oaks, CA: Sage.

Carver, A. (1978). Applying feminist approaches to learning and research: A practical curriculum model. *Women's Studies Newsletter, 7,* 24–26.

Chesler, M. A., & Zuniga, X. (1991). Dealing with prejudice and conflict in the classroom: The pink triangle exercise. *Teaching Sociology, 19,* 173–181.

Chin, J. L., & Russo, N. F. (1997). Feminist curriculum development: Principles and resources. In J. Worell & N. G. Johnson (Eds.), *Shaping the future of feminist psychology: Education, research, and practice* (pp. 93–119). Washington, DC: American Psychological Association.

Clinchy, B. M. (1989). The development of thoughtfulness in college women. *American Behavioral Scientist, 32,* 647–657.

Clinchy, B. M. (1995). A connected approach to the teaching of developmental psychology. *Teaching of Psychology, 22,* 100–104.

Collins, P. H. (2000). *Black feminist thought: Knowledge, consciousness, and the politics of empowerment* (2nd ed.). New York: Routledge.

Comas-Díaz, L. (1994). An integrative approach. In. L. Comas-Diaz & B. Greene (Eds.), *Women of color: Integrating ethnic and gender identities in psychotherapy* (pp. 287–318). New York: Guilford Press.

Comas-Díaz, L., & Greene, B. (Eds.). (1994). *Women of color: Integrating ethnic and gender identities in psychotherapy*. New York: Guilford Press.

Connell, R. W. (1993). Disruptions: Improper masculinities and schooling. In L. Weis & M. Fine (Eds.), *Beyond silenced voices: Class, race and gender in United States schools* (pp. 191–208). Albany: State University of New York Press.

Constantine, M. G. (2001). Theoretical orientation, empathy, and multicultural counseling competence in school counselor trainees. *Professional School Counseling, 4,* 342–348.

Constantine, M. G., & Gainor, K. A. (2001). Emotional intelligence and empathy: Their relation to multicultural counseling knowledge and awareness. *Professional School Counseling, 5*, 131–137.

Constantine, M. G., & Ladany, N. (2000). Self-report multicultural counseling competence scales: Their relation to social desirability attitudes and multicultural case conceptualization ability. *Journal of Counseling Psychology, 47*, 155–164.

Cook, J. A., & Fonow, M. M. (1986). Knowledge and women's interests: Issues of epistemology and methodology in feminist sociological research. *Sociological Inquiry, 56*, 2–29.

Corvin, S. A., & Wiggins, F. (1989). An antiracism training model for White professionals. *Journal of Multicultural Counseling and Development, 17*, 105–114.

Cottrell, D. (1999). Teaching through narratives of women's lives. In S. N. Davis, M. Crawford, & J. Sebrechts (Eds.), *Coming into her own: Educational success in girls and women* (pp. 77–91). San Francisco: Jossey-Bass.

Crawford, M., & Unger, R. (2004). *Women and gender: A feminist psychology* (4th ed.). Boston: McGraw-Hill.

Cross, T., Klein, F., Smith, B., & Smith, B. (1982). Face-to-face, day-to-day-racism CR. In G. T. Hull, P. B. Scott, & B. Smith (Eds.), *All the women are white, all the blacks are men, but some of us are brave* (pp. 52–56). Old Westbury, NY: The Feminist Press.

Cross, W. E. (1978). The Thomas and Cross models of psychological Nigrescence: A review. *Journal of Black Psychology, 5*(1), 13–31.

Cross, W. E. (1991). *Shades of black: Diversity in African-American identity*. Philadelphia: Temple University Press.

Crowley-Long, K. (1998). Making room for many feminisms: The dominance of the liberal political perspective in the psychology of women course. *Psychology of Women Quarterly, 22*, 113–130.

Crumpacker, L., & Vander Haegen, E. M. (1987). Pedagogy and prejudice: Strategies for confronting homophobia in the classroom. *Women Studies Quarterly, 15*(3/4), 65–73.

Culley, M. (1985). Anger and authority in the introductory women's studies classroom. In M. Culley & C. Portuges (Eds.), *Gendered subjects: The dynamics of feminist teaching* (pp. 209–217). Boston: Routledge & Kegan Paul.

Culley, M., Diamond, A., Edwards, L., Lennox, S., & Portuges, C. (1985). The politics of nurturance. In M. Culley & C. Portuges (Eds.), *Gendered subjects: The dynamics of feminist teaching* (pp. 11–20). Boston: Routledge & Kegan Paul.

Currie, D. H. (1992). Subject-ivity in the classroom: Feminism meets academe. *Canadian Journal of Education, 17*, 341–364.

D'Andrea, M., & Daniels, J. (1995). Promoting multiculturalism and organizational change in the counseling profession: A case study. In J. Ponterotto, J. Casas, L. Suzuki, & C. Alexander (Eds.), *Handbook of multicultural counseling* (pp. 17–33). Thousand Oaks, CA: Sage.

D'Andrea, M., Daniels, J., & Heck, R. (1991). Evaluating the impact of multicultural counseling training. *Journal of Counseling and Development, 70*, 143–150.

Darder, A. (2002). *Reinventing Paulo Freire: A pedagogy of love*. Boulder, CO: Westview Press.

Davenport, D. (1996). Black lesbians in academia: Visibility invisibility. In B. Zimmerman & T. McNaron (Eds.), *The new lesbian studies: Into the twenty-first century* (pp. 9–11). New York: The Feminist Press.

Davis, B. (1981). Teaching the feminist minority. *Women Studies Quarterly, 9*(4), 7–9.

Davis, F., Steiger, A., & Tennenhouse, K. (1989). *A practical assessment of feminist pedagogy.* (ERIC Document Reproduction Service No. ED 327 502). Retrieved July 26, 2002, from Eric/E*Subscribe database.

Davis, K. S. (2001). "Peripheral and subversive": Women making connections and challenging the boundaries of the science community. *Science Education, 85,* 368–409.

Davis, S. N. (1999). Creating a collaborative classroom. In S. N. Davis, M. Crawford, & J. Sebrechts (Eds.), *Coming into her own: Educational success in girls and women* (pp. 123–138). San Francisco: Jossey-Bass.

Davis, S. N., & Ratigan, V. K. (1999). Studying women's lives in an interdisciplinary context. In S. N. Davis, M. Crawford, & J. Sebrechts (Eds.), *Coming into her own: Educational success in girls and women* (pp. 92–106). San Francisco: Jossey-Bass.

Deaux, K., & Stewart, A. J. (2001). Framing gendered identities. In R. K. Unger (Ed.), *Handbook of the psychology of women and gender* (pp. 84–97). New York: Wiley.

Deay, A., & Stitzel, J. (1998). Reshaping the introductory women's studies course. In G. E. Cohee, E. Däumer, T. D. Kemp, P. M. Krebs, S. Lafky, & S. Runzo (Eds.), *The feminist teacher anthology: Pedagogies and classroom strategies* (pp. 87–97). New York: Teachers College Press.

DeDanaan, L. (1990). Center to margin: Dynamics in a global classroom. *Women's Studies Quarterly, 18*(1/2), 135–144.

Deem, R. (1980). *Schooling for women's work*. Boston: Routledge & Kegan Paul.

Denmark, F. L., Russo, N. F., Frieze, I. H., & Sechzer, J. (1988). Guidelines for avoiding sexism in psychological research: A report of the ad hoc committee on nonsexist research. *American Psychologist, 43,* 582–585.

Diamond, R., & Adams, B. (1995). *Recognizing faculty work: Reward system for the year 2000. New directions for higher education.* San Francisco: Jossey-Bass.

Díaz-Lázaro, C. M., & Cohen, B. B. (2001). Cross-cultural contact in counseling training. *Journal of Multicultural Counseling and Development, 29,* 41–56.

Dilley, P. (1999). Queer theory: Under construction. *International Journal of Qualitative Studies in Education, 12,* 457–472.

Disch, E. (1999). Encouraging participation in the classroom. In S. N. Davis, M. Crawford, & J. Sebrechts (Eds.), *Coming into her own: Educational success in girls and women* (pp. 139–154). San Francisco: Jossey-Bass.

Donovan, J. (2000). *Feminist theory: The intellectual traditions of American feminism* (3rd ed.). New York: F. Ungar.

Downing, N. E., & Roush, K. L. (1985). From passive acceptance to active commitment: A model of feminist identity development for women. *Counseling Psychologist, 13,* 695–709.

Dreher, G. F., & Cox, T. H. (1996). Race, gender, and opportunity: A study of compensation attainment and the establishment of mentoring relationships. *Journal of Applied Psychology, 81,* 297–308.

Drenovsky, C. K. (1999). The advocacy project on women's issues: A method for teaching and practicing feminist theory in an introductory women's studies course. *Women's Studies Quarterly, 27*(3/4), 12–20.

Duncombe, M. (1998). Students' fear of lesbianism. In B. S. Winkler & C. DiPalma (Eds.), *Teaching introduction to women's studies: Expectation and strategies* (pp. 99–110). Westport, CT: Bergin & Garvey.

Eichorn, J., Farris, S., Hayes, K., Hernandez, A., Jarratt, S. C., Powers-Strubbs, K., et al. (1992). A symposium on feminist experiences in the composition classroom. *College Composition and Communication, 43,* 297–322.

Eichstedt, J. (1996). Heterosexism and gay/lesbian/bisexual experiences: Teaching strategies and exercises. *Teaching Sociology, 24,* 384–388.

Elabor-Idemudia, P. (2001). Equity issues in the academy: An Afro-Canadian woman's perspective. *The Journal of Negro Education, 70,* 192–203.

Elenes, C. A. (2001). *Transformando fronteras:* Chicana feminist transformative pedagogies. *Qualitative Studies in Education, 14,* 689–702.

Elliot, L. G. (1993). Using debates to teach the psychology of women. *Teaching of Psychology, 20,* 35–38.

Ellsworth, E. (1989). Why doesn't this feel empowering? Working through the repressive myths of critical pedagogy. *Harvard Educational Review, 59,* 297–324.

Elovson, A. C., & Cockroft, I. (1977). *The reported impact of women's studies courses on students' lives.* ERIC Document Reproduction Service No. ED160944.

Enns, C. Z. (1993a). Integrating separate and connected knowing: The experiential learning model. *Teaching of Psychology, 20,* 7–13.

Enns, C. Z. (1993b). Twenty years of feminist counseling and therapy: From naming biases to implementing multifaceted practices. *Counseling Psychologist, 21,* 3–87.

Enns, C. Z. (1994). Archetypes and gender: Goddesses, warriors, and psychological health. *Journal of Counseling and Development, 73,* 127–133.

Enns, C. Z. (1997). *Feminist theories and feminist psychotherapies: Origins, themes, and variations.* Binghamton, NY: Haworth Press.

Ensher, E. A., Grant-Vallone, E. J., & Marelich, W. D. (2002). Effects of perceived attitudinal and demographic similarity on protégés' support and satisfaction gained from their mentoring relationships. *Journal of Applied Social Psychology, 32,* 1407–1430.

Espín, O. M. (1994). Feminist approaches. In L. Comas-Diaz & B. Greene (Eds.), *Women of color: Integrating ethnic and gender identities in psychotherapy* (pp. 265–286). New York: Guilford Press.

Espín, O. M. (1995). On knowing you are the unknown: Women of color constructing psychology. In J. Adleman & Enguídanos, G. (Eds.), *Racism in the lives of women* (pp. 127–136). New York: Harrington Park Press.

Espín, O. M. (1997). *Latina realities: Essays on healing, migration, and sexuality.* Boulder, CO: Westview Press.

Esterberg, K. G. (1997). *Lesbian and bisexual identities: Constructing communities, constructing selves.* Philadelphia: Temple University Press.

Estrada, A. U., Durlak, J. A., & Juarez, S. C. (2002). Developing multicultural counseling competencies in undergraduate students. *Journal of Multicultural Counseling and Development, 30,* 110–123.

Fassinger, R. E. (1997, August). *Dangerous liaisons: Reflections on feminist mentoring.* Paper presented at the 105th Annual Convention of the American Psychological Association, Chicago, IL.

Fassinger, R. E. (in press). Theoretical issues in the study of women's career development: Building bridges in a brave new world. In W. B. Walsh & M. L. Savickas (Eds.), *Handbook of Vocational Psychology* (3rd ed.). Mahwah, NJ: Erlbaum.

Ferguson, A. (1982). Feminist teaching: A practice developed in undergraduate courses. *Radical Teacher, 20,* 26–29.

Ferguson, M. (1992). Is the classroom still a chilly climate for women? *College Student Journal, 26,* 507–511.

Fiedler, F. E., Mitchell, T., & Triandis, H. C. (1971). The culture assimilator: An approach to cross-cultural training. *Journal of Applied Psychology, 55,* 95–102.

Findlen, B. (Ed.). (1995). *Listen up: Voices from the next feminist generation.* Seattle, WA: Seal Press.

Fine, M., & Burns, A. (2003). Class notes: Toward a critical psychology of class and schooling. *Journal of Social Issues, 59,* 841–860.

Fisher, B. M. (1981). What is feminist pedagogy? *Radical Teacher, 18,* 20–24.

Fisher, B. M. (1987). The heart has its reasons: Feeling, thinking, and community-building in feminist education. *Women's Studies Quarterly, 15*(3/4), 47–57.

Fisher, B. M. (2001). *No angel in the classroom: Teaching through feminist discourse.* Lanham, MD: Rowman & Littlefield.

Flaskerud, J. H., & Soldevilla, E. Q. (1986). Pilipino and Vietnamese clients: Utilizing an Asian mental health center. *Journal of Psychosocial Nursing, 24*(8), 32–36.

Forcey, L. R., & Swerdlow, A. (Eds.). (1995). Rethinking women's peace studies [Special issue]. *Women's Studies Quarterly, 23*(3/4).

Forrest, L., & Rosenberg, F. (1997). A review of the feminist pedagogy literature: The neglected child of feminist pedagogy. *Applied and Preventive Psychology, 6,* 179–192.

Frankenberg, R. (1990). White women, racism, and antiracism: A women's studies course exploring racism and privilege. *Women's Studies Quarterly, 18*(1/2), 145–154.

Franzosa, S. D. (1993). Shaking the foundation: How schools shortchange girls. *National Women's Studies Association Journal, 5,* 325–339.

Freedman, E. B. (1990). Small group pedagogy: Consciousness raising in conservative times. *National Women's Studies Association Journal, 2,* 603–623.

Freedman, E. B. (2002). *No turning back: The history of feminism and the future of women.* New York: Ballantine Books.

Freeman, J. (1979). How to discriminate against women without really trying. In J. Freeman (Ed.), *Women: A feminist perspective* (2nd ed., pp. 194–208). Palo Alto, CA: Mayfield Publishing.

Freire, P. (1970). *Pedagogy of the oppressed* (M. B. Ramos, Trans.). New York: Seabury Press.

Freire, P. (1985). *The politics of education.* South Hadley, MA: Bergin & Garvey.

Freire, P. (1994a). *Pedagogy of hope: Reliving pedagogy of the oppressed.* New York: Continuum.

Freire, P. (1994b). *Pedagogy of the oppressed* (Rev. 20th anniv. ed., M. B. Ramos, Trans.). New York: Continuum.

Freire, P. (1998a). *Pedagogy of freedom: Ethics, democracy, and civic courage.* Lanham, MD: Rowman & Littlefield.

Freire, P. (1998b). *Teachers as cultural workers: Letters to those who dare to teach.* Boulder, CO: Westview.

Friedman, S. S. (1985). Authority in the feminist classroom: A contradiction in terms? In M. Culley & C. Portuges (Eds.), *Gendered subjects: The dynamics of feminist teaching* (pp. 203–208). Boston: Routledge & Kegan Paul.

Fukuyama, M. A. (1990). Taking a universal approach to multicultural counseling. *Counselor Education and Supervision, 30,* 6–17.

Garber, L. (2001). *Identity poetics: Race, class, and the lesbian-feminist roots of queer theory.* New York: Columbia University Press.

Garcia, B., & Van Soest, D. (1997). Changing perceptions of diversity and oppression: MSW students discuss the effects of a required course. *Journal of Social Work Education, 33,* 119–129.

Gardner, S. (1993). Teaching about domestic violence: Strategies for empowerment. *National Women's Studies Association Journal, 5,* 94–102.

Gardner, S., Dean, C., & McKaig, D. (1989). Responding to differences in the classroom: The politics of knowledge, class and sexuality. *Sociology of Education, 62,* 64–74.

Gawelek, M. A., Mulqueen, M., & Tarule, J. M. (1994). Woman to women: Understanding the needs of our female students. In S. M. Deats & L. T. Lenker (Eds.), *Gender and academe: Feminist pedagogy and politics* (pp. 179–198). Lanham, MD: Rowman & Littlefield.

Gay, G. (2000). *Culturally responsive teaching: Theory, research, and practice.* New York: Teachers College Press.

Gergen, M. (2001). *Feminist reconstructions in psychology.* Thousand Oaks, CA: Sage.

Giddings, P. (1984). *When and where I enter: The impact of Black women on race and sex in America*. New York: Morrow.

Gilbert, L.A., & Rossman, K. M. (1992). Gender and the mentoring process for women: Implications for professional development. *Professional Psychology: Research and Practice, 23*, 233–238.

Gilbert, M. K., Holdt, C., & Christophersen, K. (1999). Letting feminist knowledge serve the city. In M. Mayberry & E. C. Rose (Eds.), *Meeting the challenge: Innovative feminist pedagogies in action* (pp. 319–340). New York: Routledge.

Gilligan, C. (1982). *In a different voice*. Cambridge, MA: Harvard University Press.

Ginorio, A. B. (1998). Contextualizing violence in a participatory classroom: A socially defined identities approach. *Psychology of Women Quarterly, 22*, 77–96.

Ginorio, A. B., & Martinez, L. J. (1998). Where are the Latinas? Ethno-race and gender in psychology courses. *Psychology of Women Quarterly, 22*, 53–68.

Giroux, H. A. (1987). Critical literacy and student experiences: Donald Graves' approach to literacy. *Language Arts, 64*, 175–181.

Giroux, H. A. (1992). *Border crossings: Cultural workers and the politics of education*. New York: Routledge.

Giroux, H. A. (1997). Rewriting the discourse of racial identity: Towards a pedagogy and politics of whiteness. *Harvard Educational Review, 67*, 285–320.

Giroux, H. A., & McLaren, P. (Eds.). (1994). *Between borders: Pedagogy and politics in cultural studies*. New York: Routledge.

Gloria, A. M., Rieckmann, T., & Rush, J. (2000). Issues and recommendations for teaching an ethnic/culture-based course. *Teaching of Psychology, 27*, 102–107.

Gloria, A. M., & Robinson-Kurpius, S. E. (2001). Influences of self-beliefs, social support, and comfort in the university environment on the academic nonpersistence decisions of American Indian undergraduates. *Cultural Diversity and Ethnic Minority Psychology, 7*(1), 88–102.

Goldberger, N. (1997). Ways of knowing: Does gender matter? In M. R. Walsh (Ed.), *Women, men, and gender* (pp. 252–260). New Haven, CT: Yale University Press.

Goldberger, N., & Tarule, J. M. (Eds.). (1996). *Knowledge, difference, and power: Essays inspired by "Women's ways of knowing."* New York: Basic Books.

Goldenberg, M., & Stout, B. (2000). Writing everybody in. In J. Glazer-Raymo, B. K. Townsend, & B. Ropers-Huilman (Eds.), *Women in American higher education: A feminist perspective* (2nd ed., pp. 507–515). Boston: Pearson Custom Publishing.

Goldstein, G. S., & Benassi, V. A. (1994). The relation between teacher self-disclosure and student classroom participation. *Teaching of Psychology, 21*, 212–217.

Gollnick, D. (1980). *Multicultural teacher education: Case studies of thirteen programs. Vol. 2* (Report No. BBB06621). Washington, DC: National Institute of Education.

Golumbisky, K. (2002). Gender equity and mass communication female student majority. *Journalism and Mass Communication Educator, 56*(4), 53–66.

Gonzalez, R., Biever, J. L., & Gardner, G. T. (1994). The multicultural perspective in therapy: A social constructionist approach. *Psychotherapy, 31,* 515–524.

Goodman, D. J. (2000). Motivating people from privileged groups to support social justice. *Teachers College Record, 102,* 1061–1085.

Goodwin, A. L. (1997). Historical and contemporary perspectives on multicultural teacher education: Past lessons, new directions. In J. E. King, E. R. Hollins, & W. C. Hayman (Eds.), *Preparing teachers for cultural diversity* (pp. 5–22). New York: Teachers College Press.

Gore, J. M. (1992). What we can do for you! What can "we" do for "you"? Struggling over empowerment in critical and feminist pedagogy. In C. Luke & J. Gore (Eds.), *Feminisms and critical pedagogy* (pp. 54–73). New York: Routledge.

Gore, J. M. (1998). On the limits to empowerment through critical and feminist pedagogies. In D. Carlson & M. W. Apple (Eds.), *Power, knowledge, pedagogy: The meaning of democratic education in unsettling times* (pp. 271–288). Boulder, CO: Westview Press.

Grace, A., & Gouthro, P. A. (2000). Using models of feminist pedagogies to think about issues and directions in graduate education for women students. *Studies in Continuing Education, 22,* 5–28.

Gram, A. M. (1992). Peer relationships among clinicians as an alternative to mentor–protégé relationships in hospital settings. *Professional Psychology: Research and Practice, 23,* 416–417.

Grant, C. A., & Sleeter, C. E. (2000). Race, class, gender, and disability in the classroom. In J. A. Banks & C. A. M. Banks (Eds.), *Multicultural education: Issues and perspectives* (4th ed., pp. 59–81). New York: Wiley.

Grant, C. A., & Wieczorek, K. (2000). Teacher education and knowledge in "the knowledge society": The need for social moorings in our multicultural schools. *Teachers College Record, 101,* 913–935.

Greene, B. (1997). Lesbian women of color: Triple jeopardy. *Journal of Lesbian Studies, 1*(1), 109–147.

Greene, B., & Sanchez-Hucles, J. (1997). Diversity: Advancing an inclusive feminist psychology. In J. Worell & N. G. Johnson (Eds.), *Shaping the future of feminist psychology: Education, research, and practice* (pp. 173–202). Washington, DC: American Psychological Association.

Grillo, T., & Wildman, S. (1995). Sexism, racism, and the analogy problem in feminist thought. In J. Adleman & G. Enguídanos (Eds.), *Racism in the lives of women* (pp. 171–180). New York: Harrington Park Press.

Grobman, L. (2001). *Teaching at the crossroads: Cultures and critical perspectives in literature by women of color.* San Francisco: Aunt Lute Books.

Grossberg, L. (1994). Introduction: Bringin' it all back home—pedagogy and cultural studies. In H. Giroux & P. McLaren (Eds.), *Between borders: Pedagogy and the politics of cultural studies* (pp. 1–25). New York: Routledge.

Grumet, M. (1988). *Bitter milk: Women and teaching.* Amherst: University of Massachusetts Press.

Gutiérrez, L., Fredricksen, K., & Soifer, S. (1999). Perspectives of social work faculty on diversity and societal oppression content: Results from a national survey. *Journal of Social Work Education, 35,* 409–419.

Hackney, C. E., & Bock, M. (2000, Winter). Beyond mentoring: Toward an invitational academe. *Advancing Women in Leadership Journal, 3*(1). Retrieved August 3, 2001, from http://www.advancingwomen.com/awl/winter2000/hackney-bock.html

Halpern, D. F., Smothergill, D. W., Allen, M., Baker, S., Baum, C., Best, D., et al. (1998). Scholarship in psychology: A paradigm for the twenty-first century. *American Psychologist, 53,* 1292–1297.

Hammonds, E. (1997). Black (w)holes and the geometry of Black female sexuality. In E. Weed & N. Schor (Eds.), *Feminism meets queer theory* (pp. 136–156). Bloomington: Indiana University Press.

Hardiman, R. (1982). White identity development: A process-oriented model for describing the racial consciousness of White Americans. *Dissertation Abstracts International, 43,* 104A. (University Microfilms No. 82-10330)

Hardiman, R., & Jackson, B. W. (1997). Conceptual foundations for social justice courses. In M. Adams, L. A. Bell, & P. Griffin (Eds.), *Teaching for diversity and social justice* (pp. 16–29). New York: Routledge.

Harding, S. (1986). *The science question in feminism.* Ithaca, NY: Cornell University Press.

Harding, S. (1987). Introduction: Is there a feminist method? In S. Harding (Ed.), *Feminism and methodology* (pp. 1–14). Bloomington: Indiana University Press.

Hare-Mustin, R. T., & Marecek, J. (Eds.). (1990). *Making a difference: Psychology and the construction of gender.* New Haven, CT: Yale University Press.

Harris, R. S. (1976). *A history of higher education in Canada 1663–1960.* Toronto, Ontario, Canada: University of Toronto Press.

Hartmann, S. M. (1998). *The other feminists: Activists in the liberal establishment.* New Haven, CT: Yale University Press.

Hase, M. (2002). Student resistance and nationalism in the classroom: Reflections on globalizing the curriculum. In A. A. Macdonald & S. Sánchez-Casal (Eds.), *Twenty-first-century feminist classrooms* (pp. 87–107). New York: Palgrave Macmillan.

Hawkesworth, M. (2000). Analyzing backlash: Feminist standpoint theory as analytical tool. In J. Glazer-Raymo, B. K. Townsend, & B. Ropers-Huilman (Eds.), *Women in higher education: A feminist perspective* (2nd ed., pp. 148–169). Boston: Pearson Custom Publishing.

Hawoode, T. L., & Scanlon, L. P. (1987). World of our mothers: College for neighborhood women. *Women's Studies Quarterly, 15*(3/4), 101–109.

Hayes, E. (1989). Insights from women's experiences for teaching and learning. *New Directions for Continuing Education, 43,* 55–66.

Heaney, T. (1995). Issues in Freirean pedagogy, "Freire Issues" section. *Thresholds in education.* Retrieved June 20, 2000, from http://www3.nl.edu/academics/cas/ace/facultypapers/ThomasHeaney_Freirean.cfm

Heard, D. (1999). A development model of teachers educating themselves for multicultural pedagogy. *Higher Education, 38,* 461–487.

Helms, J. E. (1990). *Black and white racial identity: Theory, research, and practice.* Westport, CT: Greenwood Press.

Helms, J. E. (1995). An update of Helms's White and People of Color racial identity models. In J. G. Ponterotto, J. M. Casas, L. A. Suzuki, & C. M. Alexander (Eds.), *Handbook of multicultural counseling* (pp. 181–198). Thousand Oaks, CA: Sage.

Helms, J. E., & Cook, D. A. (1999). *Using race and culture in counseling and psychotherapy.* Needham Heights, MA: Allyn & Bacon.

Heywood, L., & Drake, J. (1997). Introduction. In L. Heywood & J. Drake (Eds.), *Third wave agenda: Being feminist, doing feminism* (pp. 1–20). Minneapolis: University of Minnesota Press.

Higgenbotham, E. B. (1992). African American women's history and the metalanguage of race. *Signs: Journal of Women in Culture and Society, 17,* 251–274.

Hinchey, P. H. (1998). *Finding freedom in the classroom: A practical introduction to critical theory.* New York: Peter Lang.

Hollingsworth, M. A. (2000). *The role of research training environment, past research attitudes, and mentoring relationships in predicting current research attitudes and behaviors.* Unpublished doctoral dissertation, University of Maryland, College Park.

Hollingsworth, M. A., & Fassinger, R. E. (2002). The role of faculty mentors in the research training of counseling psychology doctoral students. *Journal of Counseling Psychology, 49,* 324–330.

Hoodfar, H. (1997). Feminist anthropology and critical pedagogy: The anthropology of classrooms' excluded voices. In S. de Castell & M. Bryson (Eds.), *Radical in(ter)ventions: Identity, politics, and difference/s in educational praxis* (pp. 211–232). Albany: State University of New York Press.

hooks, b. (1982). *Ain't I a woman: Black women and feminism.* London: Pluto Press.

hooks, b. (1984). *Feminist theory: From margin to center.* Boston: South End Press.

hooks, b. (1989). *Talking back: Thinking feminist, thinking black.* Boston: South End Press.

hooks, b. (1994). *Teaching to transgress: Education as the practice of freedom.* New York: Routledge.

Howe, K. (1985). The psychological impact of a women's studies course. *Women's Studies Quarterly, 13*(1), 23–24.

Hughes, H. M., Hinson, R. C., Eardley, J. L., Farrel, S. M., Goldberg, M. A., Hattrich, L. G., et al. (1993). Research vertical team: A model for scientist-practitioner training. *The Clinical Psychologist, 53,* 14–18.

Hughes, K. P. (1998). Liberation? Domestication? Freire and feminism in the university. *Convergence, 31*(1/2), 137–145.

Humm, M. (1991). *Border traffic.* Manchester, England: Manchester University Press.

Hunt, D. M., & Michael, C. (1983). Mentorship: A career training and development tool. *Academy of Management Review, 8,* 475–485.

Hyde, C. A., & Ruth, B. J. (2002). Multicultural content and class participation: Do students self-censor? *Journal of Social Work Education, 38,* 241–256.

Hyde, J. S. (1990). Meta-analysis and the psychology of gender differences. *Signs: Journal of Women in Culture and Society, 16,* 55–73.

Hyde, J. S. (1994). Can meta-analysis make feminist transformations in psychology? *Psychology of Women Quarterly, 18,* 451–462.

Ibrahim, F. A. (1985). Effectiveness in cross-cultural counseling and psychotherapy: A framework. *Psychotherapy, 2,* 321–323.

Ibrahim, F. A. (1991). Contribution of cultural worldview to generic counseling and development. *Journal of Counseling and Development, 70,* 13–19.

Ignatiev, N. (1995). *How the Irish became White.* New York: Routledge.

Ivey, A. E., Ivey, M. B., & Simek-Morgan, L. (1993). *Counseling and psychotherapy: A multicultural perspective.* Boston: Allyn & Bacon.

Jack, D. C. (1991). *Silencing the self: Women and depression.* New York: Harper Perennial.

Jackson, S. (1997). Crossing borders and changing pedagogies: From Giroux and Freire to feminist theories of education. *Gender and Education, 9,* 457–467.

Jagdose, A. (1996). *Queer theory: An introduction.* New York: New York University Press.

James, J. (1998). Gender, race, and radicalism: Teaching the autobiographies of native and African American women activists. In G. E. Cohee, E. Däumer, T. D. Kemp, P. M. Krebs, S. Lafky, & S. Runzo (Eds.), *The feminist teacher anthology: Pedagogies and classroom strategies* (pp. 234–258). New York: Teachers College Press.

Jenkins, M. M. (1990). Teaching the new majority: Guidelines for cross-cultural communication between students and faculty. *Feminist Teacher, 5*(1), 8–15.

Jenkins, Y. M. (2000). The Stone Center theoretical approach revisited: Applications for African American women. In L. C. Jackson & B. Greene (Eds.), *Psychotherapy with African American women* (pp. 62–81). New York: Guilford Press.

Jennings, L. B., & Smith, C. P. (2002). Examining the role of critical inquiry for transformative practices: Two joint case studies of multicultural teacher education. *Teachers College Record, 104,* 456–481.

Jipson, J. (Ed.). (1995a). *Repositioning feminism and education: Perspectives on educating for social change.* Westport, CT: Greenwood Press.

Jipson, J. (1995b). Teacher-mother: An imposition of identity. In J. Jipson, P. Munro, S. Victor, K. Jones, & G. Freed-Rowland (Eds.), *Repositioning feminism and education: Perspectives on educating for social change* (pp. 21–35). Westport, CT: Bergin & Garvey.

Johnson, W. B. (2002). The intentional mentor: Strategies and guidelines for the practice of mentoring. *Professional Psychology: Research and Practice, 33,* 88–96.

Johnson, W. B., & Huwe, J. M. (2002). Toward a typology of mentorship dysfunction in graduate school. *Psychotherapy: Theory/Research/Practice/Training, 39*(1), 44–55.

Johnston, B. (1999). Putting critical pedagogy in its place: A personal account. *Tesol Quarterly, 33*, 557–565.

Kailin, J. (2002). *Antiracist education: From theory to practice*. Lanham, MD: Rowman & Littlefield.

Kalbfleish, P. J., & Keyton, J. (1995). Power and equality in mentoring relationships. In P. J. Kalbfleish & M. J. Cody (Eds.), *Gender, power, and communication in human relationships* (pp. 189–212). Hillsdale, NJ: Erlbaum.

Kanpol, B., & McLaren, P. (Eds.). (1995). *Critical multiculturalism: Uncommon voices in a common struggle*. Westport, CT: Bergin & Garvey.

Katz, J. H. (1985). The sociopolitical nature of counseling. *The Counseling Psychologist, 13*, 615–625.

Kaufmann, J. (2000). Reading counter-hegemonic practices through a postmodern lens. *International Journal of Lifelong Education, 19*, 430–447.

Kaye, M. (1972). Diving into the wreck: The woman writer in the twentieth century. In N. Hoffman, C. Secor, & A. Tinsley (Eds), *Female studies VI* (pp. 68–78). Old Westbury, NY: Feminist Press.

Keim, J., Warring, D. F., & Rau, R. (2001). Impact of multicultural training on school psychology and education students. *Journal of Instructional Psychology, 28*, 249–253.

Kennedy, M., Lubelska, C., & Walsh, V. (Eds.). (1993). *Making connections: Women's studies, women's movements, women's lives*. London: Taylor & Francis.

Kenway, J., & Modra, H. (1992). Feminist pedagogy and emancipatory possibilities. In C. Luke & J. M. Gore (Eds.), *Feminisms and critical pedagogy* (pp. 138–166). New York: Routledge.

Khan, S. (1999). Teaching an undergraduate course on the psychology of racism. *Teaching of Psychology, 26*, 28–33.

Kim, N. I. (2000). The general survey course on Asian American women: Transformative education and Asian American feminist pedagogy. *Journal of Asian American Studies, 3*, 37–65.

Kimmel, E. (1999). Feminist teaching, and emergent practice. In S. N. Davis, M. Crawford, & J. Sebrechts (Eds.), *Coming into her own: Educational success in girls and women* (pp. 57–75). San Francico: Jossey-Bass.

Kimmel, E., & Worell, J. (1997). Preaching what we practice: Principles and strategies of feminist pedagogy. In J. Worell & N. G. Johnson (Eds.), *Shaping the future of feminist psychology: Education, research, and practice* (pp. 121–153). Washington, DC: American Psychological Association.

King, T. C., & Buker, E. A. (2001). "To and fro": Deepening the soul life of women's studies through play. *National Women's Studies Association Journal, 13*(1), 105–125.

Kirk, G., & Okazawa-Rey, M. (Eds.). (2001). *Women's lives: Multicultural perspectives* (2nd ed.). New York: McGraw-Hill.

Kiselica, M. S. (1991). Reflections on a multicultural internship experience. *Journal of Counseling and Development, 70,* 126–135.

Kiselica, M. S., & Maben, P. (1999). Do multicultural education and diversity appreciation training reduce prejudice among counseling trainees? *Journal of Mental Health Counseling, 21,* 240–255.

Kitzinger, C. (1996). The token lesbian chapter. In S. Wilkinson (Ed.), *Feminist social psychologies: International perspectives* (pp. 119–144). Philadelphia: Open University Press.

Knight, T., & Pearl, A. (2000). Democratic education and critical pedagogy. *The Urban Review, 32,* 197–226.

Knouse, S. B. (2001). Virtual mentors: Mentoring on the Internet. *Journal of Employment Counseling, 38*(4), 162–169.

Koocher, G. P. (2002). Mentor revealed: Masculinization of an early feminist construct. *Professional Psychology: Research and Practice, 33,* 509–510.

Kowalski, R. M. (2000). Including gender, race, and ethnicity in psychology content courses. *Teaching of Psychology, 27,* 18–24.

Krahenbuhl, G. S. (1998, November/December). Faculty work: Integrating responsibilities and institutional needs. *Change,* 18–25.

Kram, K. E. (1985). *Mentoring at work: Developmental relationships in organizational life.* Glenview, IL: Scott Foresman.

Kumashiro, K. K. (2002). Against repetition: Addressing resistance to anti-oppressive change in the practices of learning, teaching, supervising, and researching. *Harvard Educational Review, 72,* 67–92.

Ladany, N., Inman, A. G., Constantine, M. G., & Hofheinz, E. W. (1997). Supervisee multicultural case conceptualization ability and self-reported multicultural competence as functions of supervisee racial identity and supervisor focus. *Journal of Counseling Psychology, 44,* 284–293.

Ladson-Billings, G. (1998). Who will survive America? Pedagogy as cultural preservation. In D. Caroson & M. W. Apple (Eds.), *Power, knowledge, pedagogy: The meaning of democratic education in unsettling times* (pp. 289–304). Boulder, CO: Westview Press.

Lather, P. (1991). *Getting smart—Feminist research and pedagogy within the postmodern.* New York: Routledge.

Lather, P. (1998). Critical pedagogy and its complicities: A praxis of stuck places. *Educational Theory, 48,* 487–497.

Leach, M. M., & Carlton, M. A. (1997). Toward defining a multicultural training philosophy. In D. B. Davis & H. L. K. Coleman (Eds.), *Multicultural counseling competencies: Assessment, education and training, and supervision* (pp. 184–208). Thousand Oaks, CA: Sage.

Lee, C. C. (1991). Promise and pitfalls of multicultural counseling. In C. C. Lee & B. L. Richardson (Eds.), *Multicultural issues in counseling: New approaches to di-*

versity (pp. 1–13). Alexandria, VA: American Association for Counseling and Development.

Leistyna, P. (2002). *Defining and designing multiculturalism*. Albany: State University of New York Press.

Leong, F. T. L., & Kim, H. H. (1991). Going beyond cultural sensitivity on the road to multiculturalism: Using the Intercultural Sensitizer as a counselor training tool. *Journal of Counseling and Development, 7*, 112–118.

Lerner, G. (1993). *The creation of feminist consciousness*. Oxford, England: University Press.

Lewis, J. A., Lewis, M. D., Daniels, J. A., & D'Andrea, M. J. (1998). *Community counseling: Empowerment strategies for a diverse society*. San Francisco: Brooks/ Cole.

Lewis, M. G. (1990). Interrupting patriarchy: Politics, resistance, and transformation in the feminist classroom. *Harvard Educational Review, 60*, 467–488.

Lewis, M. G. (1993). *Without a word: Teaching beyond women's silence*. New York: Routledge.

Linnehan, F. (2002). The relation of a work-based mentoring program to the academic performance and behavior of African American students. *Journal of Vocational Behavior, 59, 310–325*.

Lips, H. J. (2003). *A new psychology of women: Gender, culture, and ethnicity* (2nd ed.). Mountain View, CA: Mayfield Publishing.

Litner, B., Rossiter, A., & Taylor, M. (1992). The equitable inclusion of women in higher education: Some consequences for teaching. *Canadian Journal of Education, 17*, 286–302.

Locke, D. C. (1990). A not so provincial view of multicultural counseling. *Counselor Education and Supervision, 30*, 18–25.

Locke, D. C., & Faubert, M. (1999). Innovative pedagogy for critical consciousness in counselor education. In M. S. Kiselica (Ed.), *Confronting prejudice and racism during multicultural training* (pp. 43–58). Alexandria, VA: American Counseling Association.

Lorde, A. (1984). *Sister outsider*. Trumansburg, NY: The Crossing Press.

Luchetta, T. (1996). The use of e-mail discussion in fostering a learning community in an undergraduate psychology of women course. *Feminist Collections, 17*, 7–8.

Luebke, B. F., & Reilly, M. E. (1995). *Women's studies graduates: The first generation*. New York: Teachers College.

Luhmann, S. (1998). Queering/querying pedagogy? Or, pedagogy is a pretty queer thing. In W. F. Pinar (Ed.), *Queer theory in education* (pp. 141–156). Mahwah, NJ: Erlbaum.

Luke, C., & Gore, J. M. (Eds.). (1992). *Feminisms and critical pedagogy*. New York: Routledge.

Luttrell, W. (1989). Working-class women's ways of knowing: Effects of gender, race and class. *Sociology of Education, 62*, 33–46.

Lynn, M. (1999). Toward a critical race pedagogy: A research note. *Urban Education, 33*, 606–627.

MacDermid, S. M., Jurich, J. A., Myers-Walls, J. A., & Pelo, A. (1992). Feminist teaching: Effective education. *Family Relations, 41*, 31–38.

Macdonald, A. A. (2002). Feminist pedagogy and the appeal to epistemic privilege. In A. A. Macdonald & S. Sánchez-Casal (Eds.), *Twenty-first-century feminist classrooms: Pedagogies of identity and difference* (pp. 111–133). New York: Palgrave Macmillan.

Mackie, R. (1981). Contributions to the thought of Paulo Freire. In R. Mackie (Ed.), *Literacy and revolution: The pedagogy of Paulo Freire* (pp. 93–119). New York: Continuum.

Maher, F. A. (1984). Appropriate teaching methods for integrating women. In B. Spanier, A. Bloom, & D. Boroviak (Eds.), *Toward a balanced curriculum: A sourcebook for initiating gender integration projects* (pp. 101–108). Cambridge, MA: Schenkman Publishing Company.

Maher, F. A. (1987a). Inquiry teaching and feminist pedagogy. *Social Education, 51*, 186–192.

Maher, F. A. (1987b). Toward a richer theory of feminist pedagogy: A comparison of "liberation" and "gender" models for teaching and learning. *Journal of Education, 169*, 91–100.

Maher, F. A. (1999). Progressive education and feminist pedagogies: Issues in gender, power, and authority. *Teachers College Record, 101*, 35–60.

Maher, F. A., & Dunn, K. (1984). *The practice of feminist teaching: A case study of interactions among curriculum, pedagogy, and female cognitive development* (Work in progress: No. 144). Wellesley, MA: Stone Center Working Papers.

Maher, F. A., & Tetreault, M. K. T. (1994). *The feminist classroom.* New York: Basic Books.

Maher, F. A., & Tetreault, M. K. T. (1996). "Women's ways of knowing" in women's studies, feminist pedagogies, and feminist theories. In N. R. Goldberger, J. M. Tarule, B. M. Clinchy, & M. F. Belenky (Eds.) *Knowledge, difference, and power: Essays inspired by "Women's ways of knowing"* (pp. 148–174). New York: Basic Books.

Maher, F. A., & Tetreault, M. K. T. (1997). Learning in the dark: How assumptions of whiteness shape classroom knowledge. *Harvard Educational Review, 67*, 321–349.

Maher, F. A., & Tetreault, M. K. T. (2001). *The feminist classroom: Dynamics of gender, race, and privilege* (Expanded ed.). Lanham, MD: Rowman & Littlefield.

Manese, J., E., Wu, J. T., & Nepomuceno, C. A. (2001). The effect of training on multicultural counseling competencies: An exploratory study over a ten-year period. *Journal of Multicultural Counseling and Development, 29*, 31–40.

Manglitz, E. (2003). Challenging white privilege in adult education: A critical review of the literature. *Adult Education Quarterly, 53*, 119–134.

Manicom, A. (1992). Feminist pedagogy: Transformations, standpoints, and politics. *Canadian Journal of Education, 17*, 365–389.

Margolis, E., & Romero, M. (1998). "The department is very male, very white, very old, and very conservative": The functioning of the hidden curriculum in graduate sociology departments. *Harvard Educational Review, 68*, 1–32.

Marsella, A. J. (1998). Toward a "global-community psychology": Meeting the needs of a changing world. *American Psychologist, 53*, 1282–1291.

Matlin, M. W. (2004). *The psychology of women* (5th ed.). Belmont, CA: Wadsworth/ Thomson.

Mayer, J. D., & Salovey, P. (1993). The intelligence of emotional intelligence. *Intelligence, 17*, 433–442.

Maynard, M. (1996). Challenging the boundaries: Towards an anti-racist women's studies. In M. Maynard & J. Purvis (Eds.), *New frontiers in women's studies: Knowledge, identity, and nationalism* (pp. 11–29). London: Taylor & Francis.

McCarn, S. R., & Fassinger, R. E. (1996). Revisioning sexual minority identity formation: A new model of lesbian identity and its implications for counseling and research. *The Counseling Psychologist, 24*, 508–534.

McCaughey, M., & Burger, C. J. (1998). Cybergrrrl education and virtual feminism: Using the Internet to teach introductory women's studies. In B. S. Winkler & C. DiPalma (Eds.), *Teaching introduction to women's studies: Expectations and strategies* (pp. 151–162). Westport, CT: Bergin & Garvey.

McDavis, R. J., & Parker, M. (1977). A course on counseling ethnic minorities: A model. *Counselor Education and Supervision, 16*, 146–149.

McHugh, M., Koeske, R., & Frieze, I. H. (1986). Issues to consider in conducting nonsexist psychological research: A guide for researchers. *American Psychologist, 41*, 879–890.

McKeachie, W. J. (1997). Student ratings: The validity of use. *American Psychologist, 52*, 1218–1225.

McKeachie, W. J. (2002). *Teaching tips: Strategies, research, and theory for college and university teachers.* Boston, MA: Houghton Mifflin.

McLaren, P. (1997). *Revolutionary multiculturalism: Pedagogies of dissent for the new millennium.* Boulder, CO: Westview Press.

McLaren, P. (2000a). *Che Guevara, Paulo Freire and the pedagogy of revolution.* New York: Rowman & Littlefield.

McLaren, P. (2000b). Paulo Freire's pedagogy of possibility. In S. F. Steiner, H. M. Krank, P. McLaren, & R. E. Behruth (Eds.), *Freirean pedagogy, praxis, and possibilities* (pp. 1–22). New York: Taylor & Francis.

Merta, R. J., Stringham, E. M., & Ponterotto, J. G. (1988). Simulating culture shock in counselor trainees: An experiential exercise. *Journal of Counseling and Development, 66*, 242–245.

Messmer, M. (2003). Building an effective mentoring program. *Strategic Finance, 84*(8), 17–18.

Miller, J. B. (1987). *Towards a new psychology of women* (2nd ed.). Boston: Beacon Press.

Miller, J. B., & Stiver, I. P. (1997). *The healing connection: How women form relationships in therapy and in life.* Boston: Beacon Press.

Mobley, M. (1997, March). *Cultural impasses in cross-cultural interactions on campus*. Preconvention workshop at American College Personnel Association, Chicago, IL.

Moglen, H. (1983). Power and empowerment. *Women's Studies International Forum*, 6, 131–134.

Moradi, B. (2002). Privilege exercise. *The Feminist Psychologist*, 29(1), 8.

Morgan, K. P. (1987). The perils and paradoxes of feminist pedagogy. *Resources for Feminist Research*, 16, 49–52.

Morrell, E. (2002). Toward a critical pedagogy of popular culture: Literacy development among urban youth. *Journal of Adolescent and Adult Literacy*, 46, 72–77.

Morrow, S. L. (2000). Feminist reconstructions of psychology. In M. Biaggio & M. Hersen (Eds.), *Issues in the psychology of women* (pp. 15–31). New York: Kluwer Academic/Plenum Publishers.

Moss, G. (2001). Critical pedagogy: Translation for education that is multicultural. *Multicultural Education*, 9, 2–11.

Moya, P. M. L. (2001). Chicana feminism and postmodernist theory. *Signs: Journal of Women in Culture and Society*, 26, 441–483.

Mumford, L. S. (1985). Why do we have to read all this old stuff? Conflict in the feminist theory classroom. *Journal of Thought*, 20, 88–96.

Musil, C. M. (Ed.). (1992). *The courage to question*. Washington, DC: Association of American Colleges.

Mussey, A., & Kesselman, A. (1998). Outrageous/liberating acts: Putting feminism into practice. In B. S. Winkler & C. DiPalma (Eds.), *Teaching introduction to women's studies: Expectations and strategies* (pp. 213–221). Westport, CT: Bergin & Garvey.

Myers, L. J. (1993). *Understanding an Afrocentric world view: Introduction to an optimal psychology* (2nd ed.). Dubuque, IA: Kendall/Hunt.

Nadelhaft, J. (1985). Feminism in the classroom: Through the eye of the storm. In J. Fritsch (Ed.), *Toward excellence and equity* (pp. 235–246). Orono: University of Maine.

Nadelhaft, R. (1985). Predictable storm in the feminist classroom. In J. Fritsch (Ed.), *Toward excellence and equity* (pp. 247–256). Orono: University of Maine.

National Center for Education Statistics. (2002). Postsecondary education. In *Digest of education statistics, 2001* (chap. 3). Retrieved February 25, 2003, from http://nces.ed.gov/pubs2002/digest2001/tables/dt229.asp

National Women's Studies Association. (1996). *Liberal learning and the women's studies major: A report to the profession*. College Park, MD: Author.

Nelsen, R. W. (1981). Reading, writing and relationship: Toward overcoming the hidden curriculum of gender, ethnicity, and socio-economic class. *Interchange*, 12, 229–242.

Nelson, M. L., & Holloway, E. L. (1990). Relation of gender to power and involvement in supervision. *Journal of Counseling Psychology*, 37, 473–481.

Neville, H. A., Heppner, M. J., Louie, C. E., Thompson, C. E., Brooks, L., & Baker, C. E. (1996). The impact of multicultural training on White racial identity attitudes and therapy competencies. *Professional Psychology: Research and Practice, 27,* 83–89.

Newmann, F., & Wehlage, G. (1995). *Successful school restructuring.* Alexandria, VA: Association for Supervision and Curriculum Development.

Ng, R. (1995). Teaching against the grain: Contradictions and possibilities. In R. Ng, P. Staton, & J. Scane (Eds.), *Anti-racism, feminism, and critical approaches to education* (pp. 129–152). Westport, CT: Greenwood Press.

Ng, R., Staton, P., & Scane, J. (Eds.). (1995). *Anti-racism, feminism, and critical approaches to education.* Westport, CT: Greenwood Press.

Nieto, S. (1999a). *The light in their eyes: Creating multicultural learning communities.* New York: Teachers College Press.

Nieto, S. (1999b). Multiculturalism, social justice, and critical teaching. In I. Shor & C. Pari (Eds.), *Education is politics: Critical thinking across differences, K–12: A tribute to the life and work of Paolo Freire* (pp. 1–32). Portsmouth, NH: Boynton/Cook Heinemann.

Noddings, N. (1984). *Caring: A feminist approach to ethics and moral education.* Berkeley: University of California Press.

Nuttall, E. V., Sanchez, W., & Webber, J. J. (1996). MCT theory and implications for training. In D. W. Sue, A. E. Ivey, & P. B. Pedersen (Eds.), *A theory of multicultural counseling and therapy* (pp. 123–138). Pacific Grove, CA: Brooks/Cole.

Nwachuku, U. T., & Ivey, A. E. (1991). Culture-specific counseling: An alternative training model. *Journal of Counseling and Development, 70,* 106–111.

Obidah, J. E. (2000). Mediating boundaries of race, class, and professorial authority as a critical multiculturalist. *Teachers College Record, 102,* 1035–1060.

Okin, S. M. (1999). *Is multiculturalism bad for women?* Princeton, NJ: Princeton University Press.

Omolade, B. (1987). A black feminist pedagogy. *Women's Studies Quarterly, 15*(3/4), 32–39.

Orner, M. (1992). Interrupting the calls for student voice in "liberatory" education: A feminist poststructuralist perspective. In C. Luke & J. Gore (Eds.), *Feminisms and critical pedagogy* (pp. 74–89). New York: Routledge.

Orr, C. M. (1997). Charting the currents of the third wave. *Hypatia, 12,* 29–45.

Orr, D. J. (1993). Toward a critical rethinking of feminist pedagogical praxis and resistant male students. *Canadian Journal of Education, 18,* 239–254.

Ortman, P. E. (1993). A feminist approach to teaching learning theory with educational applications. *Teaching of Psychology, 20,* 38–40.

Ossana, S. M., Helms, J. E., & Leonard, M. M. (1992). Do "womanist" identity attitudes influence college women's self-esteem and perceptions of environmental bias? *Journal of Counseling and Development, 70,* 402–408.

Ostrove, J. M. (2003). Belonging and wanting: Meanings of social class background for women's constructions of their college experiences. *Journal of Social Issues, 59*, 771–784.

Ostrove, J. M., & Cole, E. R. (2003). Privileging class: Toward a critical psychology of social class in the context of education. *Journal of Social Issues, 59*, 677–692.

Ottavi, T. M., Pope-Davis, D. B., & Dings, J. G. (1994). Relationship between White racial identity attitudes and self-reported multicultural counseling competencies. *Journal of Counseling Psychology, 41*, 149–154.

Paccione, A. V. (2000). Developing a commitment to multicultural education. *Teachers College Record, 102*, 980–1006.

Paludi, M. A., & DeFour, D. C. (1992). The mentoring experiences questionnaire: Initial psychometric analyses. *Mentoring International, 6*, 19–23.

Park, S. M. (2000). Research, teaching, and service: Why shouldn't women's work count? In J. Glazer-Raymo, B. K. Townsend, & B. Ropers-Huilman (Eds.), *Women in American higher education: A feminist perspective* (2nd ed., pp. 285–308). Boston: Pearson Custom Publishing.

Parker, W. M., Moore, M. A., & Neimeyer, G. J. (1998). Altering White racial identity and interracial comfort through multicultural training. *Journal of Counseling and Development, 76*, 302–310.

Parker, W. M., Valley, M. M., & Geary, C. A. (1986). Acquiring cultural knowledge for counselors in training: A multifaceted approach. *Counselor Education and Supervision, 26*, 61–71.

Patterson, C. H. (1996). Multicultural counseling: From diversity to universality. *Journal of Counseling and Development, 74*, 227–231.

Pedersen, P. B. (1991). Multiculturalism as a generic approach to counseling. *Journal of Counseling and Development, 70*, 6–12.

Pedersen, P. B. (1994). Simulating the client's internal dialogue as a counselor training technique. *Simulation and Gaming, 25*, 40–50.

Pedersen, P. B. (1999). Culture-centered interventions as a fourth dimension of psychology. In P. Pedersen (Ed.), *Multiculturalism as a fourth force* (pp. 3–18). Philadelphia: Taylor & Francis.

Peet, M., & Reed, B. G. (1999). Activism in an introductory women's studies course: Connected learning through the implementation of praxis. *Women's Studies Quarterly, 27*(3/4), 21–35.

Peterson, R., & Trierweiler, S. (1999). Scholarship in psychology: The advantages of an expanded vision. *American Psychologist, 54*, 350–355.

Peterson, V. S., & Runyan, A. S. (1999). *Global gender issues* (2nd ed.). Boulder, CO: Westview Press.

Philbin, M., Meier, E., Huffman, S., & Boverie, P. (1995). A survey of gender and learning styles. *Sex Roles, 32*, 485–494.

Phinney, J. S., & Rotheram, M. J. (Eds.). (1987). *Children's ethnic socialization: Pluralism and development.* Newbury Park, CA: Sage.

Plaskow, J. (2000, June). *Cultivating a critical consciousness: Jewish feminist reflections on wisdom and spirituality in the university.* Address presented at the Global Multifaith Conference of University Chaplains, Campus Ministers, and Religious Professionals, University of British Columbia, Vancouver, Canada.

Ponterotto, J. G., Gretchen, D., Utsey, S. O., Rieger, B. P., & Austin, R. (2002). A revision of the Multicultural Counseling Awareness Scale. *Journal of Multicultural Counseling and Development, 30,* 153–180.

Ponterotto, J. G., Rieger, B. P., Barrett, A., Harris, G., Sparks, R., Sanchez, C. M., & Magids, D. (1996). Development and initial validation of the Multicultural Counseling Awareness Scale. In G. R. Sodowsky & J. C. Impara (Eds.), *Multicultural assessment in counseling and clinical psychology* (pp. 247–282). Lincoln, NE: Buros Institute of Mental Measurements.

Porter, N. (1995). Supervision of psychotherapists: Integrating anti-racist, feminist, and multicultural perspectives. In H. Landrine (Ed.), *Bringing cultural diversity to feminist psychology* (pp. 163–175). Washington, DC: American Psychological Association.

Pramaggiore, M., & Hardin, B. (1998). Webbed women: Information technology in the introduction to women's studies classroom. In B. S. Winkler & C. DiPalma (Eds.), *Teaching introduction to women's studies: Expectations and strategies* (pp. 163–174). Westport, CT: Bergin & Garvey.

Quinlivan, K., & Town, S. (1999). Queer pedagogy, educational practice and lesbian and gay youth. *Qualitative Studies in Education, 12,* 509–524.

Rabinowitz, N. S. (2002). Queer theory and feminist pedagogy. In A. A. Macdonald & S. Sánchez-Casal (Eds.), *Twenty-first-century feminist classrooms* (pp. 175–200). New York: Palgrave Macmillan.

Ragins, B. R., & Cotton, J. (1991). Easier said than done: Gender differences in perceived barriers to gaining a mentor. *Academy of Management Journal, 34,* 939–951.

Ragins, B. R., & Cotton, J. L. (1999). Mentor functions and outcomes: A comparison of men and women in formal and informal mentoring relationships. *Journal of Applied Psychology, 84,* 529–550.

Ragins, B. R., Cotton, J. L., & Miller, J. S. (2000). Marginal mentoring: The effects of type of mentor, quality of relationship, and program design on work and career attitudes. *Academy of Management Journal, 43,* 1177–1194.

Rakow, L. F. (1992). Gender and race in the classroom: Teaching way out of line. *Feminist Teacher, 6,* 10–13.

Ramirez, M., III. (1999). *Multicultural psychotherapy: An approach to individual and cultural differences* (2nd ed.). Boston: Allyn & Bacon.

Reynolds, A. L. (1995). Challenges and strategies for teaching multicultural counseling courses. In J. G. Ponterotto, J. M. Casas, L. A. Suzuki, & C. M. Alexander (Eds.), *Handbook of multicultural counseling* (pp. 312–330). Thousand Oaks, CA: Sage.

Rezai-Rashti, G. (1995). Multicultural education, anti-racist education, and critical pedagogy: Reflections on everyday practice. In R. Ng, P. Staton, & J. Scane

(Eds.), *Anti-racism, feminism, and critical approaches to education* (pp. 3–19). Westport, CT: Greenwood Press.

Rice, R. E. (1991). The new American scholar: Scholarship and the purposes of the university. *Metropolitan Universities, 1,* 7–18.

Rich, A. (1979). *On lies, secrets, and silence: Selected prose—1966–1978.* New York: Norton.

Rich, A. (1980). Compulsory heterosexuality and lesbian existence. *Signs: Journal of Women in Culture and Society, 5,* 631–640.

Rickabaugh, C. A. (1998). *Sex and gender: Student projects and exercises.* Boston: McGraw-Hill.

Ridley, C. R., Espelage, D. L., & Rubinstein, K. J. (1997). Course development in multicultural counseling. In D. B. Pope-Davis & H. L. K. Coleman (Eds.), *Multicultural counseling competencies: Assessment, education and training, and supervision* (pp. 131–158). Thousand Oaks, CA: Sage.

Ridley, C. R., & Thompson, C. E. (1999). Managing resistance to diversity training: A social systems perspective. In M. S. Kiselica (Ed.), *Confronting prejudice and racism during multicultural training* (pp. 3–24). Alexandria, VA: American Counseling Association.

Riger, S. (1978). A technique for teaching the psychology of women: Content analysis. *Teaching of Psychology, 5,* 221–223.

Riger, S. (1992). Epistemological debates, feminist voices: Science, social values, and the study of women. *American Psychologist, 47,* 730–740.

Roffman, E. (1994). The personal is professional is political: Feminist praxis in a graduate school counselor training program. In S. M. Deats & L. T. Lenker (Eds.), *Gender and academe: Feminist pedagogy and politics* (pp. 79–90). Lanham, MD: Rowman & Littlefield.

Rogler, L. H., Malgady, R. G., & Rodriguez, O. (1989). *Hispanics and mental health: A framework for research.* Malabar, FL: Krieger.

Romney, P., Tatum, B., & Jones, J. (1992). Feminist strategies for teaching about oppression: The importance of process. *Women's Studies Quarterly, 20*(1/2), 95–110.

Ropers-Huilman, B. (1998). *Feminist teaching in theory and practice: Situational power and knowledge in poststructural classrooms.* New York: Teachers College Press.

Rose, E. C. (1998). The class meets in cyberspace: Women's studies via distance education. In G. E. Cohee, E. Däumer, T. D. Kemp, P. M. Krebs, S. Lafky, & S. Runzo (Eds.), *The feminist teacher anthology: Pedagogies and classroom strategies* (pp. 114–134). New York: Teachers College Press.

Rose, S. (1989). The protest as a teaching technique for promoting feminist activism. *National Women's Studies Association Journal, 1,* 486–490.

Rose, S. (1996). Integrating lesbian studies into the feminist psychology classroom. In B. Zimmerman & T. McNaron (Eds.), *The new lesbian studies: Into the twenty-first century* (pp. 108–114). New York: The Feminist Press.

Ross, B. L. (1995). *The house that Jill built: A lesbian nation in formation.* Toronto, Ontario, Canada: University of Toronto Press.

Rosser, S. V. (1998). Warming up the classroom climate for women. In G. E. Cohee, E. Däumer, T. D. Kemp, P. M. Krebs, S. Lafky, & S. Runzo (Eds.), *The feminist teacher anthology: Pedagogies and classroom strategies* (pp. 31–44). New York: Teachers College Press.

Rothenberg, P. (1996). The politics of discourse and the end of argument. In E. Friedman, W. Komar, C. B. Flint, & P. Rothenberg (Eds.), *Creating an inclusive college curriculum: A teaching sourcebook from the New Jersey Project* (pp. 59–69). New York: Teachers College Press.

Rothenberg, P. (1998). Integrating the study of race, gender, and class: Some preliminary observations. In G. E. Cohee, E. Däumer, T. D. Kemp, P. M. Krebs, S. Lafky, & S. Runzo (Eds.), *The feminist teacher anthology: Pedagogies and classroom strategies* (pp. 135–149). New York: Teachers College Press.

Rothenberg, P. (2000). *Invisible privilege: A memoir about race, class, and gender.* Lawrence: University Press of Kansas.

Rubin, L., & Nemeroff, C. (2001). Feminism's third wave: Surfing to oblivion? *Women and Therapy, 23*(2), 91–104.

Ruble, D. N., Croke, J. A., Frieze, I., & Parsons, J. E. (1975). Field study of sex-role attitude change in college women. *Journal of Applied Social Psychology, 5,* 110–117.

Ruddick, S. (1989). *Maternal thinking: Toward a politics of peace.* Boston: Beacon Press.

Rudolph, F. (1962). *The American college and university: A history.* New York: Vintage Books.

Rudy, K. (2001). Radical feminism, lesbian separatism, and queer theory. *Feminist Studies, 27*(1), 191–222.

Russo, N. (1998). Teaching about gender and ethnicity: Goals and challenges [editorial]. *Psychology of Women Quarterly, 22,* i–vi.

Ryan, M. (1990). Classrooms and contexts: The challenge of feminist pedagogy. *Feminist Teacher, 4,* 39–42.

Sabnani, H. B., Ponterotto, J. G., & Borodovsky, L. G. (1991). White racial identity development and cross-cultural counselor training. *The Counseling Psychologist, 19*(1), 76–102.

Sánchez-Casal, S., & Macdonald, A. A. (2002). Introduction: Feminist reflections on the pedagogical relevance of identity. In A. A. Macdonald & S. Sánchez-Casal (Eds.), *Twenty-first century feminist classrooms: Pedagogies of identity and difference* (pp. 1–28). New York: Palgrave Macmillan.

Sandler, B. R., & Hall, R. (1986). *The campus climate revisited: Chilly for women faculty, administrators, and graduate students.* Washington, DC: Project on the Status and Education of Women, Association of American Colleges.

Sandoval, C. (1991). U.S. third world feminism: The theory and method of oppositional consciousness in the postmodern world. *Genders, 10,* 1–36.

Santos, S. J., & Reigadas, E. (2002). Latinos in higher education: An evaluation of a university faculty mentoring program. *Journal of Hispanic Higher Education, 1*(1), 40–50.

Sapon-Shevin, M. (1999). *Because we can change the world: A practical guide to building cooperative, inclusive classroom communities*. Boston: Allyn & Bacon.

Sasaki, B. (2002). Toward a pedagogy of coalition. In A. Macdonald & S. Sanchez (Eds.), *The pedagogical relevance of identity* (pp. 31–58). New York: Palgrave Macmillan.

Saulnier, C. F. (1996). *Feminist theories and social work*. New York: Haworth Press.

Scandura, T. A. (2001). An investigation of the moderating effects of gender on the relationships between mentorship initiation and protégé perceptions of mentoring functions. *Journal of Vocational Behavior, 59*, 342–363.

Scanlon, J. (1993). Keeping our activist selves alive in the classroom: Feminist pedagogy and political activism. *Feminist Teacher, 7*, 8–13.

Scherpf, S. (2001). Rap pedagogy: The potential for democratization. *The Review of Education/Pedagogy/Cultural Studies, 23*, 73–110.

Scheurich, J. J. (2002). *Anti-racist scholarship: An advocacy*. Albany: State University of New York Press.

Schniedewind, N. (1985). Cooperatively structured learning: Implications for feminist pedagogy. *Journal of Thought, 20*(3), 74–87.

Schniedewind, N. (1987a). Feminist values: Guidelines for teaching methodology in women's studies. In I. Shor (Ed.), *Freire for the classroom* (pp. 170–179). Portsmouth, NY: Boynton/Cook.

Schniedewind, N. (1987b). Teaching feminist process. *Women's Studies Quarterly, 15*(3/4), 15–31.

Schniedewind, N. (1993).Teaching feminist process in the 1990's. *Women's Studies Quarterly, 21*(3/4), 17–29.

Schram, B. A. (1976). Women's studies as humanist education: Some concepts, activities, and curriculum. *Humanist Education, 14*(4), 157–167.

Schuster, M. R., & Van Dyne, S. R. (1985). The changing classroom. In M. R. Schuster & S. R. Van Dyne (Eds.), *Women's place in the academy: Transforming the liberal arts curriculum* (pp. 161–171). Totowa, NJ: Rowman & Allanheld.

Sciarra, D. T. (1999). *Multiculturalism in counseling*. Itasca, IL: Peacock.

Scott, R., Richards, A., & Wade, M. (1977). Women's studies as change agent. *Psychology of Women Quarterly, 1*, 377–379.

Sheared, V. (1994). Giving voice: A womanist construction. In E. Hayes & S. A. J. Colin III (Eds.), *Confronting racism and sexism in adult continuing education* (pp. 27–38). San Francisco: Jossey-Bass.

Sheffield, E. (2003). Higher education. In *The Canadian encyclopedia*. Retrieved August 17, 2003, from http://www.thecanadianencyclopedia.com/index.cfm?PgNm=TCE&Params=A1ARTA0002537

Shor, I. (1987a). *Critical teaching and everyday life*. Chicago: University of Chicago Press.

Shor, I. (Ed.). (1987b). *Freire for the classroom*. Portsmouth, NH: Boynton/Cook Publishers.

Shor, I., & Freire, P. (1987). *A pedagogy for liberation*. South Hadley, MA: Bergin & Garvey.

Shrewsbury, C. M. (1987). What is feminist pedagogy? *Women's Studies Quarterly, 15*(3/4), 6–13.

Siegel, D. L. (1997). Reading between the waves: Feminist historiography in a "postfeminist" moment. In L. Heywood & J. Drake (Eds.), *Third wave agenda: Being feminist, doing feminism* (pp. 40–54). Minneapolis: University of Minnesota Press.

Simon, R. I. (1992). *Teaching against the grain: Text for a pedagogy of possibilities.* South Hadley, MA: Bergin & Garvey.

Sinacore, A. L., Blaisure, K. R., Justin, M., Healy, P., & Brawer, S. (1999). Promoting reflexivity in the classroom. *Teaching of Psychology, 26,* 267–270.

Sinacore, A. L., Healy, P., & Justin, M. (2002). A qualitative analysis of the experiences of feminist psychology educators: The classroom. *Feminism & Psychology, 12,* 339–362.

Sleeter, C. E. (1996). *Multicultural education as social activism.* Albany: State University of New York Press.

Sleeter, C. E. (1999). *Multicultural education.* Upper Saddle River, NJ: Prentice Hall.

Sleeter, C. E., & Grant, C. A. (1987). An analysis of multicultural education in the United States. *Harvard Educational Review, 4,* 421–444.

Sleeter, C. E., & Grant, C. A. (2003). *Making choices for multicultural education: Five approaches to race, class, and gender* (4th ed.). New York: Wiley.

Sleeter, C. E., & McLaren, P. (Eds.). (1995). *Multicultural education, critical pedagogy and the politics of difference.* Albany: State University of New York Press.

Sodowsky, G. R., Kuo-Jackson, P. Y., Richardson, M. F., & Corey, A. T. (1998). Correlates of self-reported multicultural competencies: Counselor multicultural social desirability, race, social inadequacy, locus of control racial ideology, and multicultural training. *Journal of Counseling Psychology, 45,* 256–264.

Sodowsky, G. R., Taffe, R. C., Gutkin, T. B., & Wise, S. L. (1994). Development of the Multicultural Counseling Inventory: A self-report measure of multicultural competencies. *Journal of Counseling Psychology, 41,* 137–148.

Solomon, B. M. (1985). *In the company of educated women: A history of women in higher education in America.* New Haven, CT: Yale University Press.

Sparks, E. E., & Park, A. H. (2000). The integration of feminism and multiculturalism: Ethical dilemmas at the border. In M. M. Brabeck (Ed.), *Practicing feminist ethics in psychology* (pp. 203–224). Washington, DC: American Psychological Association.

Spelman, E. V. (1988). *Inessential woman.* Boston: Beacon Press.

Stake, J. E., & Gerner, M. A. (1987). The women's studies experience: Personal and professional gains for women and men. *Psychology of Women Quarterly, 11,* 277–284.

Stake, J. E., & Hoffman, F. (2000). Putting feminist pedagogy to the test: The experience of women's studies from student and teacher perspectives. *Psychology of Women Quarterly, 24,* 30–38.

Stake, J. E., & Hoffmann, F. (2001). Changes in student social attitudes, activism, and personal confidence in higher education: The role of women's studies. *American Educational Research Journal, 38,* 411–436.

Stake, J. E., & Malkin, C. (2003). Students' qualities of experience and perceptions of intolerance and bias in the women's and gender studies classroom. *Psychology of Women Quarterly, 27,* 174–185.

Stake, J. E., Roades, L., Rose, S., Ellis, L., & West, C. (1994). The women's studies experience: Impetus for feminist activism. *Psychology of Women Quarterly, 18,* 403–412.

Stark, C. (2001). Psychological climate changes for women in academic psychology: Forecasts, sources, and implications. *Canadian Psychology, 42,* 286–300.

Stein, A. (1997). *Sex and sensibility: Stories of a lesbian generation.* Berkeley: University of California Press.

Stevenson, R. R. (1989). Creating a connected classroom: Two projects that work! *Teaching of Psychology, 16,* 212–214.

Sue, D. W. (1990). Culture-specific strategies in counseling: A conceptual framework. *Professional Psychology: Research and Practice, 21,* 424–433.

Sue, D. W., Arredondo, P., & McDavis, R. J. (1992). Multicultural counseling competencies and standards: A call to the profession. *Journal of Counseling and Development, 70,* 477–486.

Sue, D. W., Carter, R. T., Casas, J. M., Fouad, N. A., Ivey, A. E., Jensen, M., et al. (1998). *Multicultural counseling competencies: Individual and organizational development.* Thousand Oaks, CA: Sage.

Sue, D. W., Ivey, A. E., & Pedersen, P. B. (1996). *A theory of multicultural counseling and therapy.* Pacific Grove, CA: Brooks/Cole.

Sue, S., Zane, N., & Young, K. (1994). Research on psychotherapy and behavior change. In A. Bergin & S. Garfield (Eds.), *Handbook of psychotherapy and behavior change* (4th ed., pp. 783–817). New York: Wiley.

Surrey, J. (1983). *The "self-in-relation": A theory of women's development* (Work in progress: No. 13). Wellesley, MA: Stone Center Working Papers.

Sutphin, C. (1992). The inclusion/exclusion issue: Including students in choosing texts. *Feminist Teacher, 7,* 31–34.

Swaffield, B. (1996, March 27–30). *What happens when male professors enact feminist pedagogies?* (ERIC Document Reproduction Service No. ED397429). Paper presented at the annual meeting of the Conference on College Composition and Communication, Milwaukee, WI.

Swank, E., Asada, H., & Lott, J. (2001). Student acceptance of a multicultural education: Exploring the role of a social work curriculum, demographics, and symbolic racism. *Journal of Ethnic & Cultural Diversity in Social Work, 10,* 85–103.

Szapocznik, J., & Kurtines, W. M. (1989). *Breakthroughs in family therapy with drug abusing and problem youth.* New York: Springer.

Szapocznik, J., Santisteban, D., Rio, A., Perez-Vidal, A., Santisteban, D., & Kurtines, W. M. (1989). Family effectiveness training: An intervention to prevent drug abuse and problem behaviors in Hispanic adolescents. *Hispanic Journal of Behavioral Sciences, 11,* 4–27.

Tannen, D. (1990). *You just don't understand.* New York: Morrow.

Tannen, D. (1997). Women and men talking: An interactional sociolinguistic approach. In M. R. Walsh (Ed.), *Women, men, and gender: Ongoing debates* (pp. 82–90). New Haven, CT: Yale University Press.

Tatum, B. D. (1992). Talking about race, learning about racism: The application of racial identity development theory in the classroom. *Harvard Educational Review, 62,* 1–24.

Tatum, B. D. (2002). *"Why are all the Black kids sitting together in the cafeteria?" and other conversations about race* (Rev. ed.). New York: Basic Books.

Taylor, E., Tisdell, E., & Hanley, M. (June, 2000). *The role of positionality in teaching for critical consciousness: Implications for adult education.* Paper presented at the Annual Adult Education Research Conference, University of British Columbia, Vancouver, Canada.

Thompson, M. E. (1993). Diversity in the classroom: Creating opportunities for learning feminist theory. *Women's Studies Quarterly, 21*(3/4), 114–121.

Thousand, J., Diaz-Greenberg, R., Nevin, A., Cardelle-Elawar, M., Bekett, C., & Reese, R. (1999). Perspectives on a Freirean dialectic to promote inclusive education. *Remedial and Special Education, 20,* 323–326.

Tisdell, E. J. (1995). *Creating inclusive adult learning environments: Insights from multicultural education and feminist pedagogy* (Information Series No. 361). Columbus, OH: ERIC Clearinghouse on Adult, Career, and Vocational Education, Center on Education and Training for Employment, The Ohio State University.

Tisdell, E. J. (1998). Poststructural feminist pedagogies: The possibilities and limitations of feminist emancipatory adult learning and practice. *Adult Education Quarterly, 48*(3), 139–156.

Tomlinson, M. J., & Fassinger, R. E. (2002). The faces of feminist pedagogy: A survey of psychologists and their students. In L. H. Collins, M. R. Dunlap, & J. C. Chrisler (Eds.), *Charting a new course for feminist psychology* (pp. 37–64). Westport, CT: Praeger Publishers.

Tong, R. P. (1998). *Feminist thought* (2nd ed.). Boulder, CO: Westview Press.

TuSmith, B. (1989–1990). The cultural translator: Toward an ethnic womanist pedagogy. *Melus, 16*(2), 17–29.

Ulku-Steiner, B., Kurtz-Costes, B., & Kinlaw, C. R. (2000). Doctoral student experiences in gender-balanced and male-dominated graduate programs. *Journal of Educational Psychology, 92,* 296–307.

Unger, R. (1983, March). *Measuring attitudes about reality: Implications for feminists.* Paper presented at the first annual New Jersey Conference on Women, Douglass College, New Brunswick, NJ.

United States Department of Health and Human Services. (2000/2001). *Mental health: Culture, race and ethnicity—A supplement to mental health: A report of the Surgeon*

General. Rockville, MD: U.S. Department of Health and Human Services, Public Health Office, Office of the Surgeon General.

Valle, M. E. (2002). Antiracist pedagogy and conscientización: A Latina professor's struggle. In A. A. Macdonald & S. Sánchez-Casal (Eds.), *Twenty-first-century feminist classrooms* (pp. 155–173). New York: Palgrave Macmillan.

Vázques, L. A. (1997). A systematic multicultural curriculum model: The pedagogical process. In D. Pope-Davis & H. Coleman (Eds.), *Multicultural counseling competencies: Assessment, education and training, and supervision* (pp. 159–183). Thousand Oaks, CA: Sage.

Vedovato, S., & Vaughter, R. (1980). Psychology of women courses changing sexist and sex-typed attitudes. *Psychology of Women Quarterly, 4*, 587–590.

Vinson, T. S., & Neimeyer, G. J. (2000). The relationship between racial identity development and multicultural counseling competency. *Journal of Multicultural Counseling and Development, 28*, 177–192.

Volpp, L. (2003). Feminism versus multiculturalism. In A. K. Wing (Ed.), *Critical race feminism: A reader* (2nd ed., pp. 395–405). New York: New York University Press.

Vontress, C. E., Johnson, J. A., & Epp, L. R. (1999). *Cross-cultural counseling: A casebook*. Alexandria, VA: American Counseling Association.

Walker, A. (1983). *In search of our mothers' gardens: Womanist prose*. New York: Harcourt Brace Jovanovich.

Walker, R. (Ed.). (1995). *To be real*. New York: Doubleday.

Wallace, B. G. (2000). A call for change in multicultural training in graduate schools of Education: Education to end oppression and for social justice. *Teachers College Record, 102*, 1086–1111.

Wallace, J. E. (2001). The benefits of mentoring for female lawyers. *Journal of Vocational Behavior, 58*, 366–391.

Wallerstein, M. (1987). Problem-posing education: Freire's method for transformation. In I. Shor (Ed.), *Freire for the classroom: A sourcebook* (pp. 33–44). Portsmouth, NH: Heinemann.

Walsh, M. R. (Ed.). (1997). *Women, men, and gender: Ongoing debates*. New Haven, CT: Yale University Press.

Ward, M. C. (2002). *A world full of women* (3rd ed.). Boston: Allyn & Bacon.

Waugh, P. (1998). Postmodernism and feminism. In S. Jackson & J. Jones (Eds.), *Contemporary feminist theories* (pp. 177–193). New York: New York University Press.

Weatherall, A. (1999). Exploring a teaching/research nexus as a possible site for feminist methodological innovation in psychology. *Psychology of Women Quarterly, 23*, 199–214.

Weber, L. (1998). A conceptual framework for understanding race, class, gender, and sexuality. *Psychology of Women Quarterly, 22*, 13–32.

Weed, E. (1997). Introduction. In E. Weed & N. Schor (Eds.), *Feminism meets queer theory* (pp. vii–xiii). Bloomington: Indiana University Press.

Weiler, K. (1988). *Women teaching for change: Gender, class and power*. South Hadley, MA: Bergin & Garvey.

Weiler, K. (1991). Freire and a feminist pedagogy of difference. *Harvard Educational Review 61*, 449–474.

Weiler, K. (2001). Rereading Paulo Freire. In K. Weiler (Ed.), *Feminist engagements: Reading, resisting, and revisioning male theorists in education and cultural studies* (pp. 67–87). New York: Routledge.

Wetzel, J. (1999). Assessment and feminist pedagogy. In M. Mayberry & E. C. Rose (Eds), *Meeting the challenge: Innovative feminist pedagogies in action* (pp. 99–119). New York: Routledge.

Whelehan, I. (1995). *Modern feminist thought*. New York: New York University Press.

Wong, N. (1991). Socialist feminism: Our bridge to freedom. In C. T. Mohanty, A. Russo, & L. Torres (Eds.), *Third world women and the politics of feminism* (pp. 288–296). Bloomington: Indiana University Press.

Wood, J. T. (1993). Bringing different voices into the classroom. *National Association for Women's Studies Journal, 5*, 82–93.

Wood, W., & Eagly, A. H. (2002). A cross-cultural analysis of the behavior of women and men: Implications for the origins of sex differences. *Psychological Bulletin, 128*, 699–727.

Worell, J., Stilwell, D., Oakley, D., & Robinson, D. (1999). Educating about women and gender: Cognitive, personal, and professional outcomes. *Psychology of Women Quarterly, 23*, 797–811.

Wright, J. (1998). Lesbian instructor comes out: The personal is pedagogy. In G. E. Cohee, E. Däumer, T. D. Kemp, P. M. Krebs, S. Lafky, & S. Runzo (Eds.), *The feminist teacher anthology: Pedagogies and classroom strategies* (pp. 191–207). New York: Teachers College Press.

Zikmund, B. (1988, September 1). The well-being of academic women is still being sabotaged—by colleagues, by students, and by themselves. *The Chronicle of Higher Education, 198*, A44.

Zimmerman, M. A., Bingenheimer, J. B., & Notaro, P. C. (2002). Natural mentors and adolescent resiliency: A study with urban youth. *American Journal of Community Psychology, 30*(2), 221–243.

Zita, J. N. (1994) Gay and lesbian studies: Yet another unhappy marriage? In L. Garber (Ed.), *Tilting the tower* (pp. 258–276). New York: Routledge.

Zuckerman, D. (1983). Women's studies, self-esteem, and college women's plans for the future. *Sex Roles, 8*, 633–642.

AUTHOR INDEX

Acker, S., 16, 27, 29
Adams, B., 165
Adams, K., 12
Adams, M., 4, 6, 10, 11, 13, 15, 16, 59, 81
Agular, M., 50
Alcoff, L., 47
Allen, K. R., 47
Allinson, C. W., 148
American Association of Colleges, 121
American Association of University Women, 27
American Council on Education, 168
American Psychological Association, 85, 90, 130, 131, 134, *141*, 169, 170, 174–175
Ancis, J. R., 90, 95, 96, 97
Andersen, M. L., 134
Anderson, A., 61
Appelbaum, P., 75
Arciniega, G. M., 89
Armstrong, S. J., 148
Arredondo, P., 88–89, 90
Asada, H., 131
Atkinson, D. R., 149
Attneave, C., 90
Atwood, J., *117*
Ayers-Nachamkin, B., 122

Bahuniuk, M. H., 149
Baker, C., 120
Ball, A. F., 76, 77, 81
Ballard, M. E., 11, 13, 15
Banks, C. A. M., 4, 127
Banks, J. A., 4, 70, 72, 74, 127
Bargad, A., 118
Basu, A., 60
Bauer, D. M., 13
Baumgardner, B., 63, 64
Beck, E. T., 12, *113*
Belenky, M. J., 29, 30, *31*, 114, 119
Bell, L. A., 4, *76*, 77
Bell, S., 66, 67, 113, *114, 115*, 117, 118, 120
Bellafonte, G., 63
Benassi, V. A., 113
Benishek, L. A., 145, 151, 152
Benismon, E. M., 167, 168

Bennett, P., 59
Bennetts, C., 78, 81, 147
Benokraitis, N. V., 169, 170
Berk, R., 6
Berkeley, K. C., 27, 54
Bernal, D. D., 22, *50*
Berry, E., 13
Betz, N. E., 27
Bezucha, R. J., *33*
Bieschke, K., 145
Biever, J. L., 86
Bignell, K. C., 113, 120
Bingenheiemer, J. B., 149
Black, E., 13
Blaisure, K. R., 47
Boatswain, S., 163
Boatwright, K. J., 111, 116
Bock, M., 148, 151
Bohan, J. S., 44, 47
Boler, M., 13, 34
Borodvsky, L. G., 91
Bourdieu, P., 82
Boverie, P., 114
Bowleg, L., 14
Boxer, M., 109
Boyer, E. L., 164, 165, 172, 175
Brawer, S., 47
Briskin, L., 110
Britzman, D., 59
Brokes, A. J., 12
Bronstein, P., 14, 127
Brown, K. H., 14
Brunner, D. D., 13
Bryson, M., 59, 67
Buker, E. A., 14
Burbules, N. C., 6
Burger, C. J., 65
Burke, R. J., 146, 148
Burn, S. M., 60, 61
Burns, A., 118
Butler, J. E., 21, 125, 128, *129, 132, 133, 137*

Cacoullos, A. R., 44
Calhoun, C., 55
Calliste, A. M., 50, 51

Carlton, M. A., 95
Carney, C. G., 94
Carter, R. T., 86, 90, 92, 94
Carver, A., 120
Casas, A., 149
Castell, S., 67
Cean, C., *113*
Chesler, M. A., 58
Chin, J. L., *10*, 13, 14, 18, 128, 136
Christopherson, K., 119
Clinchy, B. M., 13, 29, 30, *31*, 52
Cockroft, I., 111, 112, 121, 122
Cohen, B. B., 89
Cole, E. R., 118
Collins, P. H., 49, 52, 134
Comas-Díaz, L., 51, 52, 85, 95
Connell, R. W., 114
Constantine, M. G., 92, 96
Cook, J. A., 47, 85, 91
Corvin, S. A., 94
Cory, A. T., 96
Cotton, J., 146, 147, 148
Cottrell, D., 13, 14
Cox, T. H., 149
Crawford, M., 28
Croke, J. A., 118
Cross, W. E., 14, 91, 135
Crowley-Long, K., 28, 29
Crumpacker, L., 14, 58
Culley, M., 13, 30, *34, 35, 112–113, 114,
    115*, 121
Currie, D. H., 13, 120

D'Andrea, M., 90, 96, 125
Daniels, J., 96, 125
Daniels, J. A., 90
Darder, A., 7, 8, 16, 17, 19
Davenport, D., 59
Davis, B., 120
Davis, F., 122
Davis, K. S., 152
Davis, S. N., 11, 12, 14
Dean, C., *113*
Deaux, K., 95
Deay, A., 14
de Castell, S., 59
DeDanaan, L., 14
Deem, R., 36
DeFour, D. C., 148
Dei, G. J. S., 50
Denmark, F. L., 29

Diamond, R., 13, 30, 165
Díaz-Lázaro, C. M., 89
Dilley, P., 59
Dings, J. G., 92
Disch, E., 11, *12*
Dobos, J., 149
Donovan, J., 27, 29, 32, 33, 36
Downing, N. E., 94
Drake, J., *63, 64*
Dreher, G. F., 149
Drenovsky, C. K., 111
Duncombe, M., 12
Dunn, K., 114
Durlak, J. A., 96

Eagly, A. H., 38
Edwards, L., 13, 30
Eichorn, J., 114
Eichstedt, J., 15
Elabor-Idemudia, P., 163
Elenes, C. A., 12, *20, 53, 54*
Elliot, L. G., 14
Ellis, L., 111
Ellis, S., 15
Ellsworth, E., 5, 18, *19*, 46, 76, *119*
Elovson, A. C., 111, 112, 121, 122
Emery, K., 12, 59
Enns, C. Z., 13, 32, *82, 83*, 110
Ensher, E. A., 148
Epp, L. R., 86, 87
Espelage, D. L., 125
Espín, O. M., *48–49*, 56, 127, *137*
Esterberg, K. G., 56, 57, 58
Estrada, A. U., 96

Farnsworth, G. B., 47
Fassinger, R. E., 94, 111, 145, 146, 150, 151,
    152, 171
Faubert, M., 6, 8, 93
Ferguson, A., 12, *33*, 119
Ferguson, M., 116, 117
Fiedler, F. E., 89
Findlen, J. A., *63, 64*
Fine, M., 118
Fisher, B. M., 4, *9–10*, 14, 17, *27*, 28, 34
Flaskerud, J. H., 90
Fonow, M. M., 47
Forcey, L. R., 31
Forrest, L., 4, 10, 11, 13, 14, 15, 25, 109,
    110, 119
Frankenberg, R., 14
Franzosa, S. D., 27

Meier, E., 114
Merta, R. J., 89
Messmer, M., 147, 148, 151
Michael, C., 146
Miller, J. B., 31, 114, 146
Mitchell, T., 89
Mobley, M., 140
Modra, H., *110, 117, 122*
Moglen, H., 113
Moore, M. A., 92
Moradi, B., *78*
Morgan, K. P., 112
Morrell, E., 8
Morrow, M., 66
Morrow, S. L., 44, 47
Moss, G., 126, 141
Moya, P. M. L., *22, 50*, 131
Mulqueen, M., 13
Mumford, L. S., 115, 117
Musil, C. M., 110, 111, *112*, 118
Musil C. M., 119, 120, 121, 122
Mussey, A., 15
Myers, L. J., 85
Myers-Walls, J. A., 47

Nadelhaft, J., 114
Nadelhaft, R., *116*
National Center for Education, 168
National Women's Studies Association, 110, 120
Neimeyer, G. J., 92
Nelsen, R. W., *116, 117*, 118
Nelson, M. L., 149
Nemeroff, C., 65
Nepomuceno, C. A., 89
Neville, H. A., 92, 149
Newmann, F. N., 137
Ng, R., *4*, 12, 18, *19*, 51, 52, 54
Nieto, S., 4, *5, 75, 82*
Noddings, N., *30*, 31
Notaro, P. C., 149
Nuttall, E. V., 94
Nwachuken, U. T., 90

Oakley, D., 121
Obidah, J. E., 20, 79
Okasawa-Rey, 113
Okazawa, M., 44
Okazawa-Rey, M., 60, 62, 66, 105
Omolade, B., 52, 53, *54*
Orner, M., 45, 46
Orr, C. M., 63, 64

Orr, D. J., *114*
Ortman, P E., 117
Ossana, S. M., 94
Ostrove, J. M., 118
Ottavi, T. M., 92
Ottman, P. E., 120

Paccione, A. V., 125, *126*
Paludi, M. A., 148
Park, A. H., 3, 20
Park, J., 145
Park, S. M., 164, 165, 169, 170
Parker, W. M., 90, 92
Parsons, J. E., 118
Paschiera, M., 116
Patterson, C. H., 87
Pearl, A., 77
Pedersen, P. B., 85, 86, 88, 89
Peet, M., 111
Pelo, A., 47
Peterson, R., 165
Peterson, V. S., 61
Philbin, M., 114
Phinney, J. S., 72
Plaskow, J., 135
Ponterotto, J. G., 89, 91, 96
Pope-Davis, D. B., 92
Porter, N., 86
Portuges, C., 13, 30
Pramaggiore, M., 65

Quina, K., 14
Quina, Q., 127
Quinlivan, K., 59
Qureshi, A., 86, 90, 94

Rabinowitz, N. S., 57, 59
Ragins, B. R., 146, 147, 148
Rakow, L. F., 37, 114
Ramirez, M., III, 86
Ratigan, V. K., 14
Rau, R., 126
Reed, B. G., 111
Reigadas, E., 147
Reilly, M. E., 119
Reynolds, A. L., 126
Rezai-Rashti, G., 4, 5
Rice, R. E., 165
Rich, A., *47*, 54, 55, *111*
Richards, A., 63, 64, 118
Richardson, M. F., 96

Taffe, R. C., 96
Tannen, D., 31
Tarule, J. M., 13, 29, 30, *31*, 119
Tastsoglou, E., 66
Tatum, B., 15
Tatum, B. D., 73, 135
Taylor, E., 127
Taylor, M., 112
Tennenhouse, K., 122
Tetreault, M. K. T., 19, 20, 44, 45, 46–47,
    106
Thompson, C. E., 92
Thompson, M. E., 111
Thousand, J., 7, 8
Tisdell, E., 127
Tisdell, E. J., 5, 17, 18, *19*, *20*, 44
Tomlinson, M. J., 111, 171
Tong, R. P., 27, 29, 32, 36, 60, 61
Town, S., 59
Triandis, H. C., 89
Trierweiler, S., 165
TuSmith, B., 54
Twine, F. W., 12

Ulku-Steiner, B., 149
Unger, R., 28, 118
United States Department of Health and
    Human Services, 88

Valle, M. E., 51, 52
Valley, M. M., 90
Vander Haegen, E. M., 14, *58*
Van Dyne, S. R., 114
Van Soest, D., 131, *133*
Vásquez, L. A., 125
Vaughter, R., 118
Vedovato, S., 118
Vinson, T. S., 92
Vontress, C., 86, 87

Wade, M., 118
Walker, A., *48*, 63, 64
Wallace, B. G., 69, *79*
Wallace, J. E., 149
Wallerstein, M., 5, *7*, 9
Walsh, M. R., 14
Walsh, V., 110
Ward, M. C., 60, 61
Warring, D. F., 126
Waugh, P., *44*
Weatherall, A., *121*
Webber, J. J., 94
Weber, L., 134
Weed, E., 57
Wehlage, G., 137
Weiler, K., 5, 6, 15, 16, 17, *18*, 19, 36, *37*,
    133, 140
West, C., 15, 111
Wetzel, J., 111, 121, 122
Whelehan, I., 27, 29, 33, 36
Wieczorek, K., 79, *79*, 81
Wiggins, F., 94
Wildman, S., 132
Wise, S. L., 96
Wong, N., 38, *39*
Wood, J. T., 14, 31, 38
Worell, J., 10, 11, 12, 13, 14, 17, 18, 19, 109,
    110, 121
Wright. J., 12
Wu, J. T., 89

Young, K., 90

Zane, N., 90
Zimmerman, M. A., 149
Zita, J. N., 57
Zuckerman, D., 122
Zuniga, X., 58

SUBJECT INDEX

Conscientization
    development of, 134
    as foundation for critical and liberation
        pedagogy, 6
Conscientization, as foundation for critical
    and liberation pedagogy, 6
Consciousness differential, 22
Consciousness-raising
    as foundation for feminist pedagogy, 9–
        10
    self-reflection in, 10
Content, integration of critical, mult-
    icultural, feminist pedagogies and, 16
Critical, multicultural, and feminist
    pedagogy(ies)
    integration of, 16–21
        borderland pedagogies as tools in,
            19–21
        content in, 16
        converging themes among, 17–19
        dynamics of power and privilege in,
            17
        goals in, 17
        oppression and privilege in, 18–19
        personal experience in, 18
        process in, 16–17
        similarities among, 16–17
        student–teacher power differential
            in, 18
Critical consciousness
    in antiracist feminism, development of,
        52
    development of, 134
    in multicultural instruction, 134, 135
    perception for action, 6
    for social change, 37
    three-stage model of, 135
Critical multiculturalism, characteristics of,
    5
Critical multicultural pedagogies
    application to graduate psychology
        course
        intimacy and relationships in, 137–
            139
        power and privilege in, 139–140
    challenges, strategies, curricular imple-
        mentation in, 129
        cultural diversity, 128, 130–133
        pedagogical, 128, 133, 134–136
        philosophical, 128, 129, 130
        social action, 136
    Freirean, 136–137

Critical pedagogies. *See also* Critical, multi-
    cultural, and feminist pedagogies
    conscientization and, 6
    integration with feminist pedagogy, 72, 77
    and literacy education, 76–77
    multicultural approaches and
        class issues in, 82–83
        contributions of, 80
        insights of, 80
        limitations of, 80–81
        teacher preparation and, 81–82
    nomenclature for, 4
    principles and strategies associated with,
        6–9
    problem posing and participatory dia-
        logue in, 7–8
    process and outcomes of, 9
    relationship with feminist and multicul-
        tural pedagogy, 75–76
    self-reflection and praxis in, 7–9
    shared features of, 6–15
    single-studies approach and, 93
    social reconstructionist approach and,
        93
    theorists of, 5
Critical thinking, student responses in
    women's studies programs, 121–122
Crumpacker, L., 58
Culley, M., *34, 35, 112–113, 114, 115*
Cultural competence, training for effective
    level of, 96
Cultural diversity. *See also* Diversity;
    Multicultural instruction
    challenges to, 128, 130–133
    in psychology curriculum
        clarification of terms and concepts
            in, 131
        incongruence between preconceived
            biases and new information, 132–
            133
        integration of, 130
        management of, 130, 131–133
        self-disclosure in teaching of, 131
        student resistance to, 132
        students from different racial and
            ethnic backgrounds and, 133
Cultural feminism
    connections and relatedness in, 29, 30,
        31
    empowerment in, 29, 30
    feminist standpoint epistemologies in,
        32

student responses to, 122–123
Enns, C. Z., *82, 83*
Espín, G., *137*
Espín, O. M., *48–49*
Evaluation
in feminist pedagogy, 12–13
of research in faculty work, 173
of scholarship in faculty work, 172, 173
of teaching
by "the system," 170–171
in traditional institutions, 172–173
traditional systems of, 192
Exceptional and culturally different approach
comparison with human relations approach, 74
for disadvantaged groups, 70, 71
equity pedagogy in, 70
Existential counselor training, 103
acceptance of worldview in, client and counselor, 87–88
goals and strategies of shared with universal counselor training, 92
limitation of, 94
transcendence of culture in, 86–87

Faculty, on legitimacy of multiculturalism and feminism, 192–193
Faculty work
reevaluation of
research in, 173
scholarship in, 172, 173
teaching in, 172–173
Feminism(s)
global and transnational, 60–62
and pedagogy, 62
second-wave and pedagogy, 25–26
third-wave, 62–64
Feminist antiracist pedagogy, 77–78
classroom sharing and discussion in, 77–78
learning community in, 78
realist identity theory and, 77, 78
Feminist educator, goals of, 109
Feminist multicultural pedagogy, conclusions and implications for, 83–84
Feminist pedagogies. *See also* Critical, multicultural, and feminist pedagogies
Feminist pedagogy
benefits to both male female students, 116–117
centrality of sex and gender in, 100

components of, 10
consciousness-raising in, 9–10
definition of, 9
components in, 10
evaluation process in, 12–13
as form of social action, 111
integration with critical pedagogy, 72
integrative concepts in, 21
interpersonal skills training in, 11–12
limitations of, 123–124
principles and activities in, 110
collaboration and valuing of personal and academic experiences, 119–120
incorporation and attention to diversity, 113–119
integration of cognitive and affective learning, 120–123
power and authority, 112–113
social change, 110–112
principles and strategies of, 10–13
diversity, 9, 10, 14–15
holistic learning and integration of dichotomies, 13–14
power, 11–13
principles of, 109–110
self-disclosure in, 12
social action interventions in
students' responses to, 111–112
social change in, 15, 110–112
strategies and student responses, 109–124
student as expert and participant in, 11
students' responses to
class status and, 117–118
female *versus* male, 116
race and, 117
traditional students, 117
women of color *versus* White students, 117
as transformational, 110–112
transformative value of, 109
Feminist pedagogy literature, limitations of, 123
Fisher, B., *9–10*
Fisher, B. M., *27*
Focused culture-specific approach to counselor training
consistency with multicultural and feminist pedagogies, 93–94
counseling process in, 87
training tools in, 90–91

Freire, P., 6, 7
    antiracist feminist pedagogy and, 51
    liberation pedagogy and, 6, 7, 8, 17
    multicultural pedagogy and, 4
Friedman, S., 12

Garcia, B., 133
Gender
    differences in, and mentoring process,
        148–149
    in feminist social constructionist per-
        spective, 47
    in liberal feminist theory and pedagogy,
        28, 29
    in mentoring outcomes, 149
    or culture, in multicultural pedagogy
        dialogue with feminist pedagogy,
        100–101
Gender politics, and classism, 82–83
Gerner, M. A., 122
Giddings, P., 49
Giroux, H. A., 20
Global and transnational feminisms, 60–62
    cultural relativism versus respect for cul-
        ture in, 61–62
    economic issues in, 60
    exploitation of women versus oppression
        and, 60–61
    pedagogy and, 62
Goldberger, N., 30, 31
Grant, C. A., 70
Grobman, L., 20
Grossberg, L., 7

Halpern, D. F., 172
Hammonds, E., 56
Heywood, L., 63, 64
Hoffmann, F., 121
Holistic learning
    creative expression in, 13–14
    integration of cognitive and emotional
        spheres in, 13
    integration of the theoretical with the
        personal, 14
    subjective experience in, 13–14
hooks, b., 48, 49, 51–52, 77
Human relations approach
    comparison with exceptional and cul-
        turally different approach, 74
    goals and pedagogy in, 71–72
    to reduce racial tension, 72

Human relations pedagogy, 103
Humm, M., 30

Identity development models, and multicul-
        tural and feminist pedagogy, 94
Identity(ies)
    chosen versus imposed, 179, 180
    class versus race- and gender-based iden-
        tity, 118
    in cultural feminism, 31–32
    educational
        influence of multicultural and femi-
            nist theory on, 188
    individual
        in multicultural–feminist pedagogi-
            cal dialogue, 100–101
    intersections, borders, boundaries
        among, 20
    multiple, associated with privilege and
        oppression, 181–183
        as White, middle-class, heterosexual
            woman, 182–183
        White woman, wife, mother from
            working-class, 181
        as woman, lesbian, White, 181–182
    stable and changeable, 179–180
    visible and invisible, 179–180
Identity politics
    in lesbian feminism, 56
    in multicultural and feminist social jus-
        tice pedagogies, 106
Inclusiveness, of sexual minorities in lesbian
        feminist pedagogy, 58
Individual identity, in multicultural–feminist
        pedagogical dialogue, 100–101
Institutions
    changing missions of
        faculty roles in, 164–165
        late 20th and early 21st century, 165
        19th century, 164
        20th century to World War II, 164–
            165
        17th 18th centuries, 164
    changing participants in, 165–167
        desegregation and, 167
        diversity of students, 165
        ethnic and religious minority groups,
            166
        minority men, post-Civil War, 166
        women as educators, 166
        women pre-Civil War and post-Civil
            war, 166

Lorde, A., *48*
Luchetta, T., *112*
Luhmann, S., *57, 59*
Luttrell, W., *117*

Macdonald, A. A., *77, 78*
Maher, F. A., *16, 46–47*
Male bashing, female student response to, 115–116
Manicom, A., *110*
Maynard, M., *61*
McKaig, D., *113*
McLaren, P., *20*
Mentee issues
    expectation of reciprocity, 155
    finding mentor, 154–155
    interaction of non-feminist with feminist mentor, 155–156
Mentoring
    definitions of, 145
    demographic matching in, 147–148
    diffuse, decentered support network basis of, 151
    dyadic and small-group, 143–144, 147
    etymology of, 144–145
    literature review of, 150–151
    mentee in
        characteristics of, 147–148
        developmental relationships for, 152
    mentor characteristics in, 147–148
    models of, 145–146
    multicultural feminist, 156–161
        incorporation of political analysis and social advocacy in, 152
        as interactive process, 151
        models of, 150–151
        in patriarchal society, 156–158
        politics of power in, 153–156
        practice of, in patriarchal society, 158–161
        reciprocal nature of, 153
        role in changing marketplace, 151–152
    in non-feminist, patriarchal structure in, 156
    outcomes of, 149
        gender in, 149
    pedagogy as form of, 143
    and politics of change in, 152
    process of, 148–149
        gender differences in, 148–149

shared interests and cognitive style in, 148
types of relationships in, 143–144, 146–147
    facilitated, 147
    formal *vs.* informal, 146
    peer, 147
    team, 147
Mentor issues
    expectations of mentee, 153
    for female mentors, 153
    lack of model of shared power in mentoring, 154
    minority status of mentor or mentee, 153–154
    reciprocity, 153, 154
Modra, H., *110, 117*
Moradi, B., *78*
Moya, P. M. L., *22, 50*
Multicultural and feminist pedagogies
    dialogue in
        on gender or culture and ethnicity, 100
        on social location or identity and positionality, 100–101
    power sharing and mutual control in, 127–128, 130
    social justice
        dimensions of, 102–106
        empowerment and social change in, 101–103
        knowledge and knower in, 102, 103–104
        oppressions and and privileges in, 102, 104–105
        reflexivity and self-awareness in, 102, 105–106
Multicultural and feminist perspectives
    benefits of integration of
        appreciation of difference and multiple perspectives, 194
        growth of students and colleagues, 195
        institutional change, 196
        new ways of seeing and learning, 194–195
        opportunity to act on personal priorities, 195
    learning in
        in traditional institutions, 192–193
    teaching and learning in
        institutional challenges, 193

teaching from
    challenges in, 189–193
    concepts about diversity in, 193–194
    student differences and resistance in,
        190–192
    teaching about multiple social loca-
        tions, 189–190
    in traditional institutions, 192–193
Multicultural competence
    research literature on, 126
    teaching of
        research literature on, 126
Multicultural competence training
    outcomes of, 126
Multicultural counseling and therapy (MCT)
    counseling competencies in, 88–89
    theory of, 88
    training goals for, 89
Multicultural counseling literatures
    relationships with multicultural educa-
        tion literatures, 92–93
Multicultural counseling training
    approaches to
        culture-specific, 90–91
        existential or universal, 86–88
        philosophical assumptions underly-
            ing, 86
        race-based, 91–92
        ubiquitous, 87, 88–89
    future directions in, 95–96
    future needs in
        agreement in definition of terms, 95
        research on efficacy of training ap-
            proaches, 95–96
        self-reflection to understand impact
            of privilege on others, 96–97
        unifying framework, 95
Multicultural counselor training
    integration with multicultural feminist
        pedagogy, 93
    lack of interplay of social identities
        within different contexts, 95
    limitations of for feminist and
        multicultural pedagogy, 94–95
    and multicultural feminist pedagogy,
        93–95
Multicultural education
    approaches to, 70–75
        education for the exceptional and
            culturally different, 70–71, 75
        human relations, 71–72, 74, 75
        multicultural, 73–74, 75

pedagogies and, 71
single-group studies, 72–73, 75
social reconstructionist education,
    74, 75
comparison of multicultural approaches
    to, 74–75
dimensions of, 4
relationship with critical and feminist
    pedagogy, 75–76
and teacher training. See also Teacher
    training
Multicultural education approach
    comparison with social reconstruction-
        ist approach, 75
    curriculum in, 73–74
    goals of, 71
Multicultural education literature
    contributions, challenges and limita-
        tions of, 80–83
    on teacher training, 78–80
Multicultural feminist mentoring
    boundary differences in, 157
    egalitarian character of, 156
    misunderstanding of mentoring rela-
        tionships, 157
    in patriarchal society, 156–157
        burnout in, 158–159
        conflicting demands in, 159
        mentee responsibility in, 160
        organizational and systemic strate-
            gies for, 160–161
        peer mentoring in, 161
        power differentials in, 158
        process and relationship strategies
            for, 158–160
        reciprocity in, 159
        training for, 160–161
    transition out of mentoring relationship
        in, 157–158
Multicultural feminist models
    entry points in, 106–107
    multiple and multiple entry points in,
        106–107
    single-issue approaches in, 107
Multicultural feminist pedagogical dialogue
    centrality of race and ethnicity in
        multicultural approach, 100
    centrality of sex and gender in feminist
        approach, 100
    sociopolitical location of groups or in-
        dividual identity and positionality,
        100–101

246   SUBJECT INDEX

Multicultural feminist pedagogies
  basis of, 21–22
  of future, 84
  goals of, 84
  and the institutional "system"
    evaluation of teaching and, 170–171
    "hidden curriculum" and, 168–169
    monocultural androcentrisim and, 169
    research *versus* teaching and service work in, 169–170
    teaching portfolios and, 171
    traditional faculty reward system and, 165, 169
  interface between institution, educator, and student, 163
  knowledge as social construct in, 22
  multicultural counselor training approaches and, 93–95
  and "the system," 168–172
  strategies for change of, 174–175
Multicultural instruction in psychology. *See also* Cultural diversity
  cultural diversity challenges in, 128, 130–133
  pedagogical challenges in, 128, 133, 134–136
  philosophical challenges in, 128, 129, 130
Multicultural pedagogy. *See also* Critical multicultural and feminist pedagogies
  as antiracist, 5
  centrality or race and ethnicity in, 100
  description of, 4–5
  integration of social justice and critical pedagogy in, 4–5
  integrative concepts in, 21
  as a philosophy, 5
Multicultural teacher education
  critical inquiry and problem posing in, 79–80
  phases in, 79
Multicultural teacher training programs
  barriers to implementation of, 125–126
  outcomes of, 126
  personal changes and gains from, 126
  positive response to, 126
  trainee resistance to, 126–127
Multicultural training approaches, differences in, 86

Nadelhaft, R., *116*

Naming, politics of, 144–145
Nelsen, R. W., *117, 1116*
Nieto, S., *5*
Noddings, N., *30*

Omolade, B., *54*
Oppression
  conceptualization of
    in critical, multicultural, and feminist pedagogies, 18
  of dominant culture, 6
  heterosexuality as an ideology of, in lesbian feminism, 55
  issues in mentoring, 152
  multiple
    in women of color feminisms, 49, 50
  recognition of internalization of, 6
  single or multiple, 102, 104–105
Oppression and privilege
  integration of critical, multicultural, feminist pedagogies and, 18–19
  matrix of, in diversity feminisms, 66
  in multicultural and feminist social justice pedagogies, 102, 104–105
  in social justice multicultural and feminist pedagogies, 102, 104–105
Orner, M., *46*
Orr, D. J., *114*

Paccione, A. V., *126*
Participatory dialogue
  in critical pedagogies, 7–8
Participatory learning, 11
Partnership, in feminist classroom, 112
Patriarchal society
  multicultural feminist mentoring in, 156–157
Patriarchal structure
  in non-feminist mentoring, 156
Patriarchy
  and oppression
    contribution of heterosexuality to, 54–55
  and reciprocity in multicultural feminist mentoring, 159
  socialist feminism and, 36
Pedagogy
  as form of mentoring, 143
  traditions in, 3–4
Pedersen, P. B., *88*
Personal experience
  in critical pedagogies, 18

integration of critical, multicultural, feminist pedagogies and, 18

integration with academic experience
  in feminist classroom, 119
  student responses to, 120

linking with course content, 136

valuing of
  in feminist classroom, 119
  pedagogical techniques for, 119

Politics of power
  in mentoring
    mentee issues, 154–156
    mentor issues, 153–156

Positionality
  changed with change in status and perspective, 184
  characterization of, 46
  contributions of
    educators', 178
  educational training and, 187–188
  of educators, 178–179
    shifts in with identity shifts, 183
  in institutional roles with lesbian identity
    radical perspectives and, 185–186
  in multicultural–feminist pedagogical dialogue, 100–101
  multiple identities in
    association with privilege and oppression, 181–183
    contribution to educators, 180–181
    visible and invisible, imposed and chosen, stable and changeable, 179–181
  and pedagogy, personal reflections about, 178–189
  in postmodern feminism, 46–47
  radical perspectives and, 185–186
  religious influences and contradictions and, 185–187
  shifting and life transitions and changing priorities, 183–185
  of students, 178–179
  theory and role models and, 188–189

Postmodern feminism
  deconstruction in, 44, 47
  reflexivity in, 47
  social constructionism in, 47

Postmodern feminism and pedagogy
  authority and power in, 46
  knowledge in, limitations and changes of, 45

knowledge structure and construction in, 45
positionality in, 46–47
power in, 45
voice, safety, empowerment in, 45–46

Power
  and authority, collaborative, 112–113
  equalization of, in classroom, 112, 113
  in feminist pedagogy, 11–13
  in postmodern feminism and pedagogy, 45, 46
  sharing of
    in feminist and multicultural pedagogy, 18–19
    in feminist pedagogy, 11–13
    in multicultural and feminist pedagogies, 127–128
  social construction of, 106
  between teacher and student and institutional power
    in women of color feminist pedagogy, 53

Power and privilege
  in critical multicultural pedagogies
    application to graduate psychology course, 139–140
  dynamics in critical, multicultural and feminist pedagogy, 17
  dynamics of, 17

Power differential
  decreasing, 11–12
  in multicultural feminist mentoring, 158
  student–teacher
    integration of critical, multicultural, feminist pedagogies and, 18

Power issues, in mentoring literature, 150, 152

Power relationships, in critical pedagogy and social reconstructionist pedagogy, 83

Praxis, in critical pedagogies, 8

Privilege
  access to, antiracist feminism and, 48–49
  in classroom, 19
  dynamics of power and
    integration of critical, multicultural, and feminist pedagogies and, 17
  impact on others, understanding through self-reflection, 96–97

Privilege and oppression
  in critical pedagogy and social reconstructionist pedagogy, 83

integration in critical, multicultural, and feminist pedagogies, 18–19

multiple identities associated with, 181–183

single or multiple
in social justice pedagogies, 102, 104–105

Problem posing
in critical pedagogies, 7–8
definition of, 7

Queer pedagogy literature, deconstruction of concept of sexual normalcy and, 59

Queer theory
comparison with lesbian feminism, 57–58

deconstruction of categories of traditional sex and sexuality in, 57

inclusiveness of, 57

lesbians and, 56

Questions, student-generated for discussion, 11

Race, and response to feminist classroom, 117

Race-based counseling training
development of racial self-awareness, 87, 91–92

key concepts in, 87, 91

overlaps of approaches in, 94

Racial–Cultural Counseling Laboratory and, 92

stage model of antiracism training, 91

Radical feminism
implications for a feminist, multicultural pedagogy, 38

similarity to cultural feminists, 32–33

social transformation through social activism, 32

"the personal is political" in, 33

Radical feminist pedagogy
classroom in, 34

content about violence and its consequences in, 35

expression of emotion in, 34

feminist group process skills in, 33

goals of, 33

male domination and, 34, 35

teacher as change agent in, 34–35

validation of emotion and subjective perspectives in, 34

women-only classes in, 33–34

Rap pedagogy, 8

Reciprocity
in mentoring, 153, 154, 155

in multicultural feminist mentoring, in patriarchy, 159

Reflexivity
in critique of accepted knowledge, 135

in multicultural and feminist pedagogy, 102, 105–106

in postmodern feminism, 47

Religious influence on positionality, 186–187

Research
evaluation of, 173

versus teaching, 169–170

Resistance
to diversity in feminist classroom, male, 114

to integration of multicultural and feminist perspectives, student, 190–191

to multicultural teacher training programs, trainee, 126–127

Rich, A., *47, 111*

Riger, S., *47*

Rudy, K., *57*

Russo, N. F., *10*

Sanchez-Casal, S., *77, 78*

Saulnier, C. F., *51*

Scanlon, J., *33*

Schram, B. A., *35*

Second-wave feminist pedagogy
cultural feminism and, 29–32, 38

implications multicultural feminist theory and pedagogy, 38–39

liberal feminist theory and, 26–29, 38

radical feminism and, 32–35, 38

socialist feminism and, 35–39

Self-awareness
in multicultural and feminist pedagogy, 102, 105–106

in race-based counseling training, 87, 91–92

Self-care, in multicultural feminist mentoring, 160

Self-disclosure
to equalize power and authority in classroom, 112, 113

in feminist pedagogy, 12

by lesbian educators, 58–59

student participation and, 113

Self-esteem, enhancement of, through feminist pedagogical strategies, 122–123

Self-identification, influence of educational experience in, 187
Self-reflection
  about social change, 15
  in consciousness-raising, 10
  in critical pedagogies, 8
  in diversity feminisms, 67
  in multicultural and feminist pedagogies, 94
  in race-based approaches, 94
  stages in, 8
  to understand impact of privilege on others, 96–97
Shor, I., 7, 19
Sinacore, A., 113, 114
Sinacore, A. K., 135
Single-group studies perspective
  comparison with other approaches, 75
  goals of, 71, 72–73
  strategies of, 72–73
Single-studies approach in multicultural education
  commonalities with focused culture-specific approach, 92
  commonalities with race-based counselor training, 92–93
  reliance on critical pedagogy, 93
Single-studies pedagogy, 103
Sleeter, C. E., 70
Smith, C., 79
Smith, C. P., 80
Social action
  challenges of, in transformation of psychology curricula, 136
  interconnection with feminism, 112
Social action, interconnection with feminism, 112
Social activism, in lesbian feminism, 55–56
Social change
  connection of ideas to social action, 15
  in feminist pedagogy, 15
  feminist pedagogy and, 110–111
  in multicultural and feminist social justice pedagogies, 101–103
  opportunities to experience, 15
  self-reflections about, 15
Social construction, of Whiteness, 106
Socialist feminism
  implications for a feminist, multicultural pedagogy, 38–39
  similarity to radical feminism
    oppression and, 35

patriarchy and male dominance in, 36
  transformation of economic structure in, 36
Socialist feminist literature, on gender politics and social class, 82–83
Socialist feminist pedagogy
  classroom questions in, 37
  critical education theory influence on, 27
  goals in, means for meeting, 37–38
  hidden curriculum and educational politics and, 36–37
  issues that reproduce inequities and, 36
Social justice
  teaching for, 141
Social justice pedagogy(ies)
  multicultural and feminist
    dimensions of, 102
    individual empowerment and social change in, 101–103
    knowledge and the knower in, 102, 103–104
    reflexivity and self-awareness in, 102, 105–106
  single or multiple
    oppressions and privileges in, 102, 104–105
Social locations, multiple, teaching about, 189–190
Social reconstructionism
  contributions of, 83
  reliance on critical pedagogy, 93
Social reconstructionist pedagogy, 103
  comparison with multicultural education approach, 75
  comparison with other approaches, 75
  critical pedagogy in, 71
  goal of, 71, 74
Sociopolitical location
  in feminist approaches, 101
  in multicultural–feminist pedagogical dialogue, 100
Solomon, B. M., 166
Stake, J. E., 121, 122
Student experiences, as source of knowledge, 110
Students
  as change agents, 111
  positionality of, 178
  response to collaborative power and authority, 113

as social justice and change agents
ecological training models and, 187–188

Tarule, J. M., *31*
Teachers. *See* Educators
Teacher training
multicultural education literature on, 78–80
for multicultural teaching, 78–80, 81–82
Teaching
evaluation of, 172–173
multicultural
challenges inhibiting, 128
from multicultural feminist perspective challenges in, 189–193
of psychology
collaborative model for, 128
methodology of transformation in, 128, 129
tourist approach to, 127
traditional communication and styles in, 128
research literature on, 126
research *versus*, 169–170
for social justice, 141
traditional approach to, 192
traditional reward system, and, 165, 169
Tetreault, M. K. T., *46–47*
Third-wave feminisms, 62–64
changing consciousness *versus* raising consciousess in, 63
for a hybrid feminism, 63–64
on oppression, 63
and pedagogy, 64–65
the personal as political in, 64
relationship to second-wave feminists, 62–63
social activism in, 64
Third-wave feminist pedagogy
academic feminists in, 66
diversity of meanings and activities in, 65
generational dynamics in, 64–65
intersection of historical events and feminisms in, 65
Tisdell, E. J., *19, 20*
Traditional institutions
evaluation of teaching in, 172–173
teaching and learning in, 192–193

Ubiquitous approach
limitations of for feminist and multicultural pedagogy, 94–95
to multicultural counseling training, 87, 88
Ubiquitous approach, consistency with multicultural and feminist pedagogy, 93
Universal approach, limitation of, 94
Universal counselor training
commonalities with existential counselor training, 92
Universalist pedagogy, 103

Vander Haegen, E. M., *58*
Van Soest, D., *133*
Voice, in postmodern feminism and pedagogy, 45–46

Walker, A., *48*
Wallace, B. G., *79*
Wallerstein, N., *7*
Waugh, *44*
Weed, E., *57*
Weiler, K., *6, 18, 37*
Wieczorek, K., *79*
Women
as educators, 166
as students, 167
Women of color
and antiracist feminisms and pedagogy. *See* Antiracist pedagogy
versus White students
and response to feminist classroom, 117
Women of color feminism
access to privilege and power in, 48–49
activism in, 50
analysis of multiple oppression in, 49–50
inclusion of personal experiences and world views in, 49
Women of color feminisms
antiracist feminists, 50
Chicana feminists and, 49–50, 53
civil rights and feminism in, 49
differential access to power and, 48–49
differential oppression in, 48
inclusive and pluralistic, 49
inclusiveness in, 48
multiple oppressions of, 49, 50
womanist *versus* feminist in, 48

Women of color feminist pedagogy
  power between teacher and student and
    institutional power, 53
  transformational, 53

Women of color feminists, lesbians and, 56
Wong, N., 39
Working-class men, hostility of, in diversi-
    fied feminist classroom, 115

ABOUT THE CONTRIBUTORS

Vianey Acevedo is a doctoral student in counseling psychology at the University of Wisconsin—Madison. Her scholarly interests include multicultural counseling issues and domestic violence within the Latino community.

Özge Akçali is a psychologist in the Eating Disorders Program of Lakeridge Health Corporation in Oshawa, Ontario, Canada. She is also an associate in a group private practice. Özge Akçali received her doctoral degree in counseling psychology from McGill University in 2001. She combines her clinical and research interests in the areas of psychology of women, vocational psychology, and ethics in psychotherapy with an overarching focus on multicultural feminism in each of these areas. Özge Akçali also coconducts program evaluation research for the treatment of eating disorders.

Saba Rasheed Ali is an assistant professor of counseling psychology at the University of Iowa. She received her doctorate in counseling psychology from the University of Oregon in 2001. Her main research interests are in the areas of vocational psychology and empowerment, feminism and multiculturalism, and issues of social class. Her teaching interests include career counseling and development, feminist psychotherapy, and beginning and advanced clinical practicum.

Julie R. Ancis is an associate professor in the Department of Counseling and Psychological Services at Georgia State University. She teaches graduate courses in multicultural counseling, multicultural interventions, and counseling theories. Julie Ancis has published numerous articles and book chapters in the area of racial and gender attitudes, multicultural and feminist theories, cultural competency training, and the educational experiences of women and students of color. She coauthored a book published by the American College Personnel Association entitled *Promoting Student Learning and Student Development at a Distance: Student Affairs Concepts and Practices for Televised Instruction and Other Forms of Distance Learning.* In addition, she has frequently presented at national and international conferences. Dr. Ancis has served on the editorial board of the *Journal of Counseling and Development* and chaired the diversity section of the American Psychological Association (APA) Task Force for the Development of Guidelines for Psychological Practice with Girls and Women. She is also the editor and a contributing author of *Culturally-Responsive Interventions: Innovative Approaches to Working With Diverse Populations.*

Tina M. Anctil is an assistant professor of counseling psychology in the Department of Educational Leadership and Counseling Psychology at Washington State University. She received her doctorate at the University of Wisconsin—Madison. Dr. Anctil teaches graduate courses in supervised fieldwork and school counseling in addition to being a licensed professional counselor and a certified rehabilitation counselor. Her scholarly interests include the examination of the transition from high school to adult life for adolescents with disabilities, including the development of self-determination as it relates to resilience.

Nan Benally is a doctoral student in counseling psychology at the University of Wisconsin—Madison. She received her master's degree in counseling from Arizona State University. Her research interests include cultural identity, resilience, and spirituality in First Nations populations; academic persistence; and the impact of historical trauma on women and students of color.

Karyn J. Boatwright is an associate professor in the Kalamazoo College Department of Psychology and Women's Studies Program. Throughout the academic year, Dr. Boatwright uses feminist pedagogical strategies in her general psychology, counseling psychology, psychology of women and history, and systems courses. Her primary research interests include college women's leadership aspirations and student responses to feminist pedagogy.

Michele C. Boyer is a professor of counseling psychology and chairperson of the Department of Counseling at Indiana State University. Dr. Boyer teaches graduate courses in multicultural counseling, professional ethics, college teaching, and supervised fieldwork. She also conducts workshops on intercultural communication. She has received the Caleb Mills Distinguished Teaching Award, the most prestigious recognition Indiana State University gives for teaching. Her scholarly interests include religion and spirituality in psychology, sport psychology, and feminist therapy.

Angela M. Byars-Winston is an assistant professor of counseling psychology at the University of Wisconsin—Madison. She teaches courses in vocational psychology, psychology of U.S. women of color, counseling in community settings, assessment in counseling, alcohol and other drug addictions, and communication for cultural diversity. Dr. Byars-Winston's scholarly interests include the examination of cultural influences on the career development of women and girls, particularly Black Americans, and multicultural counseling with women of color.

Carolyn Zerbe Enns is a professor of psychology, chair of the Women's Studies Program, and contributor to the Ethnic Studies Pprogram at Cornell College. Cornell College is an undergraduate liberal arts institution with an innovative academic calendar, which is typically referred to as OCAAT (one-course-at-a-time). Dr. Enns teaches courses in multicultural psychology, psychology of women, feminist theory, personality, counseling, and abnormal psychology. Her scholarly interests include feminist theory and therapy in Japan and Korea, global and transnational feminisms, and social justice pedagogies.

Ruth E. Fassinger is a professor in the Counseling Psychology Program, Department of Counseling and Personnel Services (CAPS), at the University of Maryland. She is also an affiliate faculty member in Women's Studies, faculty director in the College Park Scholars program, and director of Undergraduate Studies for CAPS. She taught in public schools for 10 years before becoming a psychologist, so she has been teaching all of her life. She currently teaches undergraduate courses in diversity, advocacy, and social justice, and graduate courses in career, consultation, history of psychology, gender and sexuality, counseling theory, and group therapy. Her scholarly interests are in the psychology of women and gender, issues of sexuality and sexual orientation, career development, and the history and philosophy of science.

Linda M. Forrest is a professor in the counseling psychology program at the University of Oregon, where she also serves as the associate dean of the College of Education. She has taught graduate courses in theories, professional ethics, the psychology of women, career psychology, proseminars, and practicum. She has been active professionally, serving in various leadership capacities within APA. Her understanding of multicultural and feminist theories, as well as social justice issues, constantly informs her observations and involvement in interprofessional interactions. She is particularly interested in how leaders integrate their knowledge of multiculturalism and feminism to inform their leadership skills and choices.

Nancy F. Hensler-McGinnis is pursuing a doctorate in counseling psychology and a graduate certificate in women's studies at the University of Maryland, College Park. Her first research involvements included qualitative studies on women's career development. More recently, her clinical experiences at the Center for Posttraumatic Disorders (Psychiatric Institute of Washington) and as a campus advocate for survivors of sexual assault and relationship violence have furthered her commitment to integrating counseling practice with cross-disciplinary and culturally attuned theory and research, specifically in the areas of trauma recovery and women's health.

Heidi A. Larson is a counseling psychology doctoral student at Indiana State University and also teaches as an adjunct graduate faculty member for the master's program at Eastern Illinois University. She earned her master's degree in counseling and student development at Eastern Illinois University of Charleston. She served for two years as the director of Educational Programs at the Sexual Assault Counseling and Information Services (SACIS) in Charleston. She has also taught undergraduate students at Indiana State University of Terre Haute and at Lake Land College of Mattoon. She has also worked as a psychology intern at Clay City for Family Medicine in Clay City, Indiana.

Cecilia A. Nepomuceno is a doctoral student in counseling psychology at the University of Wisconsin—Madison. Her academic interests include the psychology of U.S. women of color, multicultural responsivity training for counselors through experiential group process, and the relationship between injustice, forgiveness, and well-being.

Ada L. Sinacore is an associate professor in the Department of Educational and Counselling Psychology at McGill University in Montreal, Quebec, Canada. McGill University is a research-intensive institution with a strong commitment to training Canadians as well as international students. She teaches courses in multicultural psychology, counseling theories, career psychology, and ethics. Her scholarly interests include the intersections of multicultural and feminist theories, social justice pedagogies, global feminism, negotiating multiple oppressions, and sexuality and gender. Dr. Sinacore has a strong commitment to social action and community-based research and practice in which she actively applies social justice, feminist, and multicultural models.

Karen W. Tao is a doctoral student in counseling psychology at the University of Wisconsin—Madison. She received her master's degrees in psychological counseling and in organizational psychology from Teachers College, Columbia University. Born and raised in Hilo, Hawaii, she is interested in how context and environment shape individuals' understanding of race and ethnicity. Currently, she is participating in research related to multicultural counseling and supervision competencies, Native Hawaiian ethnic identity development, perspectives on interracial dating and relationships, and the experience of undergraduate students on academic probation.

Georgiana Wilton is a scientist in the University of Wisconsin Medical School's Department of Family Medicine. She is the director of the Family Empowerment Network, a national program addressing Fetal Alcohol Spectrum Disorders (FASD) and is currently working to develop a family-centered research program on FASD. Dr. Wilton completed her doctorate in rehabilitation psychology and has worked in the field of developmental disabilities for over 22 years.